T0301261

European–American Trade and Financial Alliances

NEW HORIZONS IN INTERNATIONAL BUSINESS

Series Editor: Peter J. Buckley
Centre for International Business,
University of Leeds (CIBUL), UK

The New Horizons in International Business series has established itself as the world's leading forum for the presentation of new ideas in international business research. It offers pre-eminent contributions in the areas of multinational enterprise – including foreign direct investment, business strategy and corporate alliances, global competitive strategies, and entrepreneurship. In short, this series constitutes essential reading for academics, business strategists and policy makers alike.

Titles in the series include:

Multinational Enterprises, Innovative Strategies and Systems of Innovation
Edited by John Cantwell and José Molero

Multinational Firms' Location and the New Economic Geography
Edited by Jean-Louis Mucchielli and Thierry Mayer

Free Trade in the Americas
Economic and Political Issues for Governments and Firms
Edited by Sidney Weintraub, Alan M. Rugman and Gavin Boyd

Economic Integration and Multinational Investment Behaviour
European and East Asian Experiences
Edited by Pierre-Bruno Ruffini

Strategic Business Alliances
An Examination of the Core Dimensions
Keith W. Glaister, Rumy Husan and Peter J. Buckley

Investment Strategies in Emerging Markets
Edited by Saul Estrin and Klaus E. Meyer

Multinationals and Industrial Competitiveness
A New Agenda
John H. Dunning and Rajneesh Narula

Foreign Direct Investment
Six Country Case Studies
Edited by Yingqi Annie Wei and V.N. Balasubramanyam

Japanese Multinationals in Europe
A Comparison of the Automobile and Pharmaceutical Industries
Ken-ichi Ando

International Joint Venture Performance in South East Asia
Craig C. Julian

Governance, Multinationals and Growth
Edited by Lorraine Eden and Wendy Dobson

European–American Trade and Financial Alliances
Edited by Gavin Boyd, Alan M. Rugman and Pier Carlo Padoan

European–American Trade and Financial Alliances

Edited by

Gavin Boyd

Formerly Honorary Professor, Political Science Department, Rutgers University, USA and Adjunct Professor in Management, Saint Mary's University, Canada

Alan M. Rugman

L. Leslie Waters Chair of International Business and Director, IU CIBER, Kelley School of Business, Indiana University, USA

Pier Carlo Padoan

Executive Director, International Monetary Fund, USA and Department of Economics, University of Rome 'La Sapienza', Italy

NEW HORIZONS IN INTERNATIONAL BUSINESS

Edward Elgar

Cheltenham, UK • Northampton, MA, USA

Published by
Edward Elgar Publishing Limited
Glensanda House
Montpellier Parade
Cheltenham
Glos GL50 1UA
UK

Edward Elgar Publishing, Inc.
136 West Street
Suite 202
Northampton
Massachusetts 01060
USA

A catalogue record for this book
is available from the British Library

ISBN 1 84376 907 7

Printed and bound in Great Britain by MPG Books Ltd, Bodmin, Cornwall

Contents

Contributors

Daniele Archibugi, Center for European Studies, Harvard University, USA and Italian National Research Council, Italy.

Peter J. Boettke, Department of Economics, George Mason University, USA.

Gavin Boyd, Political Science Department, Rutgers University, USA (deceased).

Christopher J. Coyne, Department of Economics, George Mason University, USA.

Walid Hejazi, Rotman School of Management, University of Toronto, Canada.

Simona Iammarino, Science and Technology Policy Research, University of Sussex, UK, and University of Rome La Sapienza.

George G. Kaufman, Loyola University, Chicago and Federal Reserve Bank of Chicago, USA.

John Kirton, G8 Research Group, University of Toronto, Canada.

Stefano Manzocchi, Department of Economics, University of Perugia, Italy.

Pier Carlo Padoan, Executive Director, International Monetary Fund, USA and Department of Economics, University of Rome 'La Sapienza', Italy.

Alan Rugman, Kelley School of Business, Indiana University, USA.

Alain Verbeke, Haskayne School of Business, University of Calgary, Canada.

Foreword

This volume is the result of a conference held at Saint Mary's University in September 2003. Shortly after this event, Gavin Boyd died, so this book is dedicated to his memory and contribution to the financial/political economy literature.

Gavin was born in Australia, and, although a political scientist by training, it was more political economy that captured his interest, particularly international trade and investment issues. I first met Gavin in the early 1980s, when I joined the Business School at Saint Mary's University from the UK. We shared similar interests, and we very much complemented each other in our approach, and, although we never published papers together, we spent many productive hours together discussing and debating. I also contributed to several of his edited volumes.

Gavin could always be relied upon to know of a pertinent book or article. To some at conferences it might have been seen as an irritant to have him say 'Have you seen the latest paper by ...', but to those that knew Gavin, his knowledge of the literature and willingness to share, as well as his network of colleagues, are legendary. Although Gavin retired in 1989, he was always active with conference presentations and seminal papers and remained faithful to his use of a typewriter!

The year 1995 marks a significant date in Gavin's productivity. Halifax, Nova Scotia was host to the G7. Gavin thought that it was imperative that an academic conference be held as a precursor. The papers from that conference and the others that followed at Saint Mary's University marked a fruitful partnership with Edward Elgar. The first book was edited by Gavin Boyd and Alan Rugman, and was called *Euro-Pacific Investment and Trade* (Elgar, 1997). Gavin worked on many other projects over the last ten years, all under the Edward Elgar imprint.

Apart from his command of the literature, Gavin's standards for publication were extremely high. He would not tolerate slipshod work, and he took great care at editing, often with many suggestions for rewrites.

He enjoyed many successful partnerships with scholars in the field, held an Adjunct Professor position at the Business School at Saint Mary's University, and at Rutgers he was an Honorary Professor. He leaves a rich legacy to the academic world, not only from his own writings, but through his ability to bring together a wide range of scholars for symposiums or conferences. Many of these are icons in the literature and others newly emerging scholars that Gavin saw as future leaders.

This present volume addresses the policy issues that were very dear to Gavin's heart – a vision of greater transatlantic integration, cooperation and alliances.

J. Colin Dodds, President, Saint Mary's University
and Professor of Finance, Sobey School of Business

Preface

Our co-editor and the organizer of the September 2003 conference on which this book is based was Gavin Boyd. Gavin died in November 2003, and he is greatly missed by all of us who attended the series of excellent conferences on various aspects of international political economy that he organized over the last ten years at Halifax, Nova Scotia, with the sustained support of President Colin Dodds of Saint Mary's University.

In this, his final book, Gavin has brought together a distinguished group of experts on the nature and extent of transatlantic policy coordination and its implication for corporate strategy. The economic and financial linkage between Europe and North America, along with the trade and investment rules governing this interaction, are discussed in the remarkably relevant set of papers presented at that conference and edited for publication in this volume.

The complexities of the transatlantic relationship are analysed in chapters dealing with financial integration (Manzocchi and Padoan); transfer of knowledge and technology (Iammarino and Archibugi); transatlantic trade and corporate partnership (Kirton); transatlantic trade and investment links (Hejazi); the simultaneous intraregional as well as transatlantic trade and the implications for antitrust policy of the activities of multinational enterprises (Rugman and Verbeke); structural positioning and macroeconomic policy coordination (Boyd); international interdependence and the role of entrepreneurship (Boettke and Coyne); and the reform of international financial markets (Kaufman).

We hope that this book will be useful for policy makers, managers and students of international political economy, not only in Europe and North America, but also in other parts of the global system governed by similar challenges of international integration and policy coordination.

Alan M. Rugman
Pier Carlo Padoan
October 2004

1. The role of financial markets in economic performance: the EU and the USA

Stefano Manzocchi, Pier Carlo Padoan

INTRODUCTION

Over the 1990s, the US economy grew at an average rate of 3.7 per cent per year against an average yearly rate of more than a percentage point lower for the EU.[1] Ample evidence points to the role of new information technologies as the main determinants of US performance and to the limited role that innovation has played in explaining the more disappointing performance in the larger continental EU countries. Less attention has been devoted to the role of financial factors in explaining such differences. After a fall at the end of the 1970s, the capital income share of the private sector in major EU countries, from the mid-1980s, was very much on the rise and indeed larger than the share in the USA, which, while constantly rising, remained well below that of the other EU countries. In principle such an evolution in income distribution would suggest that conditions for sustained accumulation were present in the EU, also given the widespread view that labour market rigidities in Europe were pushing European firms to shed labour and increase capital accumulation, which, in turn, should have been associated with a higher rate of growth. However capital accumulation has been higher and more sustained in the USA. From 1992 to 2000, private investment in the USA grew at an annual rate of 10 per cent, well above the secular trend of the previous 40 years (3.6 per cent). Can differences in financial market performance explain, at least in part, such differences in investment and growth performance? This issue has usually been addressed from a slightly different perspective. To what extent do different financial systems, either market-based (prevailing in the USA, the UK and the Netherlands) or bank-based (prevailing in continental Europe), provide support to growth? In this chapter we will discuss different theoretical views on this issue, and then review some of the empirical literature, finally, we will briefly present some new empirical evidence.

1

THE ROLE OF FINANCE IN SUPPORTING GROWTH: MACROECONOMIC ASPECTS[2]

According to Allen (1993), the preferability of either a market-oriented or a bank-oriented financial structure depends on how firms are managed. When the production possibility set is known and management decisions can be easily evaluated, bank-oriented financial systems prevail. Whenever, instead, uncertainty about the production function generates uncertainty on the evaluation of management decisions, market-oriented financial systems prevail. Therefore the superiority of a system depends on the amount and the complexity of information to be taken into consideration in the decision-making process.

In sectors with many competitors, short production cycles and constant technology, the information set approaches completeness and the relationship between management decisions and the firm's value is known to all agents. In such a case, the relevant problem is to monitor the management decision and the bank-oriented system is preferable, as it guarantees efficient monitoring. In sectors with a small number of firms, long production cycles and frequent technology changes, the information set available to each agent is incomplete, and therefore the mapping between firm's values and investment decisions changes with the different information sets. In such conditions, the main problem for management is to approximate the complete information vector and, given the sectoral structure, financial markets, where a multiplicity of investors estimate their own action-value function, represent a superior alternative with respect to banking.

Allen's view, while it excludes an 'a priori' superiority of one system, suggests that market-oriented financial systems are more supportive of innovative sectors. Such a conclusion, however, is controversial. According to Mayer (1996), long-term lender–borrower relationships, peculiar to bank-oriented financial systems, are particularly supportive of innovative sectors that are characterized by long and complex production processes as confidence in the availability of external financing favours the stretching of both the shareholders' and the stakeholders' time horizon.

An intermediate view is taken by Maher and Anderson (2001). Both market-oriented and bank-oriented financial systems offer advantages and disadvantages relative to innovative sectors. In market-oriented systems, market pressure leads to a careful selection of innovative projects (positive factor). At the same time, such pressure can lead investors to concentrate on applied research, looking only at short-run returns (negative factor). In contrast, bank-oriented systems support basic research, which is not profitable in the short term but supportive of long-run growth (positive factor); in this latter case, however, risks connected with the quality of the projects increase (negative factor).

The two financing models can be compared according to the risk-spreading opportunities they offer. Allen and Gale (1994) and Ferri *et al.* (1997) suggest that market-oriented systems support static (horizontal) risk spreading while bank-oriented systems support intertemporal risk spreading. In other words, in market systems the horizontal reduction in risk between different firms, which is given by the width of the financial instruments available in the market, assumes major relevance. In bank-oriented systems, banks offer a better smoothing over the cycle and, therefore, better protection against risks affecting the financial structure of firms.

In bank-oriented systems, firms benefit both from the stabilization of the seniority degree of their liabilities, that is, the degree of priority of future payment commitments, and from a softening of the effects of shocks produced by monetary policy changes. As banks establish long-term relationships with borrowers, in adverse states of nature, firms will find it less difficult to obtain financing and to stabilize the order by which creditors are paid in bankruptcy (for instance through a better ratio between preferential debts and ordinary debts as well as a better long-run debt/short-run debt ratio). In addition, banks, by accepting a reduction in their margins, do not fully transfer increases in policy rates to loan rates. This insurance function transfers the return risk from the firm to the bank. In a multi-period perspective, the joint impact of the two factors strengthens the financial equilibrium of firms.

According to the law and finance approach (La Porta *et al.* 1996; Beck *et al.* 2001) the difference between financial systems depends on different corporate governance models, in turn determined by different legal systems. The most relevant distinctive element between the two main legal systems, the common law system, peculiar to Anglo-Saxon countries, and the civil law system, peculiar to continental Europe, is the different degree of protection they provide to the shareholders/investors vis-à-vis the state. To see this it is useful to recall that, while the Anglo-Saxon countries have developed governance models centred on public companies, continental European countries are characterized by concentrated ownership.[3]

Table 1.1 offers some evidence on the average capital share owned by the majority shareholder and the mean largest voting block in selected OECD countries. With respect to the first indicator, in contrast to Anglo-Saxon countries, European countries exhibit an absolute majority shareholder. Evidence is provided also by the voting power indicator, clearly smaller in the USA and in the United Kingdom.

The correspondence between the concentration of ownership and the structure of financial systems is a key argument in Maher and Anderson

(2001). They point out that, in the Anglo-Saxon systems, the main conflicts of interest arise between shareholders and managers. Shareholding atomization reduces the shareholders' ability to control managers. High monitoring costs discourage individual shareholders from scrutinizing management actions; furthermore, if manager's behaviour is not in line with her interest, the shareholder can sell her shares in the secondary market (exit option) rather than use the voice option. Consequently systems centred on public companies, in addition to requiring highly liquid financial markets, must rely on a strict legal framework regulating management's disclosure duties and information-spreading duties that play a key role in protecting small shareholders.[4]

Table 1.1   *International comparison of ownership and voting power concentration*

	Average largest stake[*]	Number of listed companies included	Mean largest voting block	Number of listed companies included
Germany	55.9	402	49.1	374
France	57.9	680	29.4	CAC40
Italy	48.0	214	48.0	216
Spain	38.2	394	40.1	193
UK	14.4	189	14.4	250
USA	25.4[**]	457	3.6	1 309

Note: [*] Data refer to 1996 for Germany, France, Italy, 1995 for Spain, 1992 for UK, 1980 for USA; [**] Percentage of outstanding shares owned by the largest five shareholders.

Source: Maher and Andersonn (2001).

In other cases the main conflicts of interest arise between majority and minority shareholders, and high ownership concentration allows a strict control of managers' behaviour. For the control shareholder, drawing rents to minority shareholders' detriment is more likely. As examples, one can mention strategies maximizing the majority stake value and intra-group transfers benefiting the firms whose share structure is more profitable for the controlling agent. This results in an increase in the firms' cost of direct finance, as shareholders, aware of the drawing costs, will claim for a higher premium. Bank financing, therefore, becomes more attractive. More generally this approach stresses the point that, whatever the existing legal tradition, the more rapidly the legal system adapts to changes in the economic structure the more this will benefit both the financial system and the growth process. With respect to this point, Beck *et al.* (2001) provide evidence that, being more reactive to change, legal systems based either on English common law or on German common law have supported financial development better than those based on French civil law.[5]

In conclusion, this approach suggests that changes in the legal framework ultimately bear on the evolution of the financial system. It also highlights the fact that in systems with public companies and developed capital markets, monitoring of management is less costly and allocation of resources is more efficient. In short, market-oriented financial systems are preferable to bank-oriented ones.

SOME EMPIRICAL EVIDENCE

After a period of hardly explainable silence, beginning in the early 1990s several contributions have appeared offering evidence both of the relationship between financial systems and growth, and of the superiority of either one of the two models. At the end of the 1960s, a seminal paper by Goldsmith (1969) provided initial evidence of a positive correlation between the degree of financial development, considered with respect to bank intermediaries, and growth. More importantly, Goldsmith's contribution opens the way to the analysis of a large set of issues that have led to further investigation. These include the choice of the appropriate measures of financial development and their correlation to growth, the direction of the causal relationship between the real and the financial sectors of economic systems, the extension of the sample of countries and the inclusion of previously omitted variables that could affect growth. An overview of the main results is presented below and summarized in Table 1.2.

Levine and Zervos (1998) carry out a cross section analysis of 47 countries (OECD and non-OECD) over the period 1976–93. Growth is regressed on indicators of the degree of development of the banking system and of financial markets. Two results stand out: (a) a positive and significant relationship between financial development and growth; (b) a significant effect on growth of both credit indicators and market indicators: consequently, while direct and indirect finance supply different services, both are growth-oriented.

A development of the above is provided by Leahy *et al.* (2001), where a test of the link between financial development and growth is investigated with reference to OECD countries. The authors present a panel analysis for the period 1970–97 with a sample of 19 countries. Contrary to others,[6] this paper detects a positive long-run relationship between the degree of development of the financial system and investment and GDP growth.

Table 1.2 *Selected empirical studies of the finance–growth link*

Author	Period and countries	Real growth variables	Financial variables	Method	Main findings
Goldsmith (1969)	1960–63 35 countries	Output growth	Intermediary asset	Cross-country analysis	Evidence of positive relation between bank development and growth, but no indication about causal direction
Levine & Zervos (1998)	1976–93 47 countries	Output growth Capital stock growth Productivity growth Savings	Bank credit to private sector stock market capitalization Stock market turnover Stock return volatility Integration with world financial market	Cross-country analysis	Positive relation between finance and growth; indications on causality direction (from the former to the latter); in different ways both bank and market finance boost growth
Leahy *et al.* (2001)	1970–97 19 OECD countries	Business sector fixed investment Level of output per capita	Liquid liabilities of financial intermediaries Bank credit to private sector Stock market capitalization	Panel analysis	Evidence of a positive link between financial development and investment; market development effects on growth are stronger than those of bank development
Arestis *et. al.* (2001)	1974–98 5 countries	Output growth	Stock market capitalization Domestic bank credit Stock market volatility	Vector autoregression (VAR)	Bank-oriented systems promote growth better than market-oriented ones
Rajan & Zingales (1998)	1980–90 41 countries 36 sectors	Value added growth in specific industry and country	Capitalization ratio [(domestic credit+stock capitalization)/GDP]. Accounting standards Dependence on external finance	Sector-level analysis	Evidence that financial development, by lowering the costs of external finance, affects growth positively; financial development plays a positive role in the birth of new firms and thus supports innovation
Cetorelli & Gambera (1999)	1980–90 41 countries 36 sectors	Value added growth in specific industry and country	Domestic credit Bank sector concentration Dependence on external finance	Sector-level analysis	Bank sector concentration boosts young firms' growth; nevertheless, considering all sectors and firm size, bank sector concentration has a negative effect on growth

Results highlight the impact of financial development on the real economy. Estimates suggest that 10 per cent changes in private credit and stock market capitalization lead to an increase of, respectively, 1.1 per cent and 3.3 per cent of real per capita GDP.

Different results are obtained by Arestis *et al.* (2001) who argue that bank-oriented systems are most suitable to promoting growth. Their contribution, based on time series analysis, shows that, in France, Germany and Japan, banks and, to a smaller extent, financial markets contribute to growth.[7] In contrast, they find no evidence of such a relationship in the Anglo-Saxon systems where, they argue, financial markets develop as a consequence, rather than being the cause, of real sector growth. The authors explain these results by banks' superior ability to overcome asymmetric information and to support long-term projects.

In a widely quoted paper Rajan and Zingales (1998)[8] investigate the causal link between financial development and growth. They offer an empirical test of the theoretical claim that the main causal channel of the finance–growth nexus is the reduction of cost of obtaining finance for firms.[9] The authors show that, after controlling for (trend) aggregate growth rate differences, industrial sectors that depend more on external finance[10] exhibit higher growth rates in countries with a higher degree of financial development. Financial development supports growth of new firms, which are more dependent on external finance than old ones. Therefore, the authors conclude, 'If new firms are disproportionately the source of ideas, financial development can enhance innovation, and thus enhance growth in indirect ways.'

Moving from this conclusion, Cetorelli and Gambera (1999) have investigated the link between the degree of concentration in the banking sector and innovative activities. They show that technological innovation is better supported in systems with a high degree of concentration in the banking industry. In such a context, long-run relationships are favoured and therefore young firms, subject to significant screening and monitoring costs but also with a high profitability potential, can take advantage. The authors suggest that a commitment *à la* Mayer in a principal/agent relationship produces positive effects for younger firms that can offset both the negative effect of the reduction in credit availability (generated by market imperfections) and rent drawing by banks (determined by the information monopolistic position). On the contrary, if one considers the entire universe of firms, negative effects of bank concentration more than offset the benefits of the long-run customer relationship.

In sum, the empirical analysis remains inconclusive on this issue and cross-section results (Beck and Levine, 2002) indicate that the difference in the source of external financing does not matter as regards the impact on growth. What matters is the size of financial systems as well as legal aspects such as governance rules and creditors protection. The size of financial markets is also important to the extent that it allows for a diversification, and to some extent a complementarity, of external finance sources (Davies, 2001).

IS SOMETHING MISSING?

While the empirical literature provides substantial evidence of a positive relationship between financial development and growth, most of the key questions addressed by the theoretical debate remain unanswered. There does not seem to be any compelling evidence that one finance model (bank or market) is clearly superior in supporting growth, nor does there seem to be any clear evidence on the direction of causality between real and financial development.

What seems to be emerging from the empirical literature is that something has been missing so far in the analysis of the growth–finance nexus. While differing in their results and in their focus, most available contributions have one common feature: they consider real growth from one perspective only. To put it differently, they neglect the fact that, while growth ultimately leads to higher GDP, there exist several alternative channels and mechanisms that relate GDP growth to the rest of the system. There is not just one but several growth mechanisms and, since this is the case, it is not unrealistic to think that different financial mechanisms have different impacts on observed growth (that is, on GDP growth) according to the different sources (mechanisms) of growth. Hence the inconclusive results so far available in the literature could, in part at least, be the consequence of a missing element in the analysis: taking into account different growth mechanisms.

This point is particularly relevant in the case of Europe. EU integration is characterized by several specific, yet interconnected, processes: monetary union, enlargement, the final phase of the single market programme, the impact of IT technology. Each of these processes has implications for both the supply and the demand of finance, and hence for the finance–growth nexus. Each of these processes is also associated with one dominant growth mechanism which, with some simplification, can be sketched out as follows.

Monetary union spurs growth through the elimination of transaction costs as well as of currency risk. It also supports growth indirectly through the impulse towards financial integration. In addition, common monetary policy can influence growth through monetary and price stability and its effects on long-term interest rates. The Single Market programme spurs growth through two main channels: a larger market size, which allows for the exploitation of economies of scale; and a more efficient resource allocation generated by stronger competitive pressures. Enlargement waves, especially those involving countries with an initially lower GDP per capita[11] spur growth through catching-up mechanisms, leading to higher capital accumulation as well as technology transfers from the centre to the periphery. Finally, the IT revolution spurs growth through technological innovation and diffusion.

As mentioned, these processes coexist and interact with different intensities, so it is quite possible that, over a given period of time a given sector, region or country is affected by different growth mechanisms acting simultaneously. This implies that the demand for as well as the supply of finance in any specific case reflect this interaction. A preliminary step in the analysis, therefore, is to identify factors affecting demand and supply of finance associated with each specific process.

Economic and Monetary Union (EMU)

EMU is probably the single most important factor that will speed up the convergence of different financial models coexisting in the EU, the bank-based and the market-based models. A first-hand view of the relative weight of the two systems is offered in Table 1.3. As a percentage of GDP, credit granted by European banks is more than twice as large as in the American case, while direct finance instruments are more relevant in the USA. In 1999, outstanding debt securities in Europe amounted to 80 per cent of domestic bank credit, while in the USA the same ratio was higher than 300 per cent. The contrast is more evident if only bonds issued by firms are considered. Similarly, US stocks capitalization exceeded 160 per cent of GDP while in the Euro area it was hardly more than 70 per cent. Finally, Japan's financial structure, generally considered as bank-oriented, reveals a share of direct finance instruments that is larger than the European one.

EMU is changing the European financial landscape and has the potential to do so in the future, both in terms of performance and of pressure on policy makers. As Danthine *et al.* (2000) show, since the introduction of the euro the following changes in European financial markets have emerged: the development of a corporate euro bond market, whose issuing activity in 1999 exceeded the activity of the dollar market; portfolios are beginning to be allocated along pan-European lines rather than on a country basis; the banking industry is undergoing transformation through mergers and acquisitions. Other additional direct effects of EMU include standardization and transparency in pricing, the shrinking of the exchange market, the elimination of the currency risk, the elimination of currency-related regulations and the homogenization of the public bond market and bank refinancing procedures.

Indirect effects include lower costs of cross-country transactions, increasing depth and liquidity of European financial markets, better diversification possibilities and decreasing importance of the home bias effect in investment. In addition, the emerging euro financial market has prompted new pressures on policy makers to harmonize legislation, taxation and standards. The establishment of TARGET and EURO1, the settlement systems for large transactions of the European System of Central Banks and the European Banking Association, respectively, and the implementation (in 1999) of the EU Directive 97/5/EC of January 1997 on cross-border credit transfers are some visible examples. Kraus (2001) provides additional evidence that investment in the euro area increasingly follows sectoral, rather than national, criteria, indicating a gradual elimination of country risk (in addition to the elimination of the currency risk). One implication for the demand of finance could be an increased preference for direct finance motivated by a reduction both in transaction costs and in the liquidity and return risks. A reduction in transaction costs should follow from the elimination of conversion costs and exchange risk in currency transactions. Both elements should spur growth. Along with the impact of technological innovation on information transfer processes, lower transaction costs will narrow spreads between cross-border, intra-EMU as well as domestic trade, also making finance cheaper.

Table 1.3   International capital market comparison * *(values in euro billions, reporting period June 1999)*

	Euro 11		USA		Japan	
	Value	% of GDP	Value	% of GDP	Value	% of GDP
Bank loans	6136.1	100.4	4154.8	48.4	4280.8	107.0
Outstanding debt securities	5422.7	88.8	14140.8	164.6	5061.1	126.5
of which issued by:						
corporate	202.3	3.3	2493.8	29.0	583.4	14.6
financial institution	1891.5	31.0	3900.1	45.4	753.7	18.8
public sector	3329.0	54.5	7746.8	90.2	3723.9	93.1
Stock market capitalization*	4346.0	71.1	13861.1	163.3	6275.8	137.7

Note: *reporting period October 1999.

Source: European Central Bank.

A related phenomenon is likely to be the parallel increase in both demand and supply of euro-denominated bonds. From the demand side a larger number of bonds will be regarded as substitutes with respect to the pre-EMU situation, with the effect of increasing liquidity of bonds in general.[12] As a consequence, from the supply side, this will lead to an increase in the use of direct finance instruments by firms. Evidence in this respect is provided by the increasing relevance (both in terms of amount and in single issue dimensions) of private bonds issues by firms with less than first-class ratings.[13] At the same time, the number of feasible diversification strategies, fed by higher liquidity, also increases. Reduction in country risk and the increased integration in the euro area will encourage an increasingly large number of firms to collect venture capital in financial markets.

The Single Market: Specialization, Geography and Market Size

The two main channels through which the Single Market project should operate are first, the deepening of specialization along comparative advantage lines, which improves resource allocation and therefore growth and, second, the exploitation of scale economies given a larger market size after the elimination of national barriers. More than 15 years after the Single European Act and more than a decade since the official launching of the Single Market, evidence of the 'growth effects of 1992' is far from conclusive, given the still relative short time period and also (and especially) given that, over the past 15 years, the macroeconomic policy stance in Europe has been all but expansionary. Nonetheless some evidence on the effects on growth and structural change in European industry is available. In a report prepared for the EC Commission, Midelfart-Knarvik *et al.* (2001) show that industrial specialization in EU countries decreased from 1970 to 1980 and increased from 1980–83 to 1994–7, especially in small countries. More specifically, high return to scale, high-skill and high-tech industries are increasingly located in core regions, indicating the growing importance of economic geography factors in determining location, while skill-intensive industries are more widespread and also show higher rates of growth. Other evidence (Paci and Pigliaru, 2000, Padoan, 2000) also shows that specialization in the European Union increases more at the regional than at national level and (Padoan, 2000 ch. 8) that growth performance is associated with specialization as higher growth is positively related to more technologically advanced sectors.

Changes in sectoral specialization require investment and hence finance. Finance is needed to support both entry and exit strategies in (old and new) markets. These strategies, in turn, may take different forms (indirect supply through exports, direct supply through FDI, acquisitions of local firms, joint ventures and so on) according to the degree of geographical relocation of production and/or of parts of the product cycle. Both models of finance are involved in such processes. As firms seek to enter sectors that are new with respect to their core business they may want to resort to market financing if they cannot rely on solid customer relationships with credit institutions. In the latter case, however, there is a pressure on the banking sector to increase the diversification of their asset portfolios by financing activities in new sectors. Such a process, on the other hand, increases the propensity of the banking sector to adapt to the enlarged market by increasing diversification and internationalization.

The single market process also leads to a weakening of bureaucratic barriers, as well as a stronger pressure on specific interest groups and a weakening of their ability to impose sector-specific outcomes on policies and on the regulatory process. This influences the institutional and legal environment in which investment takes place and, through this channel, affects the evolution of the financial system. When an economy faces both cross-border trade and capital flows, competition from external sources in both the product and financial markets make it hard and unprofitable for domestic incumbents to keep the domestic financial sector repressed. Therefore the extent of an economy's openness can be used as a proxy for the strength of incumbents' opposition to financial development. In this respect Rajan and Zingales (1998) find a strong negative correlation between openness and the size of bureaucratic barriers to entry in a country. To the extent that the single market process eliminates national barriers, changes in financial markets responding to stronger competition are more likely to take place. This process is possibly even stronger in transition countries as institutional changes associated with entry in the EU are likely to be substantial.[14]

Enlargement and Catching Up

The so called 'southern enlargement' of the 1980s, involving Spain, Portugal and Greece, as well as Ireland, and the eastern enlargement, involving Central and Eastern European countries, extend EU membership to countries whose per capita income is significantly lower than that of the incumbent members. As a consequence of integration a catching-up process is set in motion through which per capita output of the new entrants eventually converges on that of the incumbents.

There are several channels through which catching up takes place. The two most relevant ones are the accumulation of capital and the transfer of technology. Capital accumulation takes place in backward regions because initial capital shortage increases return to investment with respect to advanced regions. Capital is accumulated both through domestic investment and through capital flows from abroad. Technology transfers also take place through different channels, including trade, capital flows as well as patent transfers, as returns to the application of technologies that are new for the entrant but old for the incumbents are higher in the former. Growth convergence can be absolute or, more likely, conditional. In addition, convergence can involve only a part of the laggard countries and, finally, convergence is likely to affect regions much more than countries in their entirety. For instance, Padoan (2000, ch. 8) finds that convergence among EU regions of EU15 excludes some of the poorest regions in some of the Mediterranean countries, thus suggesting the presence of 'convergence clubs', it is therefore conditional rather than absolute and it depends on sector-specific rather than country-specific characteristics. Interestingly Padoan (ibid.) also finds that convergence is faster in those regions where there is a strong presence of both advanced industrial sectors and well developed financial and banking sectors.

What financial system will support catching up most efficiently? Catching up is a long process and hence financing investment requires a long-term horizon, suggesting a role for bank-oriented rather than market-oriented systems. Technology transfer implies technology diffusion rather than 'pure' innovation activities. Again intertemporal investment smoothing is involved as technology is transferred from one country to another rather than from one sector to another. Obviously, to the extent that technology transfer is carried out through direct investment flows, banking systems of investing countries must be prepared to step up their internationalization strategies to follow business strategies.

Finally, as catching up involves economies in transition towards market-based systems, much of new investment will be associated with privatization processes, both in industry and in banking sectors. This suggests that market-based financial systems also have a relevant role in supporting catching up during enlargement to the extent that they are better equipped to support the privatization process.

THE US CASE: FINANCIAL MARKETS AND INFORMATION AND COMMUNICATION TECHNOLOGY

The performance of the US economy has radically changed over the last decade, bringing about a renewed American leadership in terms of productivity and income growth, and sweeping away all arguments in favour of a natural convergence of the other industrial economies towards the USA. The high and sustained US growth rates and the concomitant deceleration of growth in continental Europe over the 1990s highlight the role of ICT-related innovation as the main engine of growth in advanced economies. Some authors (for example, Allen, 1993) have suggested that, in periods of intense technological innovations, market-oriented financial systems perform better than the bank-oriented, which are more suited to stages of mature technology and standardized production processes. Such a conjecture, however, deserves a more careful scrutiny. The main macroeconomic features of the US growth story in the 1990s are well known and can be summarized as follows: very high investment rates and declining saving rates; a rise in employment and a fall in unemployment rates, accompanied by a sustained increase in labour productivity. These developments suggest a structural transformation in the labour market, decreasing the NAIRU (non-accelerating inflation rate of unemployment), leading to a price deceleration alongside sustained growth. US productivity growth in the second half of the 1990s was strong both in ICT-producing and ICT-using sectors. However data point to a clear distinction between the role of *technical progress* in the ICT-producing sectors, and the role of *labour productivity* growth in the ICT-using sectors (Jorgenson and Stiroh, 2000; Oliner and Sichel, 2000). Moreover much of the acceleration in aggregate US productivity growth after 1995 can be ascribed to an acceleration in the pace of technical progress in ICT-producing sectors, measured as faster relative price declines in high-tech industries. No strong evidence of spillover effects has been found. Hence, according to some views, the neoclassical constant-returns-to-scale paradigm looks appropriate as a heuristic framework to analyse the New Economy (Stiroh, 2001). Finally, software capital accumulation seems to have played a relevant role in US productivity dynamics in the second half of the 1990s (OECD, 2001).

In confronting the US and EU experiences, two key issues have to be investigated. First, to what extent is the US success story accounted for by the presence of a strong ICT-producing sector, which is lacking in a number of countries in Europe? In other words, is there an explanation based on comparative advantage in high-tech industries that is consistent with a windfall of technical progress in the USA but not in continental Europe? The second issue concerns the role of structural factors in the performance of the OECD economies, and in particular the impact of national financial markets in the different outcomes on the two sides of the Atlantic (and the Pacific as well). The financing of innovation is clearly one of the key issues, as it deals with the Schumpeterian perspective on the role of financial markets that is more appropriate in a dynamic approach. In such a perspective the contribution of capital markets to the development of the New Economy is crucial. Moreover comparative advantage itself should be interpreted in a dynamic perspective, and financial markets are important for understanding the international dynamics of output and trade specialization. Given these assumptions, could it be possible for Europe to catch up with the USA in ICT industries?

To analyse the role of comparative advantage, Roeger (2001) calibrates a two-sector–two-skill growth model of the US and European economies, featuring both an ICT-producing and an ICT-using sector, and skilled and unskilled labour. His model also allows for adjustment costs in the capital and labour markets: the first are associated with government regulations, organizational frictions within firms or inefficiencies in financial intermediaries that prevent companies to take prompt advantage of new technological developments. Labour market adjustment costs depend on hiring and firing costs due to national or regional regulations, and on relative wage inflexibility across skill groups (for the sake of simplicity, only two in the model). It is widely believed that factor markets are more flexible in the USA, and this could account for the better macroeconomic performance. Roeger provides some evidence showing that capital adjustment costs are lower in the USA, as the variability of the cyclically adjusted investment to GDP ratio has been higher in the USA than in Europe. As far as the labour market is concerned, his evidence questions the idea that higher European adjustment costs may be mainly due to hiring and firing regulations, while more support is found for the hypothesis of wage inflexibility across skill groups in Europe. However the main point is that, even if one includes differential adjustment costs in Europe and the USA in the model, the productivity growth gap is not explained by the features of factor markets. The main finding of Roeger is that higher rates of total factor productivity growth or technical progress, and not lower adjustment costs, are at the core of the productivity growth leap in the USA; in turn, TFP growth is associated with the comparative advantage the USA holds in the production of high-tech goods, hence comparative advantage and not Eurosclerosis in general must be blamed for the inferior growth performance in Europe.

A comprehensive study of the OECD (2001) takes an opposite position. It underlines that, when one accounts for software expenditure as a component of enterprise investment and not as intermediate consumption, the use of ICT looks more important as a determinant of output growth. In this perspective, being a relatively large ICT producer is not a necessary, and perhaps neither a sufficient, condition to benefit from the developments of the New Economy. Capital and labour markets are again at the centre of the stage among the key elements affecting the technology and income dynamics of national systems.

One reason why Roeger (2001) could have overstated the role of comparative advantage is that assessing the magnitude of adjustment costs is very difficult. However, his findings are corroborated by the evidence of a much stronger role of TFP growth in the USA than in Europe in the second half of the 1990s (though the contribution of software expenditure was understated in those analyses). Discriminating between these two polar positions is rather difficult, but not necessary for our discussion if we admit that comparative advantage may evolve over time, and that the nature and regulation of financial markets may affect output and trade specialization over time. If this is true, Europe might create the structural conditions for recovery in high-tech industries. If, instead, comparative advantage is not so important, the questions remain of how financial markets can positively affect productivity growth and how Europe can improve on the ground of productivity growth.

One could argue that, from the viewpoint of ICT-producing sectors, the increase in TFP and technical progress can be interpreted as a wave of innovation occurring in the US economy and spreading to the other economies. If this is correct, the role of financial markets and intermediaries can be related back to the issue of which financial system is most supportive of innovation. We have seen that there are contrasting views on this matter. Moreover, from the perspective of the ICT-using sectors, the contribution of the financial system to the New Economy can be identified with the role of banks and capital markets in the process of enterprise investment, leading to capital deepening in the context of a given production function and to the subsequent rise in average labour productivity (ALP). Therefore 'innovation' is at the centre of the stage if ICT-producing sectors are the focus of the analysis, while 'investment' is crucial if we consider the ICT-using sectors: despite a certain degree of simplification, this can be a fruitful conceptual framework to analyse the relations between finance and growth in the New Economy.

Anderson (2000) suggests that 'insider systems' based on close relations between banks and firms are better suited for supporting long-term investment in mature industries, hence they could perform quite well as far as the diffusion of ICT capital goods, but definitely less so as far as the financing of innovation by young firms or of start-ups in the ICT-producing sector are concerned. In the latter case, the development of financial markets is particularly relevant for two reasons. First, it favours mergers and acquisitions (M&A) that are needed to substitute new for old managers, and implementing industrial reorganization in innovating firms. M&A are conducive to the process of creative destruction that allows for a more rapid turnover of production factors across firms and sub-sectors in innovating industries. The second reason is that the creation and development of so-called 'new markets' lead to a stronger intensity of initial public offerings (IPOs) as well as to a bigger role for venture capital (VC), which can be important financial channels for innovating firms. International benchmarking shows that the USA is clearly ahead in terms of IPOs on 'new markets' and VC, and that US financial intermediaries such as pension funds are very active in supporting innovating firms. Continental Europe is behind, both in IPOs on 'new markets' and in VC, which is mainly provided by banks.

Phelps and Zoega (2001) have provided evidence suggesting that recent investment booms could be affected by stock market variables. In particular they investigate how financial variables may have affected the investment performance of several OECD economies that experienced an investment boom in the second half of the 1990s. Phelps and Zoega classify industrial economies in two main sets: those where an investment boom occurred in the 1990s (the Anglo-Saxon countries, Canada, the Netherlands and Sweden), and those where no investment boom has taken place (continental Europe). They argue that market capitalization, as evaluated in 1988, had a positive effect on investment booms, meaning that larger stock markets were conducive to more investment in the presence of technological opportunities. They also suggest that stock market turnover (that is, a measure of the intensity of property changes in the stock market) is negatively related to investment booms, meaning that a more stable ownership of equity capital is also conducive to investment.

The dilemma between bank- or market-based financial systems can therefore be restated in the context of the New Economy as follows. Market-based systems operate more efficiently whenever 'innovation' is the central driving force of growth, but in Europe the banking system has played an important role in the financing of VC and start-ups in the ICT sector. Bank-based models should in principle work better in the capital-deepening phase of the spread of the New Economy, but successful OECD countries with a stronger stock market are also those where an investment boom has materialized.

FURTHER EMPIRICAL RESULTS

We now present some new empirical results presented in Mariani and Padoan (2003) that take into account the points raised above, with particular respect to the interaction between finance and growth when different growth mechanisms are taken into account. They estimate the role of financial variables on growth in major OECD countries, considering different growth variables: GDP, investment, productivity and technological progress. They also consider different financial variables related to both bank- and market-based finance. The basic idea is that the different growth variables (for example, investments and productivity growth), because of the different underlying growth mechanisms they rest upon, are likely to be affected by different financial variables (this view is shared by Benhabib and Spiegel, 2000). Mariani and Padoan (2003) consider country-specific growth–finance interactions. These specificities stem from two basic aspects that we have discussed: the role of growth factors varies across national economies and the relative weight of credit versus market finance affects growth differently across countries. The generic equation they use can be written as:

$$\Delta G = f\,(FIN,\ INT,\ CM,\ X),$$

where G is the growth variable, FIN is the vector of financial development variable(s), INT is the real interest rate, CM is a dummy accounting for integration effects (in the case of the EU) or country-specific effects, and X are additional variables.

Results are as follows. First, when output enters as dependent variable, finance is never significant in the long run, with the exception of France, where credit positively affects growth. On the other hand, credit is always significant in the short run for all countries considered. The variable capturing the effects of the financial market is significant in the short run in the case of the USA. Second, when investment enters as a dependent variable, credit variables are significant in the long run for the large continental EU countries, while market variables are significant for some EU countries and never significant for the UK and the USA. Third, when growth is measured by technological progress financial variables, both credit and market are significant in the long run. Exceptions to this pattern include France, for which only credit is significant, and Italy, for which only credit is weakly significant in the short term. So Mariani and Padoan (2003) reach the following general conclusions. Finance affects growth through different channels (GDP, investment, productivity, technology); both banks and markets have an impact on growth. The rise of an innovation-related bubble at the end of the 1980s increased the importance of market-based finance in boosting technology-driven growth, but credit finance has maintained a significant role in supporting investment-driven growth (which may be associated in part with enhanced process innovation). While there is evidence of similar growth finance relations across countries, the growth-finance nexus is far from homogeneous. National specificities matter both because growth is driven by different factors with different intensity in different countries and because the relative weight of credit and market finance varies across countries. In general market finance is more relevant in countries where technology-driven growth is more important. However, there is no clear evidence that financial markets have played a major role in explaining superior macroeconomic performance in the USA to that of continental EU economies.

These results are consistent with the view that financial development (irrespective of the distinction between bank-based and market-based systems) supports growth through financial efficiency, by contributing to productivity in general or to technological progress. The distinction between embodied or disembodied technological progress matters, as far as the different role of market and credit is concerned, to the extent that (IT-related) innovation and embodied technological progress require more market-based financial systems. But, to the extent that process innovation, itself partly related to new technologies, is investment-driven, credit finance might continue to play a relevant role. As we have mentioned, investment too can be considered as a vehicle of innovation both to the extent that new capital goods incorporate new technologies and to the extent that capital deepening may be associated with process innovation. These results have implications for the process of EU integration, both in financial and other markets. Giannetti *et al.* (2002) have highlighted the benefits of financial integration in the EU for overall growth. While we share this view, in assessing the benefits of financial integration we must take into account that (a) as financial integration proceeds so does real integration, especially as the benefits of innovation spread through Europe: as a consequence real growth may be affected by factors other than financial integration; (b) the direction of causality between real and financial integration remains an open issue and, as financial integration is itself influenced by growth, the impact on growth of financial integration may be larger as a virtuous circle develops; (c) comparative advantage might change in the process and so would the 'optimal' dependence on external finance, especially as Europe increasingly benefits from technology-driven growth; (d) the distinction between market-based and credit based external finance might persist in different countries and the impact on different growth factors would be different; (e) national inertia in factors driving growth and finance–industry relations may slow down the move towards a common benchmark.

CONCLUSIONS

The performance of the US economy over the past decade has been significantly better than that of continental Europe. We have looked at this issue, asking what role financial markets have played in this respect. In the first part of this chapter we have reviewed the main approaches to the role of finance in supporting growth in the literature. While several different perspectives have been taken in the theoretical debate, empirical results have not come to firm conclusions. In particular, while there is evidence that finance and growth are correlated, it is not clear which one of the two financing models, market-based or finance-based, is more conducive to growth. Evidence is even less conclusive on another related issue: to what extent the financial system shapes the 'real' system, or the opposite holds. Indeed, if anything emerges from the evidence, it is that each of the two main financing models contributes to growth as circumstances, countries and time periods change.

This leads to a more general conclusion. Investigation of the growth–finance nexus has been based on the assumption that, while several financial models exist, only one growth mechanism is available. We suggest that this is not the case: several growth models exist and each one of them interacts differently with financial systems. We have developed this point with respect to EU integration, which is characterized by several growth mechanisms. We have identified a number of growth mechanisms each associated with one specific integration and growth process: market size, geography and resource allocation (single market); lower transaction costs and financial integration (EMU); catching up (enlargement); innovation and diffusion (ICT and the new economy). If we accept the idea that several growth mechanisms coexist then the analysis of the growth–finance nexus should consider the relationship between growth and financial variables conditional upon the specific growth mechanism which is associated with different countries, sectors and time periods. We have reported evidence that this is indeed the case. Different financial models as well as different growth mechanism coexist in Europe. To some extent at least this marks a difference from the case of the US economy, where the strong performance has been largely driven by ITC-driven innovation, itself supported by market-based finance.

NOTES

1. Respectively, University of Perugia and University of Rome, 'La Sapienza' and IMF. The IMF is not responsible for the contents of this chapter.
2. What follows draws largely on Carettoni *et al.* (2001).
3. Empirical evidence of the negative relationship between investors protection and ownership concentration is provided by La Porta *et al.* (1996) who examine a sample of 49 countries divided on the basis of four different legal traditions: English common law, French civil law, German civil law and Scandinavian civil law.
4. The positive relationship between capital markets development and investors protection is investigated by La Porta *et al.* (1997).
5. Such a statement, while in principle correct, does not, paradoxically, apply to France which, on the contrary, has well adapted its legal system to the evolution of the economic environment.

6. See Andrès *et al.* (1999).
7. Estimation results indicate that banks' contribution to growth is from three to seven times greater than that of markets.
8. Referring to Levine and Zervos's contribution, Rajan and Zingales write: 'The two studies should be viewed as complementary, theirs providing information on a broader set of correlations, while ours details a mechanism.'
9. Their analysis covers 41 countries and 36 sectors and the period 1980–90.
10. Defined as the ratio (capital expenditures–cash flow)/capital expenditures.
11. This covers both the southern enlargement, involving Spain, Portugal and Greece, and the eastern enlargement, involving Central and Eastern European countries.
12. It has been argued that, within a single capital market, an equilibrium characterized by several sub-markets with different degrees of liquidity might originate (Pagano, 1989). This would result from a self-sustaining mechanism of market segmentation as the return spreads between bonds that are theoretically perfect substitutes imply different liquidity risks that, in their turn, justify and support the return spread.
13. In 1998, for instance, bond issues valued at more than one billion euros increased, while, in the first nine months of 1999, 46 per cent of new bonds exhibited a single A rating, lower than double and triple A ratings that prevailed in pre-EMU issues.
14. Wagner and Iakova (2001) note that, in transition countries, financial markets are largely bank-based.

REFERENCES

Allen, F. (1993), *Stock Market and Resources Allocation, in Capital Markets and Financial Intermediation*, Cambridge: Cambridge University Press.

Allen, F. and D. Gale (1994), 'A welfare comparison of the German and US financial systems', LSE Financial Markets Group, Discussion paper series, n.191.

Anderson, T. (2000), 'Seizing the opportunities of a new economy: challenges for the EU', Directorate for Science, Technology and Industry OECD mimeo.

Andrès, J., I. Hernando and J.D. Lopez (1999), 'The role of the financial system in the growth inflation link: the OECD experience', Banco de España working paper.

Arestis P., P.O. Demetriades and K.B. Luintel (2001), 'Financial development and economic growth', *Journal of Money, Credit and Banking*, February.

Beck, T. and R. Levine (2002), 'Industry growth and capital allocation: does having a market- or bank-based system matter?', NBER working paper no. 8982.

Beck, T., A. Demirgüç-Kunt and R. Levine (2001), 'Law, politics, and finance, World Bank, working paper.

Benhabib, J. and M.M. Spiegel (2000), 'The role of financial development in growth and investment', *Journal of Economic Growth*, 5, 341–60.

Carettoni, A., S. Manzocchi and P.C. Padoan (2001), 'The Growth–finance nexus and European integration: a review of the literature', UN-INTECH EIFC working paper 01–5, Maastricht.

Cetorelli, N. and M. Gambera (1999), 'Banking market structure, financial dependence and growth: international evidence from industry data', Federal Reserve Bank of Chicago.

Danthine, J.-P., F. Giavazzi and E.L. von Thadden (2000), 'European financial markets after EMU: a first assessment', CEPR, discussion paper n.2413.

Davies, E.P. (2001), 'Multiple avenues of intermediation, corporate finance and financial stability', IMF Working Paper 01/115.

European Central Bank (2000), *Monthly Bulletin*, May.

Ferri G., P.L. Morelli and G.B. Pittaluga (1997), Banche e Mercati: sostituibilità e complementarietà nella ripartizione dei rischi, Quaderni di Finanza, Consob.

Fischer, K. (1990), 'Hausbankziehungen als Instrument der bindung zwischen Banken und unternehmen: eine theoritische und empirische Analyse', doctoral dissertation, University of Bonn.

Giannetti, M., L. Guiso, T. Jappelli, M. Padula and M. Pagano (2002), 'Financial market integration, corporate financing and economic growth', European Commission Economic Paper, no. 179.

Goldsmith, R. (1969), *Financial Structure and Development*, New Haven: Yale University Press.

Jorgenson, D. and K.J. Stiroh (2000), 'Raising the speed limit: US economic growth in the information age', *Brookings Papers on Economic Activity*, 125–235.

King R.G. and R. Levine (1993), 'Finance, entrepreneurship and growth', *Journal of Monetary Economics*, **3**, 513–40.

Kraus, T. (2001), 'The impact of EMU on the structure of European Equity returns: an empirical analysis of the first 21 months', IMF Working Paper WP/01/84.

La Porta, R., F. Lopez-de-Silanes, A. Shleifer and R.W. Visny (1996), 'Law and finance', NBER working paper n.5661.

La Porta, R., F. Lopez-de-Silanes, A. Shleifer and R.W. Visny (1997), 'Legal determinants of external finance', *The Journal of Finance*, **52**, 1131–50.

Leahy, M., S. Schich, G. Wehinger, F. Pelgrin and T. Thorgeirsson (2001), 'Contribution of financial systems to growth in OECD countries', OECD working paper n.280.

Levine, R. (1997), 'Financial development and economic growth: views and agenda', *Journal of Economic Literature*, **35**, 688–726.

Levine, R. and S. Zervos (1998), 'Stock market, banks, and economic growth', *The American Economic Review*, **88**, 537–58.

Maher, M. and T. Andersonn (2001), 'Corporate governance: effects on firm performance and economic growth', OECD Working paper.

Mariani, F. and P.C. Padoan (2003), 'The growth–finance nexus and European integration: a macroeconomic perspective', UN-INTECH EIFC working paper, Maastricht.

Mayer C. (1996), 'Corporate governance, competition and performance', *OECD Economic Studies*, **27**, 7–34.

Midelfart-Knarvik, H., H. Overman, J. Redding and A. Venables (2001), 'The location of European industry', *European Economy*, 4.

OECD (2001), 'The impact of information and communication technology on output growth: issues and preliminary considerations', OECD Directorate for Science, Technology and Industry, SWP 2001/11.

Oliner, S. and D. Sichel (2000), The resurgence of growth in the late 1990s: is information technology the story? *Journal of Economic Perspectives.*

Paci, R. and F. Pigliaru (2000), 'Technological catching-up and regional convergence in Europe', papers of the European Regional Science Association conference.

Padoan, P.C. (2000), *Monetary Union, Employment and Growth*, Cheltenham, UK and Northampton, MA, USA: Edward Elgar.

Pagano, M. (1989), 'Trading volume and asset liquidity', *Quarterly Journal of Economics*, **104**, 255–74.

Phelps, E. and G. Zoega (2001), 'Structural booms: productivity expectations and asset valuations', *Economic Policy*, **32** (April), 85–126.

Rajan, J. and L. Zingales (1998), 'Financial dependence and growth', *The American Economic Review*, **88**.

Roeger, W. (2001), 'The contribution of information and communication technologies to growth in Europe and the US: a macroeconomic analysis', European Commission economic paper 147.

Stiroh, K.J. (2001), 'What drives productivity growth?', *Economic Policy Review*, Federal Reserve Bank of New York **7**(1), 37–60.

von Thadden, E.L. (1990), 'Bank finance and long-term investment', WWZ Discussion paper n.9010, University of Basle.

Wagner N., and D. Iakova (2001), 'Financial sector evolution in the Central European economies: challenges in supporting macroeconomic stability and sustainable growth', IMF working paper WP/01/.

2. Atlantic interdependent knowledge-based economies

Simona Iammarino and Daniele Archibugi*

International collaborations are a significant and increasingly important channel of diffusion of knowledge in both the public and the business sectors. Their importance has grown, as testified by the number of partnerships among public research centres, universities and firms (National Science Foundation, 2002). Collaboration for knowledge creation and diffusion has received a widespread consensus from analysts. It has been stressed that collaboration allows increasing the number of agents able to benefit from knowledge, and that it provides expanding learning opportunities. It permits the partners to share each other's expertise, by enriching overall know-how (Hagedoorn *et al.*, 2000). Collaborations can be seen as a positive sum game and the partners acquire more advantages than disadvantages, although the net gains are not always equally distributed among them (see Gambardella and Malerba, 1999, esp. p II).

However different propensities towards knowledge collaboration characterize different economies. Such propensities are in fact highly dependent on cultural specificities, societal norms, industrial structures and a broad range of institutions that influence economic performance (Lundan, 2003). A crucial factor in determining the propensity to knowledge collaboration is the link between firms' behaviour and institutional settings, which varies typically between 'coordinated' economies, such as many European countries and Japan, and 'liberal market' economies, such as the USA, but also the UK. It has been pointed out that, while in the former cooperation tends to be based on consensus, occurring traditionally through industry associations, and is disciplined by standardized contractual arrangements, in the latter knowledge sharing among firms is mainly conducted through market channels and under a legal system which allow 'free' contracting (ibid.). Thus cultural features, institutional change and policy orientation in the triad of the USA, Europe and Japan strongly affect corporate strategies in the use of opportunities for collaboration and alliances formation (Boyd and Rugman, 2003).

This chapter aims to analyse whether and to what extent European Union (EU) policy has influenced the scope and the trend of European international collaborations for innovative activities. We will take into account two forms of international collaborations for knowledge sharing: strategic technology agreements among firms from different countries; and international academic collaborations among researchers.[1]

We assume that collaborations can be viewed as an indicator of the vitality of a national knowledge system and that they are beneficial for the country as a whole. A country is often involved in collaboration if its institutions have an attractive knowledge base that is appealing for institutions based in other countries. At the same time, collaborations make it possible to plug into the knowledge system of other economies, allowing national institutions to upgrade or diversify their competencies (Cantwell and Iammarino, 2003).

In the next section we will provide a short overview of European science and technology policy and its main features. The following two sections will present some evidence on international collaborations for science and technology across the triad (Europe–USA–Japan), by focusing in particular on the comparison between the EU and the USA. Our data show that the USA has substantially augmented its participation in strategic technology partnering among firms, while Europe has recently lost significant positions; in academic collaboration, however, the EU has increased its role, whilst the USA has relatively declined. The last section summarizes the main findings and highlights questions for future research.

KNOWLEDGE COLLABORATION AND POLICY IN THE EUROPEAN UNION

Much collaboration has occurred without a deliberate promotion by public policies. Firms have found it convenient to split the costs and risks associated with innovative programmes, and this has often induced them to share strategic know-how with actual and potential competitors. Academic researchers – a social group that has traditionally been oriented towards knowledge sharing within and across national borders – have substantially benefited from the new information and communication technologies to work in coordination with colleagues in geographically remote locations.

Also policy makers have been keen to enhance further the propensity to share know-how. Governments have welcomed the idea to devote public resources to collaborative ventures, since it increases the number of players gaining from public support and it is very likely to multiply the benefits of investment in knowledge. It is therefore not surprising that schemes to promote collaboration within academia, among firms and between academia and firms, have proliferated. These policies have not been confined to the national level: on the contrary, more attention has been devoted to bilateral and multilateral international cooperation as an instrument for acquiring and disseminating expertise that is not available at the country level.

A straightforward example is European science and technology policy (STP), which aims at enhancing European cooperation in the activities of research and technological development (RTD). EU institutions have based their support of scientific and technological development upon the promotion of collaboration as a rather 'natural' outcome of a multi-government policy. Europe as a whole has felt the need to bridge (or at least not to widen) the scientific and technological gap with the USA. The budget and the competencies of each European country, including those of the largest ones, such as Germany, France and the UK, would not allow, in the majority of fields, competing with the USA. This has led EU institutions to fund research on a cooperative basis as a way to reach a sufficient critical mass to obtain excellence, and with the view that cooperative research, by involving a large number of players, will disseminate the results across a wider number of member countries. At the same time, this has also been conceived as an instrument to increase socioeconomic cohesion within the Union.

The idea of fostering collaboration in the EU through public policies has counterbalanced the fact that the main competitors of European firms are likely to be other firms based in Europe: the closest neighbour is likely to be the fiercest rival. Thus policies spurring intra-area inter-firm collaboration should also overcome the reluctance of competitors to share such a crucial strategic asset as technological expertise.

The main instrument used by the EU is a plan of financial aid to research projects known as the Framework Programme (FP), implemented every five years by the European Commission with the approval of the Council and Parliament. The bulk of the resources are attributed through competitive tenders which, among a range of requirements, also privilege co-participation from private and public organizations based in more than one EU member state.

In recent years European institutions have concentrated more and more their resources on 'priority' research areas, corresponding to the most innovative sectors: life-science and biotechnology, information society, energy and environment and sustainable growth. In their policy framework, they have included as well three main objectives, considered strategic for both economic and social reasons:

- support to small and medium enterprises (SME), critical for innovation and job creation;
- involvement of the least developed areas around the EU (Eastern Europe, the newly independent states, the Mediterranean countries) through a plan of international co-operation;
- upgrading of human capital, by means of an intense process of training and mobility of researchers that allows a continuous acquisition and exchange of knowledge across academia, industry and other institutions.

Cooperation among firms and public research organizations across countries would help to achieve all these goals.

The EU had to face another dilemma, namely how to make sure that the financial resources given to a single actor or a group of economic agents would not distort competition. The European integration process began as a custom union in order to develop a 'common' but also 'competitive' market, and it would have been contradictory for the EU itself to carry out any intervention that could distort competition. However, in the field of science and technology it has conventionally been more acceptable than in other traditional fields (such as agriculture or steel) to provide selected organizations only with funds, since it was expected that the benefits of RTD would have been propagated across the whole Union.

This has led to the release of funds for so-called 'pre-competitive' research. It has long been argued whether anything like 'pre-competitive' research does indeed exist (Jorde and Teece, 1990). However, as a rule of thumb, the EU Commission is probably right in assuming that, if a research grant is assigned to a consortium composed of a variety of organizations based in different countries, it is less likely that it will benefit a specific national industry and harm potential competitors. And the Commission is certainly right in supposing that the production of knowledge would generate direct and indirect benefits not only for the actors receiving EU funding.

How influential is the EU science and technology policy? Concerning the financial budget, it has grown with every FP, reaching in the current one (FP6, for the period 2002–6) the sum of 16270 million euros, with a 18 per cent rise as compared to FP5 (1998–2002) and a 36 per cent increase with respect to FP4 (1994–8). However it remains limited, accounting for no more than 5 per cent of the total EU budget and just 5.5 per cent of the total spending of member state governments for civil RTD (see Sharp, 2001, p. 243; European Commission, 2002, p. 20). For a more comprehensive assessment of EU policies, see Peterson and Sharp (1998). The impact of these resources is probably larger than their simple quantitative weight, as the EU finances additional projects, it privileges cofunded projects and it has a greater flexibility than the national budgets. Furthermore diverse but complementary forms of collaboration are enhanced through policies other than STP, such as those for industry, socioeconomic cohesion, transport, trans-European networks and so on.

As already pointed out, among the various structural factors underlying the different propensity to collaborate over knowledge in Europe and in the USA, different orientations in public policies have probably played a major role. For instance, the US antitrust policy that began in the early 1980s and continued throughout the 1990s has progressively relaxed the traditional argument of 'pre-competitive' research, at the same time tightly linking collaboration in production with that in research (Barfield and Thum, 2003). Also deregulation processes, particularly in telecommunications and services, have been far more dramatic in the USA than in Europe, strengthening the impact of regulatory policies on partnership formation in the American economy. Moreover it has to be noted that the process of harmonization of technical standards among the EU countries has occurred rather recently, and that national standards (especially for high-technology products) were much more differentiated within Europe than in the USA, giving rise to market segmentation and discouraging partnership. Other forms of regulation, policies for trade and investment and public procurement practices have tended to be comparatively more restrictive in the 'old continent', hampering in various ways knowledge collaboration within the Union, particularly among firms.

All these factors and, more in general, the coexistence of both national and supranational dimensions of the propensity of European countries to cooperate in innovative activities, should be taken into account in the interpretation of the evidence on international collaborations for science and technology provided in the following two sections.

STRATEGIC TECHNOLOGY AGREEMENTS

A strategic industrial technology agreement is defined as a partnership showing the following three characteristics: it involves a two-way relationship where knowledge is a crucial component; it is contractual in nature with no or little equity involvement by the participants; and it is strategic in the sense that it is a long term planned activity (Mowery, 1992; Mytelka, 2001).

It is well known that this form of knowledge sharing has substantially increased over the last 20 years. Figure 2.1 reports the trend of the absolute number of yearly interregional technological alliances for the USA, Europe and Japan in the period 1980–2000 (see Hagedoorn, 1996, 2002; NSF, 2002). The USA and Europe show the same trend: a uniform growth except the two falls following the Gulf war in 1990–91 and the Kosovo war in 1999. Foreign alliances of Japanese companies have kept fairly steady over the last 20 years.

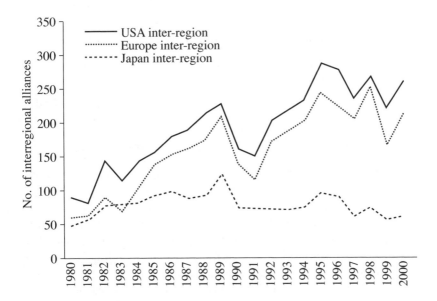

Source: National Science Foundation (2002).

Figure 2.1   Trends of interregional alliances in the triad, 1980–2000

International technology agreements are a source of knowledge and signal where companies seek expertise (Narula and Hagedoorn, 1999). Some evidence on the distribution of inter-firm technological collaboration is reported in Table 2.1. We consider the strategic technology alliances between and within the three main economic blocs.[2] International alliances have more than doubled. Alliances between blocs represent 42.4 per cent of the total in the last sub-period (1998–2000), but the share has substantially decreased over time (it was almost 53 per cent at the beginning of the 1980s).

In fact, the geographical distribution of alliances shows that the largest and fastest increasing portion is to be found within the USA: 45.8 per cent of all strategic technological alliances recorded in 1998–2000 occurred among American firms only, and this share has increased exceptionally with respect to the past (it was 34.7 per cent of the total at the beginning of the 1990s and 24.6 in the early 1980s). Of all US alliances, 54 per cent are pan-American, and 45.9 per cent involve foreign firms, yet US firms have

Table 2.1   Distribution of strategic technology alliances between and within economic blocs, 1980–2000

		Interregional alliances			
		Europe–Japan		Europe–USA	
Year	Triad total	no.	(%)	no.	(%)
1980–82	203	16	7.9	48	23.6
1989–91	404	25	6.2	101	25.0
1998–00	542	19	3.5	173	31.9

Source: Our elaboration from National Science Foundation (2002).

strong ties on both the Atlantic and the Pacific shores: in the most recent years (1998–2000), US companies have participated in as much as 84.7 per cent of all recorded technology alliances (against 69.5 per cent of the first period (1980–1982)). Inter-firm strategic technological alliances almost always imply the participation of at least one American company (see Vonortas, 1997). Among the reasons for such an outstanding involvement of US firms in overall technological alliances, a few factors seem to be particularly relevant: the significant national market in terms of both size and competition; the comparatively broader science and technology base; the larger number of leading corporations, operating in different industrial sectors and with richer tangible and intangible assets; the above-mentioned development of the antitrust regulation (Barfield and Thum, 2003).

In contrast, the share of intra-European strategic technological alliances has substantially declined: they accounted for 18.2 per cent of the total in 1980–82, and for less than 10 per cent in 1998–2000; they even decreased in absolute terms over the 1990s. On the other hand, European–US partnerships have gone up, both in relative terms (from 23.6 to 31.9 per cent) and in absolute terms (they have more than tripled as compared with two decades ago). While American companies have a weaker incentive to plug into the innovation systems of other countries, and manage to exploit their know-how abroad even in the absence of international strategic partnerships, European firms (even more than Japanese firms) need to share competencies with American counterparts (Narula and Hagedoorn, 1999).

But the most worrying result is the decline of pan-European strategic technology partnerships, all the more so in light of the policies carried out at the EU level to foster intra-area collaboration (see Narula, 1998). One possible explanation might be that the absolute amount of resources devoted to science and technology is much higher in the USA, so that

Table 2.1 (*continued*)

			Intraregional alliances						
Japan–USA		Sub-total	Europe		Japan		USA		Sub-total
no.	(%)		no.	(%)	no.	(%)	no.	(%)	
43	21.2	107	37	18.2	9	4.4	50	24.6	96
57	14.1	183	74	18.3	7	1.7	140	34.7	221
38	7.0	230	53	9.8	11	2.0	248	45.8	312

the greatest flow of alliances in the latter would be simply the outcome of the amount of investment in knowledge by US companies. In order to control for this factor, we have divided the number of alliances established by the firms of the two economies (EU and USA) with European, US and Japanese firms, by the total amount of, respectively, European and US business enterprise R&D (BERD). This provides an indicator of the European (and US) companies' propensity towards collaboration in each region. The results are reported in Table 2.2.

The data confirm that European companies have a greater propensity for forming American rather than European partnerships. In the 1998–2000 period, there are 2.03 European–US partnerships for every billion dollar($) EU-BERD, whilst the equivalent figure for pan-European alliances is just 0.62. Moreover this result is consistent over time: in fact, the European business community has always shown a greater preference for partnership with American rather than European partners. The figures were, respectively, 1.03 and 0.80 agreements for each billion dollar EU-BERD in 1980–82, and 1.41 and 1.03 in 1989–91. Looking at the agreements signed with Japanese companies, both the European and, even more, the US tendency have in fact constantly decreased. On the other hand, as already noted, US companies have a pronounced and increasing preference for intra-area strategic technical partnerships, which have more than doubled in the last 20 years.

Therefore, also keeping out the differences in investment in R&D, it turns out that intra-European inter–firm strategic technology alliances are low. These trends have occurred in spite of EU policies: although FPs have been aimed at increasing European technology partnering, the latter has decreased. Certain factors can help to explain such a decline.

First, the FP budget is very low, as compared to the requests of the business community: it should be remembered that the current budget

Table 2.2   Propensities for forming strategic technical partnerships,
1980–2000

Propensity of European firms for European, US and Japanese
technological partners

Period	Number of agreements involving European firms by EU-BERD (in billion US$ at constant dollars PPP)		
	Europe–Europe	Europe–USA	Europe–Japan
1980–82	0.80	1.03	0.34
1989–91	1.03	1.41	0.35
1998–00	0.62	2.03	0.22

Propensity of US firms for European, US and Japanese technological
partners

Period	Number of agreements involving US firms by US-BERD (in billion US$ at constant dollars PPP)		
	USA–USA	USA–Europe	USA–Japan
1980–82	0.64	0.61	0.55
1989–91	1.20	0.86	0.49
1998–00	1.54	1.07	0.24

Source: our elaboration from NSF (2002) (data from MERIT database) and from OECD
Statistics, Main Science and Technology Indicators, 2001–2.

amounts to 16 270 million euros for four years, so approximately 4000
million a year, when the annual BERD in Europe has a magnitude of
about 100 000 million euros (OECD, 2002).

Second, the EU funds have different destinations: in the main research
areas, they are principally devoted to finance 'pre-competitive' research
projects, which, as already pointed out, do not always coincide with the
aims of industrial research, more inspired by criteria of competitiveness.
Furthermore a significant share of resources is destined to non-industrial
purposes (development of backward regions, upgrading of human resources
and so on).

Eventually what remains for European collaborative industrial projects
is relatively tiny, so that the choice European firms effectuate about the
partners is fundamentally dictated by managerial criteria. On the one hand,
partners in the USA seem to be more reliable generators of knowledge than

those in Europe. On the other hand, they are less likely to compete directly on the EU market. The deepening and widening of economic integration in Europe has increased competition, and this has made companies less keen to share technology (Narula, 1998; Molero and Heys, 2001).

More generally, the development of alliance capitalism in the EU has been constrained by cultural barriers and political differences between member states, which are reflected in their structural political rivalries not only with reference to innovation policy but in a variety of other fields of public intervention (Barfield and Thum, 2003; Boyd and Rugman, 2003). Yet the weight of fragmented national interests (along with the central position still occupied by national systems of innovation) cannot fully explain the difficulties of achieving an actual integration of European research. It has been pointed out that the systematic institutionalization of the EU S&T policy in the framework programme since the 1980s, with its strong distributive accent, may have represented a powerful source of 'institutional inertia', preventing the Commission from taking effective reforms towards greater partnership in innovative activities among firms, public laboratories and universities within the Union (Banchoff, 2002).

As far as the sectoral aspects are concerned, it is well known that the bulk of these technology alliances have taken place in emerging fields, and in particular in Information Technology (IT) and biotechnology. Table 2.3 shows that these two sectors concentrate two-thirds of the total agreements which occurred in recent years. Bearing in mind that these fields involve the highest costs and risks, the result is not a surprise. Biotechnology shows the highest growth rate over the last decade, climbing from 12 to 29 per cent of total alliances. From a geographical perspective, Europe is involved in alliances in biotechnology as much as in IT, while Japan and USA show a great prevalence in IT. This suggests that Europe is relatively stronger in biotechnology and weaker in IT with respect to the other two triad economies. The amount of the FP funds in the key areas of research in some sense confirms this evidence. Overall both the USA and Japan collaborate much more heavily in the high-tech sectors of biotechnology, ICT and new materials. Thus, as noted above and clearly highlighted by Lundan (2003), it might be argued that European firms would be less inclined to engage in alliances among themselves, and would rather engage in partnerships with US firms, whose knowledge base is sufficiently different also owing to the greater availability of venture capital and heavier emphasis on entrepreneurship. Indeed empirical research has confirmed that Europe suffers relative to the USA from having smaller and more fragmented markets for innovation and a lower overall knowledge base (Eaton et al., 1998).

*Table 2.3   International strategic technology alliances, by technology field
and selected region/country, 1980–2000*

Total	1980–82	(%)	1989–91	(%)	1998–00	(%)
Total	228	*100*	464	*100*	607	*100*
Information technology	68	*30*	206	*44*	228	*38*
Biotechnology	41	*18*	54	*12*	179	*29*
New materials	20	*9*	34	*7*	30	*5*
Aerospace and defence	14	*6*	47	*10*	21	*3*
Automotive	12	*5*	24	*5*	42	*7*
Chemicals (non-biotechnology)	32	*14*	57	*12*	49	*8*
Other	42	*18*	43	*9*	58	*10*
United States						
Total	156	*100*	321	*100*	499	*100*
Information technology	49	*31*	159	*49*	192	*39*
Biotechnology	32	*21*	39	*12*	154	*31*
New materials	12	*8*	23	*7*	22	*4*
Aerospace and defence	9	*6*	29	*9*	16	*3*
Automotive	5	*3*	15	*5*	29	*6*
Chemicals (non-biotechnology)	20	*13*	34	*11*	37	*7*
Other	28	*18*	22	*7*	49	*10*
Europe						
Total	109	*100*	230	*100*	264	*100*
Information technology	32	*29*	83	*36*	80	*30*
Biotechnology	13	*12*	29	*12*	79	*30*
New materials	12	*11*	18	*8*	14	*5*
Aerospace and defence	8	*7*	29	*13*	12	*4*
Automotive	8	*7*	9	*4*	24	*9*
Chemicals (non-biotechnology)	15	*14*	34	*15*	32	*12*
Other	20	*19*	29	*12*	24	*9*
Japan						
Total	71	*100*	97	*100*	75	*100*
Information technology	23	*32*	44	*45*	37	*50*
Biotechnology	12	*17*	8	*8*	11	*15*
New materials	5	*7*	9	*9*	8	*11*
Aerospace and defence	3	*4*	4	*4*	2	*2*
Automotive	4	*5*	11	*11*	7	*9*
Chemicals (non-biotechnology)	11	*16*	15	*15*	3	*4*
Other	14	*20*	7	*7*	7	*9*

Note: Total alliances are less than the sum of the alliances of USA, Europe and Japan
because the transnational alliances are counted once for each region involved.

Source: our elaboration from National Science Foundation (2002).

Finally another interesting indicator of inter-firm research cooperation across national boundaries can be derived by looking at the internationalization of multinational corporation (MNC) technological operations, as measured by the patents of the world's largest industrial firms attributable to research undertaken in foreign locations (outside the home country of the parent company). Indeed, in order to give an account of different performances in different countries or areas, it is crucial to consider the dynamics brought about by multinational activity, all the more so as large MNCs are the most active partners in strategic technological alliances.

Table 2.4a shows that the number of USPTO patents granted to foreign MNCs for research carried out in European countries has grown substantially since the 1980s: in the case of Japanese-owned firms (whose absolute figures, however, remain fairly small) it has more than doubled, while EU multinationals have increased by almost 60 per cent their internationalization of research within the area. US-owned affiliates have invested comparatively less in innovative activities located in the EU: the variation of patent numbers between 1983–6 and 1991–5 has been around 20 per cent. Also in this case, however, the relative preference of European firms to tap into the US national knowledge base appears to be confirmed: the number of patents granted to European subsidiaries for innovative activities located in the USA is the highest in absolute terms in all periods, and its average change between the early 1980s and the first half of the 1990s is above 70 per cent. Turning to the breakdown of such investments by technological field (Table 2.4b), it is interesting to note the greater sectoral dispersion of US research located in Europe: indeed other studies have indicated that both the US and Japanese MNCs are relatively more 'Europeanized' and their asset-seeking strategy is likely to have been relatively more sensitive to the distinctiveness of regional environments across Europe, rather than to opportunities offered by specific sectors (Cantwell and Iammarino, 2003). Instead MNCs from European countries seem to assume a more sectorally oriented perspective in the process of rationalization of their innovative operations, both within the integrated area and, even more, when investing in US locations.

ACADEMIC COLLABORATIONS

Partnerships and collaborations promoted by public research institutions and universities equally play a crucial role in the international dissemination of knowledge. The scope, complexity and cost of some of today's scientific problems suggest and often compel international collaborations among institutions of different countries. They can take a variety of forms: joint

Table 2.4a   Patents of the world's largest firms attributable to research undertaken in foreign locations by nationality of the parent firm (1983–1995)

Nationality of the parent firm and location of research activity	1983–86	1987–90	1991–95	Average change (%) 1991–5/1983–6
US-owned firms in Europe	3860	3857	4631	20.0
Japanese-owned firms in Europe	64	87	146	128.1
European-owned firms in Europe*	3607	4740	5706	58.2
European-owned firms in the USA	4381	5686	7504	71.3
European-owned firms in Japan	370	592	609	64.6

Note: * Investment in research by European-owned firms outside their home countries but in other European locations.

Source: John Cantwell's database on USPTO patents by MNCs.

Table 2.4b Patents of the world's largest firms attributable to research undertaken in foreign locations by technological field, 1983–95

Tech18	European-owned firms in the US (% on total)	Tech18	US-owned firms in Europe (% on total)	Tech18	European-owned firms in Europe* (% on total)
Chemicals	34.2	Mechanical engineering	21.0	Chemicals	24.0
Electrical equipment	15.8	Electrical equipment	18.0	Electrical equipment	22.8
Mechanical engineering	13.5	Chemicals	17.6	Mechanical engineering	18.0
Pharmaceuticals	11.7	Professional instruments	10.6	Professional instruments	10.2
Professional instruments	7.2	Pharmaceuticals	9.1	Pharmaceuticals	7.0
Office equipment	4.9	Metals	6.5	Office equipment	4.8
Metals	3.3	Office equipment	6.2	Metals	4.6
Non-metallic mineral products	2.9	Non-metallic mineral products	2.3	Non-metallic mineral products	2.8
Coal & petroleum products	1.4	Other transport equipment	2.1	Coal & petroleum products	0.9
Rubber products	1.2	Motor vehicles	1.8	Rubber products	0.9
Other manufacturing	1.2	Rubber products	1.2	Other manufacturing	0.8
Food products	1.0	Food products	0.8	Motor vehicles	0.8
Motor vehicles	0.6	Other manufacturing	0.8	Nuclear reactors	0.6
Other transport equipment	0.5	Power plants	0.7	Food products	0.6
Power plants	0.4	Coal & petroleum products	0.7	Power plants	0.4
Textiles	0.1	Textiles	0.4	Other transport equipment	0.4
Nuclear reactors	0.1	Nuclear reactors	0.2	Textiles	0.1
Aircraft	0.1	Aircraft	0.0	Aircraft	0.1
Total (abs. nos of patents) = 10017571		Total (abs. nos of patents) =10012348		Total (abs. nos of patents) = 10014053	

Note: *Investment in research by European-owned firms outside their home countries but in other European locations.

Source: John Cantwell's database on USPTO patents by MNCs.

research centres, exchange of scholars and students, sharing of scientific information. One way to measure these collaborations is by looking at internationally co-authored scientific papers. A dramatic increase in the internationally co-authored papers, also facilitated by the diffusion of Internet and e-mail, is evident for all countries.

Table 2.5 reports the internationally co-authored scientific papers in absolute terms for the years 1986 and 1999. The number of internationally

Table 2.5   Internationally co-authored papers, totals and growth rates, 1986 and 1999

	Internationally co-authored articles in 1986	Internationally co-authored articles in 1999	Annual growth rate from 1986 to 1999 (%)
United States	17 187	39 669	6.6
Japan	2 509	9 275	10.6
Austria	687	2 369	10.0
Belgium	1 313	3 733	8.4
Denmark	1 025	2 813	8.1
Finland	589	2 214	10.7
France	4 932	13 905	8.3
Germany	5 805	18 340	9.3
Greece	362	1 250	10.0
Ireland	243	753	9.1
Italy	2 620	8 551	9.5
Netherlands	1 830	5 654	9.1
Portugal	160	1 129	16.2
Spain	911	5 569	14.9
Sweden	1 935	4 887	7.4
United Kingdom	6 554	16 806	7.5
Canada	4 375	8 665	5.4
Norway	568	1 589	8.2
Switzerland	2 174	5 385	7.2

Notes: Article counts are on a whole-count basis where each country author receives a whole count on internationally co-authored papers. Internationally co-authored papers consist of papers that have at least one international co-author. We could not calculate the EU total because the sum of EU countries would contain multiple countings (a paper co-authored by a French and a Belgian would be counted twice, and so on).

Source: Institute for Scientific Information, Science Citation and Social Citation Indexes; CHI Research, Inc., Science Indicators database; and National Science Foundation, Division of Science Resources Statistics (2002).

co-authored papers has at least doubled, and in some countries even tripled. It is interesting to examine the geographical evolution. The USA is still the country with the highest participation in internationally co-authored papers, and this is not surprising taking into account the size of its scientific community. But if we look at the dynamics, the situation changes abruptly: in the last 15 years USA and Canada have shown the lowest growth rates. This has led to a decrease in the US world's share of internationally co-authored scientific papers. From Figure 2.2, it is possible to infer that,

Internationally co-authored articles, 1986

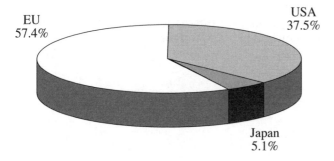

Internationally co-authored articles, 1999

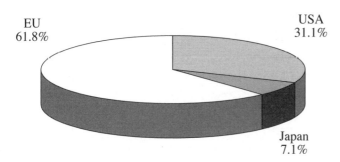

Note: Articles are assigned to every country on a fractional basis (one-half if it is co-authored between two countries and so on).

Source: our elaboration from National Science Foundation (2002).

Figure 2.2   Distribution of internationally co-authored articles across the triad, 1986 and 1999

between 1986 and 1999, both EU and Japanese shares rose at the expense of the USA.[3]

Table 2.6 presents the same data as in Table 2.5, from a different perspective: internationally co-authored articles are divided by total scientific articles for 1986 and 1999. In this way, it is straightforward to compare the evolution of both total scientific articles and internationally co-authored ones. The percentage doubles in most cases in the considered period, and this represents a clear signal of globalization in the generation

Table 2.6　Internationally co-authored scientific papers as a percentage of all scientific papers, 1986 and 1999

	Internationally co-authored in 1986 (%)	Internationally co-authored in 1999 (%)	Annual growth rate from 1986 to 1999 (%)
USA	9.2	21.6	6.8
Japan	7.5	17.6	6.7
Austria	25.2	47.6	5.0
Belgium	29.9	52.5	4.4
Denmark	24.4	48.5	5.4
Finland	18.7	42.0	6.4
France	21.0	39.6	5.0
Germany	20.1	38.4	5.1
Greece	26.6	42.1	3.6
Ireland	26.7	44.7	4.0
Italy	22.9	39.4	4.3
Netherlands	19.8	41.2	5.8
Portugal	34.8	52.8	3.3
Spain	17.0	36.2	6.0
Sweden	22.2	44.1	5.4
UK	15.7	34.1	6.1
Canada	18.9	35.4	5.0
Norway	21.9	44.9	5.7
Switzerland	32.2	52.4	3.8

Note:　National rates are based on total counts: each collaborating country is assigned one paper (a paper with three international co-authors may contribute to the international co-authorship of three countries and so on). We could not calculate the EU total, as it would contain multiple counting.

Source:　our elaboration from National Science Foundation, 2002 (data from ISI – Institute for Scientific Information).

of knowledge. It emerges that European countries have a higher share of articles in international collaboration than the USA and Japan. This fact is not surprising given the smaller size of the scientific community in each individual European country (Pianta and Archibugi, 1991; Archibugi and Pianta, 1992), but it also indicates that the academic community in Europe as a whole is perceived as a valuable asset for the acquisition of knowledge and expertise.

From a dynamic viewpoint, however, the rate of growth has been slightly higher in USA and Japan than in European countries. This finding deserves attention: from 1986 to 1999, the USA has grown more than Europe and Japan in the percentage of internationally co-authored articles in total articles (Table 2.6); but its absolute number has increased less (Table 2.5). This means that the USA has not only decreased its world share with regard to internationally co-authored articles (as Figure 2.2 shows) but also with respect to total scientific articles. In addition, the loss of shares in total scientific output has been greater than the loss of shares in the portion constituted by the internationally co-authored scientific articles.

A way to represent graphically the relation between absolute and relative size of the academic collaborative phenomenon is to place the countries in a two-dimensional space where, on the horizontal axis, we measure the absolute number of internationally co-authored articles[4] and on the vertical one their percentage of total articles. In Figure 2.3, referring to 1999, the

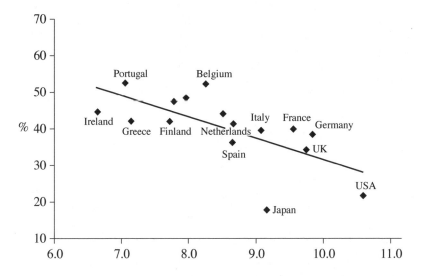

Figure 2.3   Relation between the absolute dimension of international co-authored articles and their ratio to the total articles, 1999

Table 2.7 Distribution of internationally co-authored papers across collaborating countries, 1986–8 and 1995–7

Country	Year	USA	Jap	EU	UK	Ger	Fra
USA	1986–8		8.2	54.9	12.7	11.8	8.3
USA	1995–7		9.6	60.3	12.4	12.8	8.9
Japan	1986–8	54.0		33.3	7.0	10.2	5.1
Japan	1995–7	45.6		39.4	9.1	9.9	5.7
EU	1986–8	31.9	3.1	56.6	10.3	10.4	9.0
EU	1995–7	29.0	4.5	69.4	12.1	12.1	10.9
UK	1986–8	33.9	2.9	46.3		10.2	8.2
UK	1995–7	30.6	4.7	60.2		12.6	10.7
Germany	1986–8	31.1	4.1	47.9	10.2		9.5
Germany	1995–7	30.0	4.9	58.6	11.9		11.5
France	1986–8	28.9	2.7	54.7	10.7	12.5	
France	1995–7	26.1	3.5	66.7	12.7	14.4	
Italy	1986–8	35.7	2	64.3	14.5	13.1	15.5
Italy	1995–7	32.6	3.5	76.3	15.4	14.8	16.7
Netherlands	1986–8	31.1	2.7	73.7	16.4	17.5	10.4
Netherlands	1995–7	29.2	3.9	85.4	18.4	17.6	11.8
Sweden	1986–8	36.1	2.7	61.2	12.0	12.1	7.4
Sweden	1995–7	28.8	4.5	73.2	12.6	13.5	8.8
Denmark	1986–8	29.6	2	73.2	15.4	14.8	7.3
Denmark	1995–7	29.0	3.4	94.1	17.9	16.4	9.6
Finland	1986–8	33.1	2.4	71.3	11.2	14.7	5.6
Finland	1995–7	32.1	4.8	89.0	12.4	14.9	9.3
Belgium	1986–8	25.9	3	83.7	11.8	13.8	22.8
Belgium	1995–7	22.9	2.9	97.6	14.1	14.8	23.8
Austria	1986–8	25.8	3	78.5	8.4	38.6	7.0
Austria	1995–7	25.1	2.8	82.1	10.1	34.5	8.5
Ireland	1986–8	22.3	1.8	78.2	42.6	7.9	8.8
Ireland	1995–7	21.8	2.5	101.3	40.6	12.3	10.2
Spain	1986–8	28.9	1.9	79.6	18.2	12.6	22.5
Spain	1995–7	25.4	1.9	84.5	16.9	13.1	19.5
Greece	1986–8	42.0	1.1	69.2	22.5	14.5	14.9
Greece	1995–7	31.2	2.5	122.1	23.5	23.3	21.0
Portugal	1986–8	24.2	0.4	88.4	29.3	11.6	20.8
Portugal	1995–7	21.0	2.1	126.5	25.9	15.8	22.2

Note: Row percentages may add to more than 100 because articles are counted in each contributing country and some may have authors in three or more countries. With regard to the European Union, internationally co-authored articles also include those among member countries. (Rows report the percentage of the total number of international co-authorships of the country; columns indicate the relative prominence of a country in the portfolio of internationally co-authored articles of every country.)

Source: National Science Foundation (2000).

Table 2.7 (*continued*)

Ita	Neth	Swe	Den	Finl	Belg	Aus	Irel	Spa	Gre	Por
5.7	3.4	4.1	1.7	1.2	1.9	1.0	0.3	1.7	0.9	0.2
6.7	4.2	3.5	2.0	1.6	2.0	1.4	0.4	3.1	0.9	0.4
2.1	2.0	2.0	0.8	0.6	1.5	0.8	0.2	0.8	0.2	0.0
3.5	2.7	2.6	1.1	1.1	1.2	0.7	0.2	1.1	0.3	0.2
5.8	4.7	4.0	2.4	1.5	3.4	1.7	0.6	2.7	0.8	0.5
7.6	5.8	4.1	2.9	2.1	3.7	2.0	0.8	5.0	1.1	1.6
6.1	4.8	3.7	2.4	1.1	2.4	0.9	1.6	2.8	1.3	0.8
7.8	6.5	3.8	3.0	1.5	3.1	1.4	1.8	5.0	1.7	1.3
5.5	5.1	3.7	2.3	1.4	2.8	4.1	0.3	1.9	0.8	0.3
7.1	5.9	3.8	2.7	1.7	3.0	4.5	0.5	3.7	1.6	0.7
8.6	4.0	2.9	1.5	0.7	6.0	1.0	0.4	4.6	1.1	0.7
10.1	5.0	3.1	1.9	1.4	6.2	1.4	0.5	6.9	1.8	1.3
	4.3	3.9	2.0	0.9	3.6	1.7	0.4	3.6	0.6	0.2
	5.7	3.6	2.7	1.7	3.5	2.1	0.6	6.5	1.9	1.1
6.2		3.9	2.3	2.0	9.4	1.9	0.7	2.2	0.4	0.4
8.1		4.6	3.5	2.3	9.5	1.8	1.0	4.6	1.0	1.2
5.4	3.7		8.8	5.8	2.5	1.2	0.2	1.2	0.7	0.2
6.0	5.4		9.1	7.3	3.7	1.4	0.5	3.1	0.9	0.9
5.5	4.4	17.2		3.4	1.6	1.0	0.2	1.6	0.4	0.4
8.1	7.3	15.9		4.5	3.0	2.1	0.7	5.5	2.3	0.8
4.1	6.1	18.0	5.4		2.6	1.8	0.4	0.9	2.4	0.2
7.1	6.7	17.7	6.3		3.8	2.1	0.8	3.7	1.1	1.8
7.5	13.7	3.8	1.3	1.3		2.0	0.6	3.3	1.1	0.7
8.2	15.5	5.0	2.4	2.2		1.4	1.0	5.3	2.1	1.8
6.5	5.1	3.4	1.4	1.6	3.7		0.3	2.3	0.2	0.0
7.6	4.8	3.0	2.6	1.9	2.2		0.5	4.3	1.7	0.4
4.1	5.2	1.5	0.9	1.0	2.9	0.9		1.4	0.4	0.6
7.4	8.1	3.2	2.9	2.3	5.0	1.5		4.8	1.6	1.4
9.9	4.2	2.4	1.6	0.5	4.3	1.6	0.3		0.3	1.2
11.1	5.5	3.1	3.2	1.6	3.9	2.0	0.7		1.7	2.2
4.4	2.3	3.6	1.0	0.5	3.7	0.4	0.3	0.9		0.2
13.8	5.1	3.9	5.6	4.1	6.6	3.3	1.0	7.0		3.9
3.4	4.8	1.8	2.5	0.7	5.4	0.2	0.9	6.6	0.4	
11.5	8.9	5.6	2.9	4.4	7.9	1.1	1.3	13.4	5.6	

regression line shows an inverse relationship between the two variables since, as expected, the propensity to collaborate is inversely related to the size of a country. It is interesting to note how individual countries have different propensities to collaborate. Those below the line are relatively less internationally open, or more self-referent, while those above the line show a greater propensity to favour international collaboration. Japan is well below the line, with a negligible share of internationally co-authored articles; the USA is at the extreme right of the line, because of its large dimension, and below it, although less than Japan. Slightly below the line we also find Spain, Finland, Ireland and Greece, but the distances are negligible. The scenario for 1986 is not very different. Globally, this confirms what Table 2.6 has shown: European countries are more open internationally than the other two members of the triad, and this is due not only to their smaller size, but also to a greater tendency towards academic collaboration.

To complete the picture we look at the geographical distribution of internationally co-authored articles across collaborating countries in the triad. This allows a comparison with the analysis on the industrial side. Does the European academic community have the same preference of European firms for American rather than for European partners? From Table 2.7, we note that Europe is by far the greatest collaborator for the American academic community. In 1995–7, as much as 60.3 per cent of US internationally co-authored papers involved a European partner; Europeans, instead, have a stronger propensity to use intra-area collaboration.

Interestingly, turning to the dynamics of the phenomenon, by comparing the period 1986–8 to the period 1995–7 it emerges that the share of intra-EU collaborations has significantly increased (from 56.6 to 69.4 per cent of all EU internationally co-authored papers), while the share of collaborations with the USA has decreased for the EU as a whole (from 31.9 to 29 per cent) as well as for each EU member state. If we look at Japan, we note that it has increased its percentage of collaborations with the EU (from 33.3 to 39.4) and decreased those with the USA (from 54 to 45.6). Finally the USA has increased its share of international collaborations with both Japan (from 8.2 to 9.6 per cent) and the EU (from 54.9 to 60.3 per cent).

Thus the attractiveness of the American innovation system, so evident for industrial collaborations, seems to experience a drastic reduction regarding academic production. Data supports the decline of the US share in international article co-authorship; in contrast, it reveals that European academia has strengthened its weight in international collaborations.

With respect to the composition by field of academic collaborations, the sector in which scientific articles are more internationally co-authored is Earth and space sciences, followed by Physics and Mathematics (Table 2.8). Academic partnership is also important in Biomedical research and

Biology. If we turn from international co-authorship to total co-authorship, which includes co-authoring within a country (in this case data reflects substantially the position of the USA, which is the country with the greatest number of internal articles), the sector most co-authored turns out to be Clinical medicine, followed by Biomedical research and Earth and space sciences. With respect to the growth in the period examined, the greatest progress is shown by Physics and Psychology.

We would like to stress the existence of an opposite trend in industrial and academic collaborations. Regarding the American slowdown in the latter, the figures partly reflect the reduced attention that public research institutions have received from the federal government, which has mainly devoted its resources to business priorities. Furthermore it should be borne in mind that the academic journals which included the Science Citation Index (on which the data are based) are more and more open to non-English speaking countries, and this has somewhat reduced the dominion of the Anglo-Saxon academic community. Thus, overall, it is possible to conclude that the European academia has become more attractive and has increased its significance at the worldwide level.

Table 2.8   Co-authorship and international co-authorship by field, 1986–8 and 1995–7

World	% co-authored		% internat. co-authored	
	1986–8	1995–7	1986–8	1995–7
Total science & engineering	*38.6*	*50.1*	*7.8*	*14.8*
Physics	32.2	49.0	11.1	22.4
Chemistry	26.7	38.5	6.7	12.8
Earth & space sciences	39.7	54.3	13.3	24.1
Mathematics	28.6	38.2	14.4	20.6
Biology	31.4	44.5	7.4	13.9
Biomedical research	41.5	54.9	9.1	16.2
Clinical medicine	52.4	61.3	6.3	11.5
Engineering	29.9	39.8	7.1	12.7
Psychology	30.6	38.6	4.1	8.5
Social sciences	23.4	29.2	5.4	8.6
Health & professional fields	29.6	36.7	3.3	6.4

Source: National Science Foundation (2000).

Can these positive trends be associated with the EU policies? All FPs have dedicated a whole expenditure chapter to improving human capital endowments (1280 million euros in FP5, up to 1580 in FP6). The EU Commission has undertaken an intense process of training of researchers and acquisition of knowledge, through various measures: by sustaining the intra-area mobility of researchers (by means of fellowships), by fixing awards for achieving excellent results in research, by enhancing the access to infrastructures (for an assessment of the EU impact on university research, see Geuna, 1999). The principal aim of FPs has been to build a European 'knowledge society' and a European Research Area (ERA) that could link academy, industry and institutions. At least the goal to increase cooperation in academia seems to have been achieved: a further sign of such a process has been the interrelationship of academic networking between the EU and accession countries, grown considerably between 1990 and 2000 (Wagner and Leydesdorff, 2003).

A complementary piece of evidence is represented by collaboration between academia and firms. Preliminary information from Pavitt and Patel (2002) has indicated that European firms are keener to collaborate (as measured by jointly co-authored scientific papers) with American rather than with European universities. The willingness, and ability, of US universities to cooperate with firms may have diverted some energy from typical academic collaborations. At the same time, the evidence also suggests that in the 'old continent' there is a potential, and dangerous, divergence between the trajectories followed by 'public science' and 'business technology'. As pointed out above, several structural factors may explain such a divergent trend: preliminary empirical evidence has shown, for instance, that average firm size and degree of openness to the external environment have a significant impact on both the extent of and propensity for university–firm collaboration (Fontana *et al.*, 2004).

CONCLUSIONS

This chapter has commented on a significant degree of divergence in international collaborations for knowledge. On the one hand, American companies have considerably increased the recourse to strategic technology agreements as a source of innovation, and this has also affected European firms, which have become more willing to collaborate with American partners and less interested in sharing know-how with other European companies. European firms have looked for partnerships in those countries where they could share more easily the costs and risks of research and absorb a greater flow of know-how, minimizing the danger of 'sleeping with the enemy', that is, collaborating with the most relevant market competitors. On the other hand, European academia has increased its attractiveness as measured by international co-authorship, and European scholars have augmented their collaborations, not only within the continent, but also with American scholars.

We have assumed that partners are more often sought when they have a substantial knowledge dowry: the institutions of a country are often attractive as partners if the overall national knowledge system is dynamic. Certainly the attractiveness for potential collaborators is only one of the many ways to assess the strengths of a national scientific and technological (S&T) system. However it is sensible to assume that it is positive when an S&T system increases its links with other parts of the world. It is more difficult to explain how in the last decade Europe has become more attractive in 'public science' and less attractive in 'business technology', while precisely the opposite trend has occurred in the USA.

Can these trends also be associated with deliberate public policies carried out in Europe and in the USA? We have referred to the impact of the EU R&D policy, which has increased its importance in the last decade as a tool for creating and diffusing innovation. By means of the Framework Programmes, European institutions have financed cooperation across industry and academy. Four main reasons induce us to consider collaborations so important, especially for a union of different states such as the EU: they permit sharing of the high costs and risks of research, they allow individual member countries to absorb expertise and know-how available in other member countries, they facilitate the expansion of the market by generating standardized products, and they can accelerate the process of integration in a wider sense.

However EU budget and instruments, although growing, continue to be very limited and subject to many constraints (Pavitt, 1998, p. 567). The share effectively directed towards industrial research of a collaborative nature has always been very slight as compared with actual needs. Thus EU policy does not deliver the expected results, and there is an impressive variability in its effectiveness across countries and industries. It still has not been able to make Europe become a junction of technological exchange. European firms should probably call for more help from national sources and policies, but it emerges that the EU should use a wider battery of instruments than the (limited) financial ones (Barry, 2001; Pavitt, 1998). Regulations, standards, procurements, competition, real services and large-scale cooperative civilian projects seem to be more important tools for creating a European Research Area than the (limited) financial support currently available in the Union (Lundvall, 2001). Moreover several authors (see, among others, Geuna, 2001) have stressed the need for a better balance between the allocation mechanisms based on 'quasi-market' schemes and more distributive policy orientations. Greater attention should be devoted to institutional innovation, which can also mitigate the tension between purely commercial and short-term interests and long-term collective benefits.

Nevertheless what has happened in the academic sector is significant. It testifies that Europe owns human capital which is able to allow future growth. But it has also been pointed out that European academia is becoming more and more isolated from the business sector, to the point that European companies prefer to contract research and to collaborate with American, rather than European, universities (Pavitt and Patel, 2002). Indeed a greater integration between business and academia appears essential if Europe wants to become (as policy makers have reiterated since the Lisbon Summit of 2000) the greatest knowledge society of the twenty-first-century.

Future research should be aimed at exploring in greater depth the role of structural variables in determining the propensity to favour knowledge collaboration, trying to provide answers to critical questions such as whether the European business model, largely based on the ownership of large firms by financial institutions, is giving way to one more resembling the American model of shareholder capitalism. What influence is the growth of acquisitions and alliances in Europe over the last decade likely to have on the EU business system? What is the role of industrial structures (firm size, R&D intensity, degree of turbulence, appropriability of returns to innovation, sectoral specialization and so on) in explaining different patterns of technology collaboration? Is there a trade-off between short-term efficiency resulting from the quasi-market approach to S&T funding and long-term advantages?

NOTES

* The authors wish to thank Alberto Coco for assistance in data collection and calculations.
1. We will not consider collaborations between firms and academia since data are not yet easily available (see Pavitt and Patel, 2002).
2. We do not include alliances involving countries outside the triad, which constitute around 10 per cent of the total.
3. To build Figure 2.2, we had to sum the internationally co-authored scientific articles of each country by avoiding multiple counting. We first considered the total number of scientific articles for each country in which every internationally co-authored paper is counted on a fractional assignment basis (counted one-half if co-authored between two countries, and so on); these figures are provided by NSF (2002, table 5.41). We then subtracted the number of national scientific articles for each country (obtained from the table 5.48 as the difference between the number of total articles and the number of internationally co-authored articles, in which each internationally co-authored article is on a whole-count basis; that is, counted one independently from the number of foreign partners). By doing so, we obtained the number of internationally co-authored articles for each country on a fractional assignment basis: each article is assigned to a country only for the fraction that involves it, so that no article can be counted more than once when we aggregate the countries we want to analyse.
4. We considered the logarithm of the number of articles.

BIBLIOGRAPHY

Archibugi, D. and B.-Å. Lundvall (eds) (2001), *The Globalising Learning Economy*, Oxford: Oxford University Press.

Archibugi, D. and J. Michie (1995), 'The globalisation of technology: a new taxonomy', *Cambridge Journal of Economics*, **19**, 121–40.

Archibugi, D. and M. Pianta (1992), *The Technological Specialisation of Advanced Countries. A Report to the EC on International Science and Technology Activities*, Dordrecht: Kluwer.

Banchoff, T. (2002), 'Institutions, inertia and European union research policy', *Journal of Common Market Studies*, **40**(1), 1–21.

Barfield, C.E. and C. Thum (2003), 'American alliance capitalism', in J.H. Dunning and G. Boyd (eds), *Alliance Capitalism and Corporate Management*.

Barry, A. (2001), *Political Machines. Governing a Technological Society*, London: Athlone Press.

Boyd, G. and A.M. Rugman (2003), 'Corporate alliances and competition policies', in J.H. Dunning and G. Boyd (eds), *Alliance Capitalism and Corporate Management*.

Cantwell, J. and S. Iammarino (2003), *Multinational Corporations and European Regional Systems of Innovation*, London and New York: Routledge.

Dodgson, M. (1993), *Technological Collaboration in Industry*, London and New York: Routledge.

Dunning, J.H. and G. Boyd (eds.) (2003), *Alliance Capitalism and Corporate Management*, Cheltenham UK and Northampton, MA, USA: Edward Elgar.

Eaton, J., E. Gutierrez and S. Kortum (1998), 'European technology policy', *Economic Policy*, 405–38.

European Commission (1997), *Second European Report on S&T Indicators*, Brussels: EUR 17639.

European Commission (2002), *Science, Technology and Innovation. Key Figures 2002*, Luxembourg.

Fontana, R., A. Geuna and M. Matt (2004), 'Firm size and openness: the driving forces of university–industry collaboration', in Y. Caloghirou, A. Constantelou and N.S. Vonortas (eds), *Knowledge Flows in European Industry: Mechanisms and Policy Implications*, London and New York: Routledge.

Framework Programs, FP6 (Sixth), FP5 (Fifth Framework Program) and FP4 (Fourth Framework Program), from www.cordis.lu.

Gambardella, A. and F. Malerba (eds) (1999), *The Organization of Economic Innovation in Europe*, Cambridge: Cambridge University Press.

Geuna, A. (1999), 'Patterns of university research in Europe', in A. Gambardella and F. Malerba (eds), *The Organization of Economic Innovation in Europe*.

Geuna, A. (2001), 'The changing rationale for European university research funding: are there negative unintended consequences?', *Journal of Economic Issues*, **XXXV**(3), 607–32.

Geuna, A., P. Llerena, M. Matt and M. Savona (2003), 'Collaboration between a research university and firms and other institutions', SPRU Working Paper, SEWPS no. 108, October.

Hagedoorn, J. (1996), 'Trends and patterns in strategic technology partnering since the early seventies', *Review of Industrial Organisation*, **11**, 601–16.

Hagedoorn, J. (2002), 'Inter-firm R&D partnership: an overview of major trends and patterns since 1960', *Research Policy*, **31**, 477–92.

Hagedoorn, J. (2003), 'Growth patterns in R&D partnership: an exploratory statistical study', *International Journal of Industrial Organisation*, **21**, 517–31.

Hagedoorn, J., A. Link and N. Vonortas (2000), 'Research partnerships', *Research Policy*, **29**, 567–86.

Jorde, T.M. and D.J. Teece (1990), 'Innovation and cooperation: implications for competition and antitrust', *Journal of Economic Perspectives*, **4** (3).

Lundan, S.M. (2003), 'Alliance capitalism in Europe', in J.H. Dunning and G. Boyd (eds), *Alliance Capitalism and Corporate Management*.

Lundvall, B.-Å., (2001), 'Innovation Policy in the Globalising Learning Economy', in D. Archibugi and B-Å. Lundvall (eds), *The Globalising Learning Economy*.

Molero, J. and I. Alvarez (2002), 'Multinational enterprises and systems of innovation assessment. Consequences for national and European S&T policies', paper presented at the Mesias Final Meeting, Brussels, 1–2 July.

Molero, J. and J. Heys (2001), 'The differentiated impact of innovative strategies of MNCs and national firms on European systems of innovation', paper presented at the Mesias Meeting, Budapest, 8–10 March.

Mowery, D. (1992), 'International collaborative ventures and the commercialization of new technologies', in N. Rosenberg, R. Landau and D. Mowery (eds), *Technology and the Wealth of Nations*.

Mytelka, L.K. (1991), *Strategic Partnership. States, Firms and International Competition,* London: Pinter Publishers.

Mytelka, L.K. (2001), 'Mergers, acquisitions, and inter-firm technology agreements in the global learning economy', in D. Archibugi and B-Å. Lundvall (eds), *The Globalising Learning Economy*.

Narula, R. (1998), 'Strategic technology alliances by European firms since 1980s: questioning integration?', STEP Group, Oslo, April.

Narula, R. and J. Hagedoorn (1999), 'Innovating through strategic alliances. Moving towards international partnerships and contractual agreements', *Technovation*, **19**, 283–94.

National Science Foundation (NSF) (2000), *Science and Engineering Indicators 2000*, Washington, DC: US Government Printing Office.

National Science Foundation (NSF) (2002), *Science and Engineering Indicators 2002*, Washington, DC: US Government Printing Office.

OECD (2000), 'International strategic alliances in industrial globalization', STI Working Papers Series, from www.oecd.org/dsti/sti.

OECD (2002), *Main Science and Technology Indicators 2002*, Paris: OECD.

Pavitt, K. (1998), 'The inevitable limits of EU R&D funding', *Research Policy*, **27**, 559–68.

Pavitt, K. and P. Patel (2002), 'Unpublished statistics on business and academic joint publications', paper presented at the Mesias Final Meeting, Brussels, 1–2 July.

Peterson, J. and M. Sharp (1998), *Technology Policy in the European Union*, Houndmills: Macmillan.

Pianta, M. and D. Archibugi (1991), 'Specialization and size of scientific activities: a bibliometric analysis of advanced countries', *Scientometrics*, **22**, 341–58.

Rodriguez, M.J. (ed.) (2002), *The New Knowledge Economy in Europe*, Cheltenham, UK and Northampton, MA, USA: Edward Elgar.

Roijakkers, N. and J. Hagedoorn (2003), 'Inter-firm R&D partnering in high technology industries', in J.H. Dunning and G. Boyd (eds), *Alliance Capitalism and Corporate Management*.

Rosenberg, N., R. Landau and D. Mowery (1992), *Technology and the Wealth of Nations*, Stanford: Stanford University Press.
Sharp, M. (2001), 'The need for new perspectives in European commission innovation policy', in D. Archibugi and B-Å. Lundvall (eds), *The Globalising Learning Economy*.
Vonortas, N. (1997), 'Research joint ventures in the US', *Research Policy*, **26**, 577–95.
Wagner, C. and L. Leydesdorff (2003), 'Mapping the network of global science: comparing international co-authorships from 1990 to 2000', Amsterdam School of Communications Research (ASCoR), mimeo.

3. Atlantic commerce

John Kirton

INTRODUCTION

To many casual observers, the United States (US)–European economic relationship, continually in a condition of intense competition, has erupted into acute conflict yet again.[1] In the field of trade, the past few years have featured a succession of high-profile, bitter disputes over old practices such as subsidies, old sectors such as steel and agriculture, and newer, domestically grounded, values and ideology-based issues such as beef hormones, genetically modified organisms (GMO), biotechnology and food safety as a whole (Mills, 2004; May 2001). In the field of foreign direct investment (FDI), the 1997 French-led collapse of the American-pioneered negotiations to create a Multilateral Agreement on Investment (MAI) at the Organisation for Economic Co-operation and Development (OECD) has been followed by European–American differences over the investment provisions in the World Trade Organization's (WTO) Doha development agenda and by the failure to reach any formal agreement on this issue at the unsuccessful mid-term ministerial review of the round at Cancun in September 2003 (Rugman, 1999; Rugman and Verbeke, 2003). In the field of corporate competition, Cancun's failure even to launch multilateral negotiations is equally apparent, despite the growing tendency of the European Union (EU) to block American multinational corporations (MNCs) from acquiring, as part of their global strategies, European, or even other American, firms (Boyd and Rugman, 2003).

More broadly, the end of the cold war in the 1990s has removed the incentive for US–European political–strategic solidarity to ride to the rescue of economic quarrels that threaten the overall relationship (Gardner and Stefanova, 2001; Hufbauer and Neuman, 2002). The advent of rapid globalization has placed a premium on new opportunities in the big, booming emerging markets outside the Atlantic world. The events of 11 September brought a particularly severe shock, as a terrorist attack on America, incubated in an Al-Quaeda cell in Hamburg, has led to a year of decreasing international trade and investment, and permanent security-bred increases in transaction costs on container shipping, civil aviation and much else. More recently the 2003 war on Iraq has fostered transatlantic, as well as intra-European and intra-North American, divisions, fuelled by the spectacle of Americans refusing to buy or sell French wines and the other products of a now 'disloyal' Europe. With such political as well as economic difficulties, it is little wonder that many see the US–European economic relationship as destined to decline, and even disappear as a consequential force in the globalized economy of the twenty-first century world.

During the past decade, policy makers on both sides of the Atlantic have powerfully reinforced this prevailing impression of a transatlantic economic relationship in decay. Along with firing protectionist salvos and aggressive litigation across the Atlantic, American leaders since 1994 have been preoccupied with creating full free trade agreements and economic communities, regionally and plurilaterally, in North America through the North American Free Trade Agreement (NAFTA), in the vast Asia–Pacific region through the Asia Pacific Economic Co-operation (APEC) forum, in the emerging markets of the western hemisphere through the Free Trade Agreement of the Americas (FTAA) and Summit of the Americas (SOA), and now bilaterally with several smaller countries around the world. For its part, the EU has long been preoccupied with absorbing the newly freed countries in Central and Eastern Europe, with building a direct relationship with Asia through its leaders-level Asia–Europe Summit Meeting (AESM), with modernizing its special relationships with its African, Caribbean and Pacific (ACP) partners through the Cotonou agreements, and with building its own full free trade agreements in places such as the Mediterranean and Arabian Gulf. Indeed a careful count of preferential trade agreements around the world shows that the EU leads the USA, and the world, by a large margin in this sphere (Bhagwati and Panagariya, 2003).[2]

Amidst this frenzy of plurilateralism, regionalism and bilateralism, the transatlantic economic space has been largely left out. Earlier initiatives, in the immediate wake of the cold war victory, to create a US–EU, or broader NAFTA–EU, free trade area have fallen off policy makers' priority lists. Even the traditional economic institutions that have long connected the old transatlantic partners and kept their economic cooperation moving forward have been fraying. Bilaterally little of consequence has been built on the annual US–EU summits, the TransAtlantic Business Dialogue and older mechanisms such as the 'Brucke' and similar informal consultative forums. In the plurilateral realm, the OECD has been held on a tight budgetary leash. The trade ministers' Quadrilateral has met less frequently (Cohn, 2002) and the Group of Seven (G7) and now Group of Eight (G8) Summit has turned from its traditional focus on trade and investment to other topics on an ever-expanding list (Bayne, 2001, Ullrich, 2001). Whenever the leaders of the triad do venture beyond regionalism to forge the sinews that might eventually generate a genuine globalization, everywhere but across the Atlantic is the direction in which they head. Indeed, with the Doha round in deep distress after its failure at Cancun, it is telling that no-one of consequence has suggested a transatlantic free trade agreement as a plausible response to keep the trade liberalization 'bicycle' moving ahead. Rather the divisions bred by the 2003 Iraq war have persisted into the postwar period over contracting for Iraqi reconstruction and the write-off of Iraq's formidable debt, while booming US economic growth and productivity in the face of a still stagnant Europe have further widened the transatlantic divide. Thus far the European monetary authorities have accommodated the US desire for a sustained drop in the value of its dollar, with more of an eye to the re-election of President Bush in November 2004 than an ideological belief in the value of market-driven free-floating exchange rates (Tavlas, 2003) Yet, as the euro reached historic highs against the US dollar as 2003 ended, there were signs that European tolerance was about to break.

This strong sense that the transatlantic economic relationship is in trouble or tatters is shared by scholars as well. One school, the transatlantic pessimists, see only decay and decline as the destiny for the post cold war years (Mearsheimer, 1990). Others suggest that America's international economic future lies in China, or with the rising powers of Asia and the Americas, and that the American relationship with the 'old', now stagnant and declining, Europe can be dispensed with, with little regret. Similarly scholars studying Europe's future in the emerging global economy focus on deepening the Union in the fields of finance, foreign policy and security policy, driving eastward as far as the ultimate great prize of Russia, and capturing opportunities in distant fields such as Africa and the Middle East (Gardner and Stefanova 2001).[3] In both North America and Europe, 'deepening' the existing, regionally-confined, continental community is a popular choice as well. That shrinking set of scholars who still care enough to take a close look at the transatlantic economic relationship focus increasingly on the difficulties, disputes and deeply domestically embedded differences, rather than the stability, opportunities and potential new partnership that might be present across the Atlantic in a rapidly globalizing, twenty-first century world (Kirton, 2003; Boyd, 2003a, 2003b). And even those who see stable continuity, rather than disputatious decline, as the dominant trend, offer 'mature stability' rather than any great growth or deeper partnership as the prospect for the years ahead (Hufbauer and Neuman, 2002, Kohler, 2002).[4]

In contrast, this chapter argues that the transatlantic economic relationship is not diminishing either because of divisions within or of opportunities without, in a globalizing world. Rather, it is strengthening, becoming more salient to the world and to its more interdependent members, and waiting to be politically modernized so its full potential can be secured. This argument for transatlantic optimism rests on three component claims. First, the US–EU trade, FDI and corporate relationship is a substantial, stable and slowly strengthening share of the global economy, even after a decade of intense globalization that has brought more distant regions into the long Atlantic-centred global economic core. Second, the transatlantic economic relationship has become steadily more important to the economic fortunes of both its US and its EU members, especially as each has increasingly opened to the other, as well as to outsiders, in this globalizing age. Third, there is in the relationship an ever deepening interdependence that is moving into intervulnerability and even into a single identity, especially as one moves 'downward' from traditional trade to the structural, firm-level foundations of FDI and corporate partnerships. All that has lagged is the task of building the big, broad political structures appropriate to seize the abundant transatlantic opportunities in this new 'after victory' age (Ikenberry, 2001).

This chapter explores the underlying economic case for taking up this task, by examining the actual trends in the real economy of the transatlantic area in the three defining pillars of trade, FDI and corporate partnerships. It looks, first, at long-term trends in transatlantic trade, FDI and corporate partnering in a global context; second at the importance of this activity to each partner; and, finally, at how the corporate and policy communities are responding to these trends. In doing so, it treats the EU as a collectivity, given its formal supranational authority over its members for traditionally defined trade policy and its dominant role in competition policy as well. Where important, intra-EU national differences are noted, most importantly in regard to 'the British exception' in the FDI and corporate partnership field.[5]

1 THE TRANSATLANTIC ECONOMIC RELATIONSHIP IN A GLOBALIZING WORLD

On the core issue of whether Atlantic commerce has been on the rise over the past few decades, and whether it has come to matter more to a fast changing world, the basic story is one of stable continuity, enriched by a slowly strengthening trend.

Trade

US–EU trade represents a large, steadily growing relationship and a substantial, strengthening share of world commercial flows. A 2002 analysis showed that the total US–EU trade volume had doubled, from $273 498 million in 1990 to $557 146 million in 2000 (Hufbauer and Neuman, 2002). As a share of world trade, it increased during this decade by almost 25 per cent, from 6.4 per cent in 1990 to 8.1 per cent in 2000 (after a mid-decade dip to 6.0 per cent in 1995). This increase in global share was, perhaps paradoxically, especially strong in merchandise trade (5.4 per cent to 6.9 per cent), although it arose in service trade (10.7 per cent to 12.7 per cent) as well.

A longer, more detailed, updated analysis largely confirms this portrait. As Figure 3.1 in part illustrates, in 1981 US exports to the EEC area totalled some $48 billion, while the reciprocal EEC exports to the US (US imports from the EEC15) amounted to $42 billion.[6] By 1990, these figures had more than doubled. By 2000, they had more than tripled from their levels in 1986. The size of the US–EU commercial flows has increased proportionally with the concomitant increase in worldwide trade. While the trade-diminishing effects of the economic slowdown from 11 September are evident in the decrease in trade from 2000 to 2001, the resilience of the relationship is evident in the bouncing back in EU exports to a recovering USA in 2002.

Furthermore the global significance of this relationship has not diminished, but actually increased, under the twofold pressure from globalization and trade regionalization. As Figure 3.2 shows, US exports to the EU have been a sizable and remarkably steady share of total world exports from 1981 to 1999, fluctuating between 2 per cent and 2.5 per cent. Moreover, there has been a small, steady rise since 1996.

The reciprocal EU exports to the USA have followed a more dynamic trend. They soared from a low of 2 per cent in the late 1970s, to a peak of nearly 4 per cent in 1986, then fell to a level of 2.75 per cent in the late 1990s. But, since 1996, their global share has risen even more strongly and steadily than that of US exports to the EU.

These data also show that the US–EU trade relationship has long been in general balance in the annual differences of exports and imports exchanged between the two partners. Indeed the 1990s brought to an end the big US deficit *vis-à-vis* Europe in the 1980s. The new decade began with a perfect balance and has seen only a small, steady surplus in the EU's favour since 1993.[7] This has meant that the EU has been off the US political radar screen, even as America has become concerned with its increasing overall trade deficit, led by China and Japan. This stable balance has done much to diminish transatlantic trade tensions during the past decade. It is hardly surprising that the transatlantic economic dialogue of late has focused on exchange rates, relative interest rates, fiscal policy and structural impediments to growth, rather than trade. Looking ahead, it is likely that the EU trade surplus will endure and even strengthen, given the return of booming growth and aggregate demand in the US economy in 2003 and projections for the years ahead. At the same time, Europe's trade surplus is likely to be limited by the rise in the exchange value of the euro to record levels against the US dollar. Indeed the major risk is for the disappearance of the European surplus, driven by further falls in the value of the US dollar that the US global current account deficit and serious fiscal deficit are likely to produce. The overall technological lead of US MNCs, the spread of corporate corruption from the USA to European firms, most visibly in the case of Parmalat, and any revival of European growth should extend this American advantage. There is thus an incentive for the Europeans to move now to lock in a vital and favourable trade relationship through a stronger liberalization agreement, well before the major dollar-driven shifts arrive. The general equality between the USA and the EU in global trade shares and in GDP suggests that a balanced deal could be readily struck, if economically inconsequential but politically difficult difference over agriculture and social regulation can be overcome.

Two broader conclusions can be drawn from this data. First, contrary to popular impressions that the advent of post-cold war globalization meant the decay of the transatlantic relationship, the stable upward trend of the US–EU share of global trade since 1996 shows the strength and resilience of the transatlantic bonds. Indeed, if anything, after an initial post-cold war diversion, deepening globalization seems to have had a positive effect on US–EU trade. Even at the high point of globalization, and of the steady succession of global financial crises that went with it from 1997 onward, both US–EU exports and imports were on the rise. The transatlantic trade relationship proved to be a safe harbour in a globalizing financial storm.

Second, the strong trend towards trade regionalization on both of the Atlantic sides of the triad has not arrested the steady upward trend (Rugman, 2000). It has often been suggested that the increasing salience of regional trade for the United States (NAFTA) and the European Union (Eastern Europe, Cotonou) would gradually push transatlantic commercial ties to the background. In fact, the share of US–EU trade in global commerce did fall in the early 1990s, reflecting the diversions from the initial momentum of the Canada–US Free Trade Agreement and NAFTA and the newly-opened Eastern European economies. But this dip was small and short-lived, rather than a structurally underpinned trend. By the mid-1990s, transatlantic commerce had rebounded to resume its upward trend. By the late 1990s, following the brief interregnum of a retreat to regionalism on both sides of the Atlantic, the US–EU dyad once again resumed its central importance in world trade.[8]

Foreign Direct Investment

The trends in FDI tell a similar story in even stronger terms. The 2002 analysis showed the total stock of US FDI in the EU, and the EU FDI in the USA rising from $412 422 million in 1990 to $1 376 128 million in 2000, an increase of over 300 per cent (Hufbauer and Neuman, 2002). Looking at the components, during the decade the stock of EU FDI in the USA almost quadrupled, to reach $802 712 million by 2000. The US stock in the EU tripled, to reach $573 416 million. The small net lead that the EU had in the USA over US FDI in Europe at the start of the decade had become a much larger US$220 billion gap by decade's end.

The global explosion of FDI during the 1990s, driven by the beckoning big, now available, markets in the developing world, did diminish this booming transatlantic FDI stock somewhat as a share of global FDI. Over the decade the two-way total fell, from 26.4 per cent to 21.8 per cent of the global total, and both components shrunk as well. But again there was an important mid-decade breakpoint. The global share of the US–EU total rose from 1995 to 2000, driven by a strong rebound in the value of the EU FDI stock in the USA flowing in to take advantage of America's 'goldilocks' economy and 'dot-com' boom. This suggests that 'globalization' began only as a post-cold war, short-term move into the newly opened former communist countries, and ended in 1996.

A more detailed, longer and updated analysis confirms this exponential increase in the value of transatlantic direct investment flows, the strongest evidence of the strength of the US–EU bond. As Figure 3.3 suggests, in 1982, the outflow investment position of the USA in the EEC area was estimated at over $76 billion (nominal). Within 10 years that figure nearly tripled to $213 billion in 1991, ultimately reaching a staggering $632 billion in 2001. The reciprocal flow of direct investments from the EEC into the USA followed a parallel pattern. In 1984, the European Communities' outward direct investment in the USA had amounted to 11.5 billion ECU, compared to less than 2 billion ECU in Japan.[9] In 1989, the EEC's outward direct investment in the USA was already twice that, at 23.7 billion ECU.

As a share of global investment, foreign direct investment across the Atlantic has been essentially stable over the past two decades, punctuated by the now familiar small-scale cadence of decline in the 1980s, a dip in the mid-1990s and a strong rise up to 2000. However, as Figure 3.4 illustrates, there has been a discernible twenty-first century drop.[10] This is likely to be a result of the boom–bust nature of the market-driven economy, and the

2000–2002 recession and slow growth that it brought. Looking ahead, the terrorist attacks of 11 September 2001 may provide a longer-term incentive for European firms to locate more production within the United States, rather than depending on timely transported exports from Europe itself. For the moment, there are few signs of any structural decline.

Corporate Partnerships

An assessment of the twenty-first century structural foundations of the transatlantic economic relationship can be obtained by exploring corporate mergers and acquisitions. Here, once again, the story is one of overall stability with a post-1996 rise.

As Figure 3.8 suggests, US and EU firms have since 1987 dominated global activity in the service sector, together accounting for over 80 per cent of the global activity by 1999. Since 1996, US firms' cross border services sector M&As have steadily risen. They were joined in 1998 by a much stronger spike on the part of firms from the EU.

2 THE TRANSATLANTIC ECONOMIC RELATION- SHIP WITHIN A GLOBALIZING EU AND USA

The US–EU economic relationship thus still matters as much as, or even somewhat more than, ever for the world as a whole. But, more importantly, it matters more than ever for both the USA and the EU. For each transatlantic partner has opened much more to the other, as well as to regional neighbours and more distant outsiders, in this globalizing age.[11] The overall story here is one of cumulative change towards greater interdependence, to the point where each partner is now economically vulnerable to the other should the ties be severed.

Trade

In the field of trade, the 2002 study showed that, as a share of each other's total trade, the transatlantic partner had more than held its own. Total US trade with the EU, as a portion of total American trade, was virtually constant, at 23.8 per cent in 1990, 22.2 per cent in 1995, and 22.2 per cent again in 2000. The EU, taken as a totality, remained America's number one trade partner during this time.

For Europe, the American trade relationship became more important over the decade. The US share rose steadily from 15.2 per cent of the EU total in 1990, to 17.3 per cent in 1995, and to 18.8 per cent in 2002. During the rapidly growing, 'goldilocks' 1990s, the USA offered a market like none other. It continues to do so to this day and, under current projections, will in the years ahead.

A longer, more detailed and updated analysis underscores the singularity, stability and strength of this trend. As Figure 3.5 shows, exports to the EU as a percentage of the US total have been essentially stable from 1986 to 2002, with a slow steady rise from 1994 to 2000, and a predictable dip, driven by economic slowdown and 11 September in the following two years. The same is true on the import side.[12] America still needs its market in the EU.

FDI

Of even more interest is the trend in FDI, where macroeconomic conditions and political shocks may matter less in the short term. The 2002 study showed that, as a percentage of both inward and outward stock (with one exception), the USA and EU mattered more to each other as the decade of the 1990s wore on. Even more striking was how much more each mattered to the other's domestic economy as the post-cold war globalization decade unfolded. For America, the total two-way investment volume with Europe almost doubled in importance, from 7.1 per cent of US GDP in 1990 to 13.9 per cent in 2000. For Europe the increase was even more dramatic, as it rose from 6.6% in 1990 to 17.6 per cent by 2000.

A longer look shows the power of these trends. As Figure 3.6 on FDI stocks shows, consistent with the post-cold war globalization–regionalization argument, the American share of the total investments of the EU 15 dropped from a commanding peak of 63 per cent in 1988 to below 56 per cent by 1992. But, from 1995, it started, at first slowly, then strongly, to rise back up to the 60 per cent level again. For European FDI, the US market has always been number one, and is now becoming so by an increasing margin once again (see Figure 3.7 for the converse).

Even more striking is the trend for US outward FDI stock. For over a decade and a half, the EU has steadily risen as a preferred destination for US FDI, from a share of 35 per cent in 1985 to almost 42 per cent in 2001. There are few signs of a slowdown or 11 September effect here. As Kohler (2002) puts it: 'the EU has become a more important FDI-partner for the US, while the US has lost some of its importance as an FDI-partner for the EU'. This growing US dependence on Europe in structurally-grounded FDI, at a minimum, offsets the growing EU dependence on the USA for exports. Together they produce an overall portrait of the two countries becoming more dependent on each other.

Corporate Partnerships

The growing importance and dependence of the USA and EU to and on each other is shown more strongly at the deepest structural level – the corporate partnerships among individual firms. For many years, the USA had led the list of merger and acquisition partners for EU firms, while within Europe, Britain has stood out as number one. As the 2001 report of the European Commission's Directorate General for Economic and Financial Affairs put it: 'As in previous periods, the USA heads the list of both bidders and targets for International M&A involving Community firms, followed by Switzerland ... Amongst EU countries, the UK accounts for by far the largest number of international operations, as both target and bidder' (EC, 2001).

A closer look, through the data in Figure 3.9, confirms this pattern. It shows that, in 2001, US firms led the list of those who made foreign acquisitions in Europe, doing 697 deals, worth $42.4 billion overall. The next ranked countries (in order, Australia, Canada and Japan) were far behind.

Reciprocally, in 2001, foreign acquisitions of US companies in the US were led by firms from Canada, who did 313 deals worth $20.2 billion.[13] But Canadian firms were followed fairly closely by those from, in order, Britain, Germany, France, the Netherlands and Switzerland. Together they did over 150 deals, worth $69 billion. Indeed, by value, France stood first, beating even Canada, with deals worth $24 billion, on its own. Taken in total, the EU dominated NAFTA partners Canada and Mexico, or any outsiders, as far as the USA and its firms were concerned.

It is in the realm of corporate partnerships that the 'transatlantic exception' to what might be termed the 'Rugman regionalism rule' arises in its strongest form.[14] For the striking surge in British FDI in the USA from 1997 to 1999 was driven by a few large corporate mega-mergers, notably the $48.2 billion British Petroleum takeover of Amoco, and the even larger $60.3 billion Vodaphone acquisition of Airtouch (Rugman and Kudina, 2002). Similarly the less intense, reciprocal pattern of US investment in Britain and Europe was defined by a few takeovers, such as the $10.8 billion Walmart purchase of ASDA.

While these transatlantic mega-mergers might retain a national identity for the few years 'after victory', the broader trend may be for such a continentally specific identity to slowly dissipate, as a new definition of 'transnationality' or at least 'transatlanticism' takes hold. For the Rugman list of the world's top 20 most genuinely transnational, trans-triad companies in 1997 shows that a full 18 of the 20 are from Europe, 13 from the EU and eight from the big three of Britain, Germany and France (even if none are from the USA)

(Rugman, 2000, p. 211). Although American firms may be slow to move in this direction, actual atlanticization, if not genuine globalization, is already the reality for several large, once essentially European, firms. The future points to the emergence of all-Atlantic mega-firms with a transatlantic identity, rather than ones grounded in either or even both of the two parts. At the level of the global mega-firm, this shift from interdependence through intervulnerability to a single identity seems to be already under way.

3   THE TRANSATLANTIC ECONOMIC RELATIONSHIP'S CORPORATE–POLITICAL DIVIDE

Does this ever-deepening structural independence between the USA and the EU, evident as one moves from trade to FDI to corporate partnerships, dampen the past and present propensity to economic and even political conflict, and provide a foundation for a stronger, politically produced and protected economic partnership in the years ahead? The evidence would seem to suggest the answer to both questions is 'yes'. Indeed, at present, the Atlantic is already unified by its corporations, but divided only by its political leaders and by the gulf between them and their corporations and stakeholders below.

The prevailing, inaccurate impression of transatlantic division and decline is driven in the first instance by its highly publicized, seemingly never-ending, trade, investment and competition policy disputes. Over the past decade, the major and most bitter disputes have arisen, not only from traditional trade-related actions, but also from policies on FDI practices and, prospectively, competition policy as well. Yet this high political drama is often trumped up to impress political constituencies within each continent. It is in large measure a result, not of the reality of the relationship, but of the dispute-inspiring, litigation-attracting convenience created by the new Dispute Settlement Mechanism (DSM) of the WTO born in 1995.[15] Even so, these disputes actually touch only a tiny fraction of US–EU trade, FDI and MNC life. The vast submerged mass of the iceberg that is the US–EU economic relationship in reality constitutes a substantial, stable and slowly strengthening share of the global economy.

The conflict-dampening impact of transatlantic corporate unity is first evident in assessing the number of trade conflicts as a portion of overall trade. The number of actual disputes, despite the headlines, is a very small and stable share of the overall volume of trade. In the year 2000, US-initiated disputes over EU barriers to merchandise trade covered only 5 per cent of total trade (Hufbauer and Neuman, 2002). Europe's reciprocal complaints covered only 5 per cent as well. Others have put the portion of dispute-affected trade as low as 1 per cent (May, 2001, p. 178).[16]

In the field of FDI, the growth in the volume and importance to each other of the transatlantic stock and flow has not yet generated a commensurate rise in the number of FDI-related disputes, or the emergence of a new generation of a more subtle, behind-the-border kind. The investment-related disputes of the 1990s and of the twenty-first century still largely revolve around the same instruments and political issues (notably trade with Cuba, as in the Helms–Burton legislation) that flourished in earlier decades.

Perhaps the most surprising trend in the ratio of corporate economic cooperation to government political conflict comes in regard to competition policy and M&A. For here there has been no upsurge in conflict, or even any defining disputes as bitter and protracted as those in trade and FDI, even as the pace and importance of the activity have surged. Yet a disturbing cadence is becoming clear. In 2000, the EU stopped a merger between two American companies in the Worldcom–Sprint case. In 2001, the EU again prevented a merger between two American firms, General Electric and Honeywell, even though it had already been approved by regulators in the USA.[17] The absence of transatlantic conflict over this de facto EU extraterritoriality is all the more surprising, given the failure of the MAI and the absence of a multilateral regime or institution to govern competition globally. Thus far the USA has been content to let the EU serve as the global governor of competition policy for American firms taking over European entities, and even for American firms taking over ones within the USA itself. As more and larger mergers and acquisitions come to dominate the transatlantic relationship, this condition is unlikely to last, especially given the different approaches to competition policy that EU and US regulators have (Boyd and Rugman, 2003). Preventive action would be appropriate now.

CONCLUSION: BUILDING A TWENTY-FIRST CENTURY TRANSATLANTIC PARTNERSHIP

Several possible conclusions flow from this current configuration. Perhaps the most powerful is that corporate managers and political leaders on both sides of the Atlantic realize that their economic fortunes are so interconnected at this deep structural, firm and sector-specific level that they cannot allow themselves the luxury of conflict, whatever the short-term political rewards it might bring abroad or at home. That is, interdependence has turned into an intervulnerability and single identity that all players on both sides of the Atlantic recognize and respect.

A second possible conclusion is that no new generation of political construction, narrowly confined to investment, is needed, following the failure of the MAI negotiations, on a plurilateral, global or even bilateral plane. The MAI's corpse and OECD's codes can be left as they are. Cancun's failure to move towards multilateral rules on investment and competition policy needs no lament or rapid remedial action. And America's post-Cancun penchant for building bilateral arrangements can remain directed anywhere but across the Atlantic, as it has been for decades before.

But there may be a problem brewing, one that warrants appropriate preventative EU–US action now. For globalization could well breed an integrated global economy where ever more sectors are dominated by ever fewer, ever larger, firms. Here neither new entrants nor the emergence of China or other economies and new MNCs from beyond the triad are likely to disturb the trend, and restore real competition, increased choice and lower prices, to consumers in North America, the EU and across the world.[18] It could well be time to build an American–EU partnership, bilateral in the beginning, to deal with this deeper economic challenge of a globalizing world.

Beyond the looming threat is the available opportunity. A 1996 analysis concluded that transatlantic free trade would annually increase two-way trade, in a balanced fashion, by between 20 and 30 per cent or $70–100 billion in five years, raise US economic output by 1.6 per cent to 2.8 per cent of GDP, or $142–239 billion, and raise European economic growth by 1.0 per cent to 1.9 per cent or $94–184 billion (the GDP equivalent of another Finland) (Prestowitz *et al.*, 1996). A more recent analysis concluded that there were 'large opportunities': an annual increase of US exports to the EU of $48 billion, of EU exports to the USA of $44 billion, a 19 per cent or $109 billion increase in the stock of US FDI in the EU, and a 15 per cent or $118 billion increase in the stock of EU FDI in the USA (Hufbauer and Neuman, 2002). A subsequent analysis has reinforced this view (Kohler, 2002).

Any assessment of how best to build the transatlantic partnership in the future requires, not just an analysis of past trends and present transactions, but an understanding of the broader structural conditions and unfolding steps that will do much to determine the degree and direction of the probable and prospective path ahead.

At the most basic level, the three defining features of the post-cold war, rapidly globalizing, 11 September era all point to the possibility of aiming at a big and broad advance towards a bold new transatlantic partnership. First, the long, now long gone, cold war did more to create than contain transatlantic divisions, which reached their deepest, most durable bitterness with US–European disagreements over the way to deal with the communist pillars of Cuba, China and the USSR itself. While the legacy of the cold war lives on in the little case of Cuba, as the Helms–Burton dispute attests, the much larger issues over trading with China, the Soviet gas pipeline into Europe in the early 1980s and economic sanctions on the Soviets for their invasion of Afghanistan have now disappeared. If such cold war-generated, geopolitically and ideologically grounded disputes no longer arise in the first place, there is no need to lament the lack of cold war-created glue to contain them when they threaten to destroy so much else.

Second, rapid globalization has now begun to breach its still dominant intra-triad regional reality, with the US–EU economic relationship being the first to make the trans-triad leap in a larger process of 'going global' still to come. For reasons of history, as well as current corporate and political culture, it is easy to understand why, beyond each triad, the American–British and larger American–continental Europe relationship would be the first to break out. The intensification of this relationship during the 1990s, as each partner built ever-expanding regional economic partnerships, suggests it is the defining base of an ever-broadening, more global partnership to come (Schott and Oegg, 2001).

Third, the shock of 11 September, after the immediate move to closure and downturn, has done less to impose trade and FDI-inhibiting transaction costs on transatlantic commerce than to inspire the transaction-reducing common regulatory systems, from terrorist finance to container security, that will foster more intense trade in the long run. Its impact is much more pervasive than just the launch of the Doha round in November 2001. As the war against terror is a global one, the cooperation begun across the Atlantic, and largely through the G8, with Canada, Russia and Japan already in from the start, is likely to 'go global' with speed and ease. More broadly, with both US and European troops in constant combat or combat situations, most notably in Afghanistan, the 11 September inspired war on terrorism is likely to bring the intense transatlantic cooperation bred by the real, shared, wars of 1917–18, and 1941–45, rather than the theoretically-centred divisions of the cold war years.

Beyond this basic foundation there are five further factors that generate a very big potential for partnership in the years ahead. The first is the essential economic equality between the USA and the EU, in a bilateral and global context, in trade, FDI, home MNCs, GDP, currency strength (in current exchange rates and prospectively as a share of global foreign exchange reserves) and even growth rates, with the American downturn in 2001–2002. The second is the economic balance between the two, best seen in the absence of politically noticeable trade and payments imbalances (as in the 1960s), and, more broadly, in the symmetrical policies for macroeconomic management, notably fiscal deficits and freely floating exchange rates. The third factor is the intensifying interdependence, giving way to intervulnerability, and even a common identity, with the rise of merged all-Atlantic mega-firms. A fourth is the common, cooperation-inducing outside challenges centred on keeping a rising Russia on a democratic course, and inducing a still politically closed communist China to pursue the same path. The fifth factor is the current collapse of alternative economic institutional arrangements, first with the demise of APEC's free trade target and timetable, now with the post-Cancun WTO, the FTAA's deadline for completion, and the collage of bilaterals containing no likely candidates of any real economic weight.

Against this backdrop the several promising steps already taken in the immediate past provide much optimism about the future, defined by a direction already launched. The first step is the post-Iraq invasion coming together of the USA and the major European powers across a wide range of issues at and after the G8 Evian Summit.[19] The second step is their coming to agreement on agricultural protectionism and access to affordable medicines, as the Cancun ministerial meeting and their G8 commitment deadline loomed. A third step is their coming together at Cancun on a more common approach to the Singapore issues of investment and competition policy, in order to allow the Doha round to proceed. The fourth step is their coming together in a common approach to currencies, with both calling, at the September 2003 G8 finance ministers meeting in Dubai, on China, Japan and other Asians to move to fully flexible exchange rates.

With this favourable foundation and momentum, it is appropriate to plan for a future transatlantic partnership on an ambitious scale (Rugman and Boyd, 2003, Padoan *et al.*, 2003). The task of constructing a more meaningful political forum than those devised during the 1990s should serve as a minimum first step. The key move should be, in the immediate wake of the Cancun failure, to construct a transatlantic full free trade agreement, with modern provisions for FDI, competition policy and corporate governance, with NAFTA-like provisions for labour and the environment, and with the USA and the EU's existing free trade partners included from the start (Siebert, 1996; Stokes, 1996; Reinicke, 1996; Kirton and Maclaren, 2002).

NOTES

1. The author gratefully acknowledges the comments of colleagues at a conference on 'Alliance Capitalism in the New Trans-Atlantic Economy', at St Mary's University in Halifax on 26–27 September 2003, the excellent research assistance of Nikolai Roudev and the financial support of the Social Sciences and Humanities Research Council of Canada through its grants to the 'EnviReform' and the 'After Anarchy' projects at the University of Toronto.

2. These political choices and policy-driven preferential arrangements could at least in part be the cause, as well as the consequences, of the strong trend towards intra-triad regionalism on the part of MNCs that Rugman has identified (Rugman, 2000).

3. In the North American as well as the European case, 'deepening' the existing regional continental communities is the focus of policy thinking and summit-level action.

4. In the words of Bernhard May (2001, p. 178): 'Europe and the United States became two superpowers who depend upon each other. They have common interests and to a certain degree a common value system, they are both important actors in a complex system of interdependence.' May does not proceed to identify the depth of this interdependence or what might be built upon this core.

5. Unless otherwise noted, currencies are in US dollars.

6. Data cited here is from USTR Statistics, nominal value, customs reported.

7. This should give the EU, now sporting a sluggish or stagnant economy at home, an incentive to engage in a Transatlantic Free Trade Area (TAFTA), in order to protect its sizable trade, and trade surplus, in the rich and now rapidly growing US marketplace.

8. These results are confirmed by Kohler, who writes: 'there is also no aggregate sign of EU-trade diversion from the cross Atlantic route to eastern Europe. Thus the share of EU exports going to the US rose from 14.2 percent in 1990 to 21.1 percent in 2000, although if expressed as a share in US imports the same figures amount to a small reduction from 22.1 to 20.9 percent. EU imports coming from the US have remained stable at 16.6 percent if expressed as a share of total EU imports, but have fallen slightly from 25.6 percent to 24 percent if expressed as a share of overall US exports' (Kohler, 2002, pp. 4–5). While Kohler sees in these figures signs of the trade effects from NAFTA, the differences are sufficiently small to suggest the 'NAFTA effect' is overwhelmed by that from exchange rate changes and growth differentials.

9. Data source: EUROSTAT Yearbook.

10. This suggests that it is transatlantic FDI that needs immediate policy attention to fuel further liberalization and new flows, more than trade, as traditionally defined, does.

11. As Kohler (2002) notes, external trade as a share of GDP for the EU rose during the 1990s from 15.3 per cent to 18.3 per cent for exports, and from 13.3 per cent to 19.6 per cent for imports. The US share also rose, reaching 10.8 per cent for exports and 14.6 for imports by decade's end. While the EU remains more open and trade-dependent than the USA, both have become more so over the 1990s. In this regard, the impact of post-cold war globalization is real.

12. For a more detailed look at the importance of transatlantic trade to each partner see note 8.

13. There is thus a case for including Canada in any US–EU-centered TAFTA that includes provisions for FDI and competition policy. The recent takeover by Canada's most genuinely transnational MNC, Alan, of France's Pechiney, well illustrates the point that an integrated all North Atlantic–US economic space is coming to exist at the level of leading firms. In regard to trade, the need to avoid distortions and transactions costs arising from rules of origin is another reason for including Canada from the start.

14. Rugman has argued powerfully that it is regionalism, not globalism, that dominates, as trade, FDI and the activity of the world's largest MNCs are concentrated in their home regions of the triad, rather than spread more broadly and equally across all three legs of the triad, let alone the globe as a whole. Yet the EU–US relationship was always a bit of an exception, and the British–US relationship the biggest exception of all. See Rugman (2000), Rugman and Kudina (2002) and Moore and Rugman (2003).

15. Whereas the old GATT averaged two or three disputes a year brought to its Dispute Settlement Mechanism, the WTO's much more elaborate and legalized version is attracting about a dozen a year.

16. At the same time, their harmful effects may be much larger (Kohler, 2002). This suggests a need for a new mechanism, beyond an increasingly disregarded WTO, for effective transatlantic dispute prevention and resolution.
17. Figures generously provided by Alan Rugman and Cecilia Brain show that, at the time, GE had $126 billion in annual sales, 59.1 per cent of which were in the North America and only 10 per cent in the EU. Honeywell had $23 billion in annual sales, 73.7 per cent in the USA and only 18 per cent in Europe. Much more gently, in early 2002, US authorities made their approval of an alliance between an American and European firm, American Airlines and British Airways, contingent on the latter giving US carriers several Heathrow landing slots.
18. These questions of contestability and competition are complex. See Boyd (1999).
19. One sign was the Evian Summit's creation of an historically high 206 concrete commitments, covering an unusually comprehensive array of issues, from the economic, global/transnational and political security spheres.

REFERENCES

Bayne, Nicholas (2001), 'The G7 and multilateral trade liberalization: past performance, future challenges', in George Von Furstenberg and John Kirton (eds), *New Directions in Global Economic Governance: Creating International Order for the Twenty First Century*, Aldershot: Ashgate, pp. 171–88.

Bhagwati, Jagdish and Arvind Panagariya (2003), 'Defensive play simply won't work', *Economic Times (India)*, 20 August.

Boyd, Gavin (1999), 'Contestability and Concentration in World Markets', in Gavin Boyd and John Dunning, *Structural Change and Cooperation in the Global Economy*, Cheltenham, UK and Northampton, MA, USA: Edward Elgar.

Boyd, Gavin (2003a), 'The American political economy', in Alan Rugman and Gavin Boyd (eds), *Alliance Capitalism for the New American Economy*, Cheltenham, UK and Northampton, MA, USA: Edward Elgar, pp. 1–18.

Boyd, Gavin (2003b), 'American structural and policy interdependencies', in Alan Rugman and Gavin Boyd (eds), *Alliance Capitalism for the New American Economy*, Cheltenham, UK and Northampton, MA, USA: Edward Elgar, pp. 41–65.

Boyd, Gavin and Alan Rugman (2003), 'Corporate alliances and competition policies', in John Dunning and Gavin Boyd (eds), *Alliance Capitalism and Corporate Management*, Cheltenham, UK and Northampton, MA, USA: Edward Elgar, pp. 154–70.

Cohn, Theodore (2002), *Governing Global Trade: International Institutions in Conflict and Convergence*, Aldershot: Ashgate.

EC (2001), 'Supplement A: economic trends', *European Economy*, **12** (December).

Gardner, Hall and Radoslava Stefanova (eds) (2001), *The New Transatlantic Agenda: Facing the Challenges of Global Governance*, Aldershot: Ashgate.

Hufbauer, Gary and Frederic Neuman (2002), 'US–EU trade and investment: an American perspective', paper presented at a conference titled 'Transatlantic Perspectives on the US and EU Economies: Convergence, Conflict and Cooperation', Kennedy School of Government, Harvard University, 11–12 April.

Ikenberry, John (2001), 'Strengthening the Atlantic political order', in Hall Gardner and Radoslava Stefanova (eds), *The New Transatlantic Agenda: Facing the Challenges of Global Governance*, Aldershot: Ashgate pp. 17–30.

Kirton, John (2003), 'Problems of governance in the USA', in Alan Rugman and Gavin Boyd (eds), *Alliance Capitalism for the New American Economy*, Cheltenham, UK and Northampton, MA, USA: Edward Elgar, pp. 19–40.

Kirton, John and Virginia Maclaren (2002), *Linking Trade, Environment and Social Cohesion: NAFTA Experiences, Global Challenges*, Aldershot: Ashgate.

Kohler, Wilhelm (2002), 'Issues of US–EU Trade Policy', Comment on 'Hufbauer, Gary and Frederic Neuman (2002), 'US–EU Trade and Investment: An American Perspective', paper presented at a conference titled 'Transatlantic Perspectives on the US and EU Economies: Convergence, Conflict and Cooperation', Kennedy School of Government, Harvard University, 11–12 April.

May, Bernhard (2001), 'New challenges for transatlantic economic relations', in Hall Gardner and Radoslava Stefanova (eds), *The New Transatlantic Agenda: Facing the Challenges of Global Governance*, Aldershot: Ashgate, pp. 173–90.

Mearsheimer, John (1990), 'Back to the future: instability in Europe after the cold war', *International Security* (Summer), 5–56.

Mills, Lisa (2004), 'Terminating agricultural biotechnology? Hard law, voluntary measures, and the demise of the life sciences industry', in John Kirton and Michael Trebilcock (eds), *Hard Choices, Soft Law: Voluntary Standards in Global Trade, Environment and Social Governance*, Aldershot: Ashgate.

Moore, Karl and Alan Rugman (2003), 'Canadian multinationals are regional, not global', *Policy Options*, **24** (August), 44–7.

Padoan, Pier Carlo, Paul Brenton and Gavin Boyd (2003), *The Structural Foundations of International Finance*, Cheltenham, UK and Northampton, MA, USA: Edward Elgar.

Prestowitz, Clyde, Lawrence Chimerine and Andrew Szamossegi (1996), 'The case for a transatlantic free trade area', in Bruce Stokes (ed.), *Open for Business: Creating a Transatlantic Marketplace*, New York: Council on Foreign Relations, pp. 20–31.

Reinicke, Wolfgang (1996), *Deepening the Atlantic*, Gutersloh: Bertelsmann Foundation Publishers.

Rugman, Alan (1999), 'Negotiating multilateral rules to promote investment', in Michael Hodges, John Kirton and Joseph Daniels (eds), *The G8's Role in the New Millennium*, Aldershot: Ashgate, pp. 143–57.

Rugman, Alan (2000), 'From globalisation to regionalism: the foreign direct investment dimension of international finance', in Karl Kaiser, John Kirton and Joseph Daniels (eds), *Shaping a New International Financial System: Challenges of Governance in a Globalizing World*, Aldershot: Ashgate, pp. 203–19.

Rugman, Alan and Gavin Boyd (2003), *Alliance capitalism for the new American economy*, Cheltenham, UK and Northampton, MA, USA: Edward Elgar.

Rugman, Alan and Alina Kudina (2002), 'Britain, Europe and North America', in Michele Fratianni, Paolo Savona and John Kirton (eds), *Governing Global Finance: New Challenges, G7 and IMF Contributions*, Aldershot: Ashgate, pp. 186–95.

Rugman, Alan and Alain Verbeke (2003), 'The World Trade Organization, multinational enterprise and civil society', in Michele Fratianni, Paolo Savona and John Kirton (eds), *Sustaining Global Growth and Development: G7 and IMF Challenges and Contributions*, Aldershot: Ashgate, pp. 81–97.

Schott, Jeffrey and Barbara Oegg (2001), 'Europe and the Americas: toward a TAFTA-South?', *World Economy*, **6**, pp. 745–59.

Siebert, Horst (1996), *TAFTA: Fuelling Trade Discrimination or Global Liberalization?*, Washington, DC: AICGS.

Stokes, Bruce (ed.), (1996), *Open for Business: Creating a Transatlantic Marketplace*, New York: Council on Foreign Relations.

Tavlas, George (2003), 'The economics of exchange-rate regimes: a review essay', *The World Economy* (August), 1215–46.

Ullrich, Heidi (2001), 'Stimulating trade liberalization after Seattle: G7 leadership in global governance', in George Von Furstenberg and John Kirton (eds), *New Directions in Global Economic Governance: Creating International Order for the Twenty First Century*, Aldershot: Ashgate, pp. 219–42.

APPENDIX I

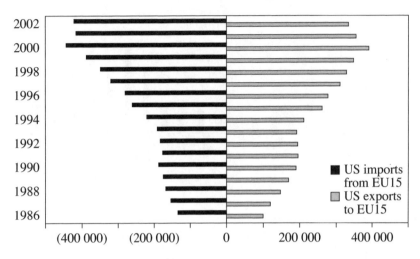

Source: US Department of Commerce, Bureau for Economic Analysis.

Figure 3A.1   Total volume of EU–US trade (billions of nominal US$;
customs reported per EU15)

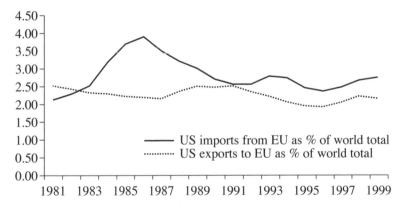

Source: Global Financial Market Database, http://www.euromonitor.com.

Figure 3A.2   US–EU trade as percentage of world trade (nominal value;
customs reported per EU15)

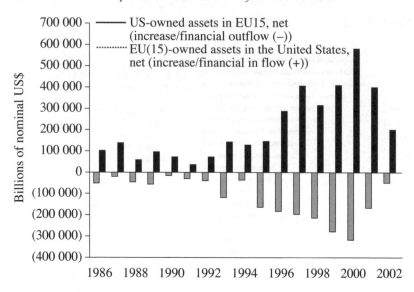

Source: US Department of Commerce, Bureau for Economic Analysis.

Figure 3A.3   *History of US–EU foreign direct investment transactions*
(billions of nominal US$; net outflows from US B.O.P.
perspective; reported per EU15)

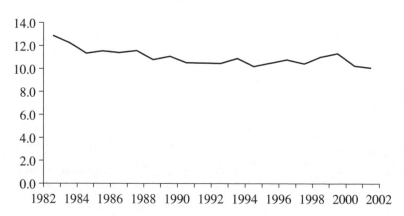

Source: US Department of Commerce, Bureau for Economic Analysis; UN Common
Database; UNCTAD Stat, calculated per nominal US$; data for some countries may differ
on inclusion of reinvested earnings.

Figure 3A.4   *US direct investment outflow to the EU15 area as percentage*
of world total FDI

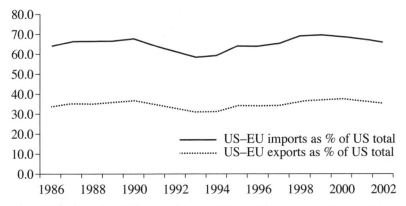

Source: US Department of Commerce, Bureau of Economic Analysis, calculated per nominal US$ value; customs reported per EU15.

Figure 3A.5   US–EU trade as percentage of US total trade

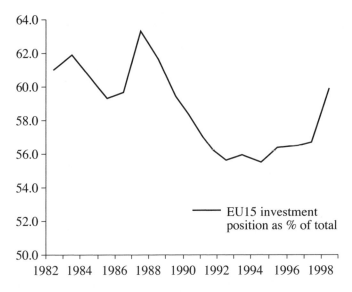

Source: OECD Source Database; UN Common Database, harmonized data, where available; calculated per nominal value; may differ on inclusion of reinvested earnings.

Figure 3A.6   (EU15) direct investment position in the US as percentage of EU total outward direct investment stock

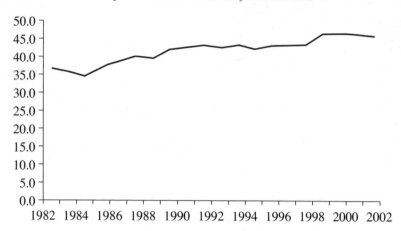

Source: US Department of Commerce, Bureau of Economic Analysis; OECD Source, calculated per nominal US$.

Figure 3A.7   US direct investment position (stock) in the EU15 area as percentage of US total outward direct investment position (stock)

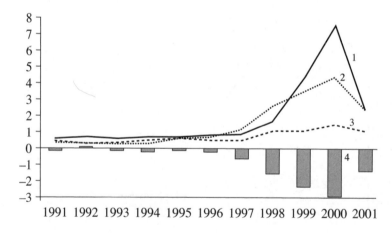

Notes:
1. Intra-EU flows.
2. EU outward flows to non-EU countries.
3. EU inward flows from non-EU countries.
4. Net inflows.

Figure 3A.8   EU foreign direct investment flows: extra-EU, intra-EU and net as % of GDP

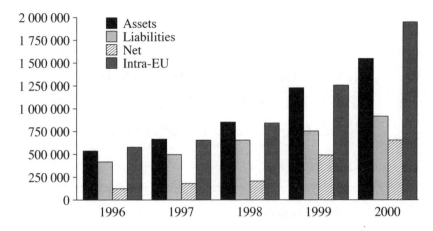

Figure 3A.9   EU foreign direct investment stocks, 1996–2000, (million ECU/EUR)

4. Structural potentials in Atlantic trade: measuring the impact of a US–Europe free trade agreement

Walid Hejazi

1. INTRODUCTION

A majority of the world's trade and foreign direct investment (FDI) is concentrated in three regional trading blocks: North America, Europe and Asia. Although two of these regions have formal regional trade agreements (North America and Europe), the third (Asia) does not. Although there have been serious discussions involving a potential free trade agreement (FTA) among some Asian economies, no major agreement is yet forthcoming.

In addition to having successful agreements in North America and Europe, there continues to be progress in expanding these agreements, including adding new members to an existing free trade area, such as the recent admission of ten new members into the European Union. There is also discussion about having an FTA among all countries in North and South America, the Free Trade Area of the Americas (FTAA). There are also examples of one country within a free trade area establishing an FTA with an outside member, including Canada–Chile, Canada–Costa Rica, Canada–Israel, the United States–Israel, United States–Jordan, United States–Australia and the United States–Singapore.

At a much more comprehensive level, there has been discussion of establishing a transatlantic trading area, namely a United States–Europe or perhaps a North America–Europe FTA. In addition to the elimination of tariffs on a broad spectrum of goods and services, such an agreement would also require identifying which sectors would be exempt, as well as defining the protections that would be afforded FDI from members of the expanded area. Such protection may be similar to the National Treatment provisions within the NAFTA.

Many empirical analyses have identified clearly that the United States trades far less with Europe than is predicted by comparative advantage, and in contrast has more of its FDI in Europe than many models would predict. A natural explanation for these patterns of US trade and FDI with Europe is that the presence of trade barriers between the United States and Europe limit their bilateral trade, and induce FDI into each other's region; that is, much of the FDI is tariff induced. To avoid tariffs imposed on goods imported into each area, MNEs locate production facilities inside the free trade area itself, thus jumping the tariff wall. The less than optimal amount of trade, and tariff induced FDI, are inefficiencies that result in significant reductions in social welfare. The corollary of this, however, is that an FTA would eliminate many of these inefficiencies, and would allow MNEs to service markets within North America and Europe in the most efficient way possible. It must be noted also that, although regional welfare is expected to increase as a result of both trade and FDI adjustments that follow an FTA, national welfare is definitely expected to rise, given the trade adjustment, but may not rise and may actually fall as FDI relocates. If, as a result of an FTA, MNEs decide to locate more inside a country, this would likely raise the host country's welfare. On the other hand, if the FDI reallocations involve moving production abroad, this may reduce welfare of the country experiencing the fall in FDI, although the extent of the fall is limited by the fact that the FDI was tariff-induced, and not the most efficient outcome on a regional basis.

There are many economic, political and social issues that need to be addressed before any such FTA can be implemented. Furthermore, although few would disagree with the view that there will be net economic benefits from such an agreement, the length of time before these benefits are achieved can be substantial. Often there are significant economic adjustment costs involved, which have important political and social implications. Through time, however, as local economies expand production in industries for which they have a comparative advantage, and contract in others, the benefits begin to emerge. This adjustment period must be well understood so that arrangements can be made to allow for flexibility in light of such significant adjustment costs.

The objective of this chapter is to look beyond these issues and measure the impact that an FTA between the United States and Europe would likely have on US trade and FDI patterns with Europe. Of course there are many approaches one could take to answer this question, including the sample of data that could be used and the year coverage. The analysis below will focus on the United States' trade and FDI patterns, with particular focus on how these patterns may change with respect to Europe: the United States is the hub and there are 52 countries that serve as spokes. A natural extension would involve using Europe's trade patterns with the United States, that is, have each European country trade with many other countries. To make the analysis more manageable, the analysis below will use the former, measuring the predicted impact that a FTA between the United States and Europe would have on US trade patterns with Europe. The United States' trade and FDI relations with many other countries will also be included to make the analysis as robust as possible.

The data trends presented below show several important results that should be pointed out. First, although the United States trades as much with Europe as it does with Canada, Europe receives almost 60 per cent of US outward FDI, whereas Canada receives less than 15 per cent. These results are found to be consistent with the estimates of our gravity model, which show robustly that the USA trades far less with Europe than is predicted by comparative advantage. The second important result is the persistent trend seen in the USA's trade patterns with the world. Specifically the share of the USA's exports and imports from developed countries has been steadily falling and the developing countries' shares have been increasing. If current trends continue, a larger share of US imports and exports will be with developing countries within the next few decades.

The empirical analysis presented below simulates the impact of a Europe–USA FTA on US trade patterns. The results show that any such agreement would have large impacts on the amount and the share of US trade with Europe. This result is true even under conservative assumptions. The impact of such an agreement affects not only trade and FDI patterns within the free trade area, but also other countries, with the result depending on the overlap in trade by industry, as well as the role of MNEs. That is, the larger the overlap in trade a region has with Europe vis-à-vis the USA, the larger the negative impact an FTA between the USA and Europe would have on that region. These issues are discussed in detail below in the context of the simulations implemented.

The format of this chapter is as follows. Section 2 discusses briefly the gains to be had from trade and FDI. Section 3 describes the data used. Section 4 provides the empirical results of the gravity model. Section 5 simulates the impact of a USA–Europe FTA on US trade and FDI patterns with the world. Section 6 concludes.

2.   THE GAINS FROM TRADE AND FDI

The gains that flow from globalization in general and more specifically FTAs are well documented. The gains vis-à-vis trade are broken down in terms of the static gains and the dynamic gains. The static gains are simply the increased amounts of goods and services that result from each country specializing in the production of goods and services for which they have a comparative advantage. These are one-time impacts that follow trade liberalization, and often involve a significant period in which each country adjusts its production away from the goods and services for which it has a comparative disadvantage toward those for which it has a comparative advantage. These static gains do not result in increased growth rates for economies, but rather simply increase the amount of goods and services available for consumption.

The dynamic gains, on the other hand, do result in increased growth rates of economies. Furthermore the dynamic gains are thought to be much more significant than the static gains: they have been estimated to be more than four times as great. These dynamic gains stem from increased growth rates that result from increased competition that follow the reduction or elimination of protection afforded domestic firms. That is, as a result of the elimination of protection for domestic firms, they are forced to be more innovative or face a loss in market share to more efficient foreign firms that would have better access to local markets with any FTA.

In addition to pursuing trade-liberalizing policies, governments have also sought to implement policies to attract FDI because of the perceived benefits that accompany such investment. These benefits include the following. First, inward FDI is an important source of R&D diffusion (Hejazi and Safarian, 1999a; van Pottelsberghe and Lichtenberg, 2001); second, foreign firms have higher levels of productivity and trade propensities than Canadian firms (Baldwin and Sabourin, 2001; Trefler, 1999; Tang and Rao, 2001); third, inward FDI contributes to domestic capital formation (Hejazi and Pauly, 2002, 2003); and finally, many studies have found complementarity between international trade and FDI (Brainard, 1997; Graham, 1993; Hejazi and Safarian, 1999b; Lipsey and Weiss, 1981, 1984; Rao *et al.* 1996; Safarian and Hejazi, 2001). In short, FDI has been shown to be important in many dimensions for both home and host economies.

This discussion indicates therefore that a discussion of trade liberalization cannot be thought of independently of FDI liberalization, and that both trade and FDI are associated with significant gains. Since these two modes used by MNEs are inexorably linked, there are often explicit protections extended to FDI in trade agreements, such as the national treatment provisions embedded in the NAFTA. That is, there is often liberalization that applies to both of these modes of international business.

A majority of international trade is in fact mediated by multinational enterprises. Rugman (2000) estimates that the top 500 MNEs account for over half of the world's trade. As FTAs reduce the direct costs of trade vis-à-vis tariff reductions, the immediate first order effect may at first glance seem to be for MNEs to reduce the amount of foreign production and increase trade. However the analysis is not that straightforward. The impact on trade and FDI could be the opposite – the MNE may now locate a production facility in the foreign market and supply both the home and host markets from an expanded or even new production in a host; such horizontal investment reallocation would depend on the locational advantages within each country. There is added complexity when there is vertical disentangling of the production process, where part of the production process is located at home and other parts abroad: the FTA would make such outcomes viable given that the movements of intermediates also face reduced or no tariffs. These complications indicate that net impacts of an FTA on trade and FDI patterns are very much specific to countries and industries and the nature of production therein.

In short, governments have sought trade liberalization policies in general because of the gains that accompany increased trade (see Coe and Helpman, 1995; Dobson, 2002; Trefler, 2004). Such developments on the trade side, however, have significant impacts on FDI, and policies on FDI are usually addressed within the FTA. Free trade has therefore been identified as an important source of growth for participating countries.

This chapter measures the impact an FTA between the United States and Europe would likely have on US trade and FDI patterns with Europe and the rest of the world. The analysis is limited in the sense that it does not make explicit estimates of the impact of such an agreement on growth rates, employment or welfare. Such extensions are beyond the scope of the chapter. Rather, it draws on results from other analyses and incorporates those results into the simulations undertaken below. Thus the analysis provided gives keen insights into the likely impact of such an agreement on a narrow dimension of the economies of the United States and Europe: their bilateral trade and FDI patterns, as well as with the rest of the world.

3. DESCRIBING THE DATA

The data used in the analysis presented here include US bilateral trade and FDI with each of 52 countries over the period 1970 to 2000. These countries account for over 90 per cent of US total trade and FDI with the world. The 52 countries and definitions of regional groupings are listed in Table 4.1. The data sources for these data as well as the additional data needed to estimate the gravity model are provided in the data appendix at the end of the chapter. There is also a short data appendix describing the FDI stock data.

There is a significant change that is taking place in terms of the United States' trading patterns with the global economy (Figure 4.1). Specifically there has been a steady decline in the share of US exports and US imports destined for and originating in developed countries. If these trends continue,

Table 4.1   Countries used and regional groupings

	Europe	East Asia	Latin America		Europe	East Asia	Latin America
Argentina			X	Italy	X		
Australia				Jamaica			X
Austria	X			Japan		X	
Bahamas			X	Korea		X	
Belgium–Luxembourg	X			Malaysia		X	
Brazil			X	Mexico			X
Canada				Netherlands	X		
Chile			X	New Zealand			
China		X		Nigeria			
Colombia			X	Norway	X		
Costa Rica			X	Panama			X
Denmark	X			Peru			X
Dominican Republic			X	Philippines		X	
Ecuador			X	Portugal	X		
Egypt				Saudi Arabia			
Finland	X			Singapore		X	
France	X			South Africa			
Germany	X			Spain	X		
Greece	X			Sweden	X		
Guatemala			X	Switzerland	X		
Honduras			X	Trinidad and Tobago			X
Hong Kong		X		Thailand		X	
India				Turkey			
Indonesia		X		United Arab Em.			
Ireland	X			United Kingdom	X		
Israel				Venezuela			X

more US imports will come from and US exports will go to developing countries by the year 2020.[1] In contrast to the trade side, the distribution of US outward FDI has not seen dramatic changes between developed and developing countries. As seen in Figure 4.2, the share of US outward FDI in developed countries has remained around 75 per cent throughout the period 1966 to 2002.

Figure 4.3 breaks the distribution of US exports and imports into three regions: intra-North American, Europe and Japan. The patterns point to dramatic differences in the way that the US economy interacts with these three regions. Although the global GDP share of Europe is far larger than that of Canada (Figure 4.4), the United States trades as much (both exports and imports) with Canada as it does with Europe. That is, although Europe has almost 25 per cent of the world's GDP and Canada about 3 per cent, the United States sends about 25 per cent of exports and receives about 20 per cent of its imports from each of Canada and Europe. Japan has about

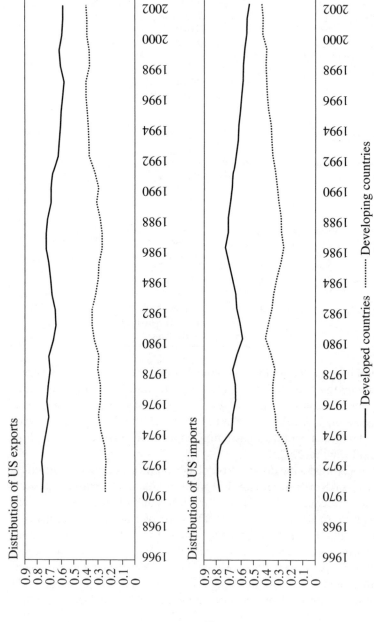

Figure 4.1   Distribution of US trade between developed and developing countries

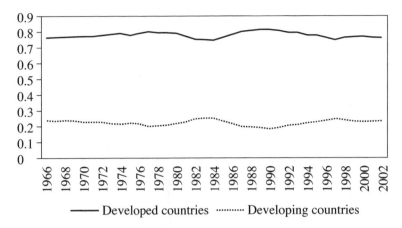

Figure 4.2   Distribution of US outward FDI stocks

10 per cent of the world's GDP share and receives about 10 per cent of US exports and imports.

In sharp contrast to the trade side, the United States has almost 60 per cent of its outward FDI in Europe, about 15 per cent in Japan and about 10 per cent in Canada (Figure 4.5). That is, despite trading as much with Canada as it does with Europe, the United States has far more FDI in Europe. This points to a significant difference in the way US MNEs service North American as opposed to European economies.

These patterns are easily explainable from a free trade perspective. As can be seen in Figure 4.6, Canada's share of U.S. FDI has fallen steadily over the past 30 years, from 35% to about 10%. Despite beginning well in advance of the Canada-U.S. FTA and the NAFTA, these trends have accelerated around the periods of FTA implementation and hence have been linked statistically to these FTAs. As a result of these agreements, the United States has relied less on production within Canada with its affiliates, opting rather to concentrate production within the United States, thus capturing economies of scale, and simply exporting to Canada.[2]

Although the analysis presented in this chapter will be at the level of US trade and FDI, something should be said about the micro strategies of US MNEs: that is, the strategies implemented by US, European and Japanese MNEs operating vis-à-vis trade with the United States. These MNEs have strikingly different strategies. The data presented in Table 4.2 indicate that US parents mediate 26.8 per cent of US exports to Europe but only 15.9 per cent to Japan. On the other hand, European MNEs operating inside the USA mediate 8.7 per cent of US exports to their parents whereas the similar statistic for Japan is 54.2 per cent. In other words, European MNEs

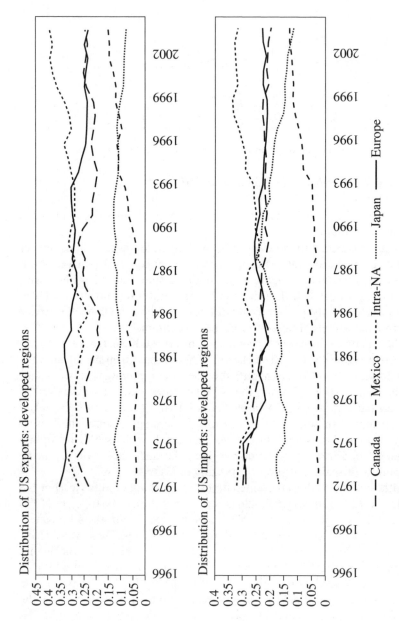

Figure 4.3　US exports and imports: developed regions

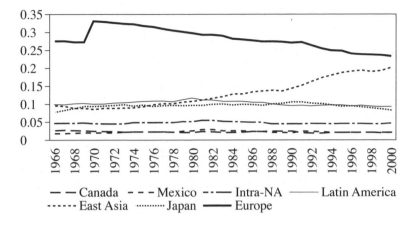

Figure 4.4   GDP shares

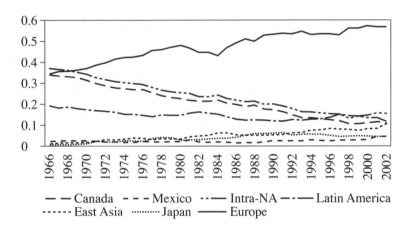

Figure 4.5   Distribution of US outward FDI stocks, by region

underperform both US and Japanese MNEs in mediating US exports. A similar story obtains on the import side. Although US MNEs mediate 11.5 per cent of imports from Europe, they only mediate 2 per cent of imports from Japan. In contrast, European MNEs mediate 34.8 per cent of imports from Europe, but this is a much smaller percentage than the 69 per cent of imports from Japan that are mediated by Japanese parents. These data indicate therefore that, although the Europeans do better than the US MNEs in terms of mediating imports from Europe into the United States, they do less well than Japanese MNEs in mediating imports from Japan.

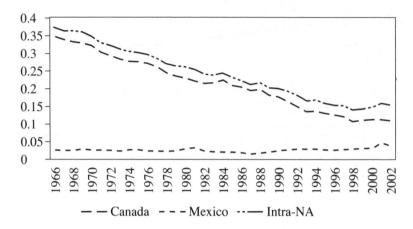

Figure 4.6   Distribution of US Outward FDI stocks within North America

Table 4.2   Role of MNEs in mediating US trade, 1992

	US exports which are intra-firm			US imports which are intra-firm		
	Percentage of all exports	Between US parents and their majority-owned foreign affiliates	Between US affiliates and their foreign-owned parents	Percentage of all imports	Between US parents and their majority-owned foreign affiliates	Between US affiliates and their forcign-owned parents
All countries	33.4	22.5	10.9	41.5	15.6	25.9
Canada	41.4	37.4	4.00	46.7	37.1	9.6
Mexico	26.3	24.9	1.5	34.7	30.5	4.2
Europe	35.5	26.8	8.7	46.3	11.5	34.8
Japan	70.1	15.9	54.2	71.3	2.00	69.2
Latin America	20.8	18.6	2.2	29.1	20.3	8.8
Asia	38.5	14.7	23.8	42.6	7.7	34.9

4.   THE GRAVITY MODEL

There are several models that have been used to explain bilateral trade patterns across countries. Each of these models appeal to a different source of comparative advantage. Specifically the monopolistic competition model appeals to increasing returns to scale and product differentiation as the source of comparative advantage. The Heckscher–Ohlin model appeals to relative factor endowments while the gravity model appeals to transactions costs (broadly defined). It has been shown by Deardorff (1995) that the gravity model can in fact be derived from alternative trade models. That is, the gravity equation is a testable implication of both the Heckscher–Ohlin and the monopolistic competition models of international trade. This is good motivation for the use of the gravity model in the context of the present chapter because the objective is to use a model that explains trade patterns well as opposed to estimating the model that is most appropriate to explain US trade.

The approach adopted here extends the gravity model used to explain trade by incorporating FDI. That is, the analysis measures the relation between trade and FDI, and this extension is linked to the transactions costs which underlie the gravity model. The gravity model has transactions costs as its source of comparative advantage. The presence of FDI stocks abroad facilitates the flow of information, technical and otherwise, on a broad front. It does so intra-firm, as internalization approaches to FDI have long argued. MNEs, moreover, are deeply involved in the spreading alliance forms of business organization. In addition, spillovers of knowledge through FDI often rival national production of knowledge locally (Hejazi and Safarian, 1999a; Hejazi, 2001). This reduction in information and transactions costs between home and host countries reduces the costs involved in conducting business between them, thus leading to increases in international trade. Also a large part of international trade is intra-firm and such trade may respond differently to price and exchange rate changes than would arm's-length trade (Zeile, 1997). As a result, one would expect the presence of MNEs to be an important determinant of trade patterns. For a thorough discussion of internalization and the MNE, see Rugman (1980, 1988).

The gravity model has been used to explain bilateral trade flows among large groups of countries and over long periods of time (Feenstra *et al.*, 2001; Frankel *et al.*, 1995; Hejazi and Trefler, 1996). The gravity model is used here to explain trade flows between the United States and 52 other countries over the period 1970 to 2000, the period for which bilateral FDI and trade data exist. Table 4.1 provided a list of countries and regional groupings used. The analysis is extended to take into account FDI as an additional determinant of international trade. Such an analysis will indicate whether, after controlling for comparative advantage (the gravity model), international trade and FDI are substitutes or complements.

Let t indicate years, i the exporting country, j the importing country, and let X_{ijt} denote bilateral exports from country i to country j in year t. Let T_{ijt} denote transactions costs broadly defined. Also let D_{ij} denote regional dummy variables. The gravity model can therefore be written as follows:

$$\log(X_{ijt}) = \alpha + \log(T_{ijt})\,\beta + D_{ij}\,\delta + \in_{ijt} \qquad (4.1)$$

The transactions cost and dummy variables (with GDP denoting gross domestic product) are listed in Table 4.3.

Table 4.3   The gravity model

	Variable description	Expected sign in trade regression
$GDPPC_{it} \times GDPPC_{jt}$	product of per capita GDPs in countries i and j	+
$GDP_{it} \times GDP_{jt}$	product of GDPs in countries i and j	+
distance$_{ij}$	a measure of distance between countries i and j	–
language$_{ij}$	a dummy variable equal to unity if countries i and j have the same language	+
exchange rate$_{ijt}$	value of the US dollar in terms of foreign currency (on a real PPP basis)	– for exports + for imports
	Dummy variables	
Adjacency$_{ij}$	Equal to 1 for Canada and Mexico, 0 otherwise	+
Europe$_j$	Equal to 1 for countries in Europe, 0 otherwise	?
East Asia$_j$	Equal to 1 for countries in East Asia, 0 otherwise	?
Latin America$_j$	Equal to 1 for countries in Latin America, 0 otherwise	?
Japan$_j$	equal to 1 for Japan, 0 otherwise	?

The idea is that countries of similar size and per capita GDP have similar needs both in terms of both intermediate inputs (Ethier, 1982) and consumption patterns. Also two countries' trade should be positively related to the two countries' incomes. In addition countries that are close geographically and countries with similar language will have small transactions costs of doing business and correspondingly large levels of bilateral trade. The exchange rate is expected to have an opposite impact in the export and import regressions: increases in the US dollar are expected to increase US imports but reduce exports.

Dummy variables are also included for the following regional groupings: Europe, East Asia, Latin America and Japan. We also include an adjacency dummy to take into account the special geographic relationship the United States has with Canada and Mexico. It is important to point out that these dummy variables are capturing residuals in the model. If the standard gravity model variables captured all of the determinants of international trade, these regional and adjacency dummy variables would be statistically insignificant. Adding the dummy variables captures persistent unexplained trade between the United States and the regional grouping that is not explained by the standard gravity model variables.

Since we are concerned with US exports to other countries, $i = U$, denoting the United States:

$$\log(X_{Ujt}) = \alpha + \log(T_{Ujt}) \beta + D_{Uj} \delta + \in_{Ujt}. \tag{4.2}$$

The reader familiar with the literature will recognize that in this section we are trying to follow as closely as possible the work of Frankel *et al.* (1995) and Hejazi and Trefler (1996). This allows for simple comparisons with previous work.

After estimating the gravity model, outward FDI is included as an additional determinant of trade:

$$\log(X_{Ujt}) = \alpha + \log(T_{Ujt}) \beta + D_{Uj} \delta + \log(FDI_{Ujt})\lambda + \in_{Ujt}. \tag{4.3}$$

Intuitively FDI fits nicely into the gravity model. According to the gravity model, the source of the comparative advantage is transactions costs, broadly defined. The presence of FDI would indicate that the links or networks in the foreign country have already been established, and hence the costs associated with exporting should be lower. As a result, exports should be higher. According to this hypothesis, therefore, trade and FDI are complementary.

The theory indicates that there is an interaction between FDI and trade. That is, FDI patterns are highly dependent upon patterns of trade, and vice versa. It is typically the case that MNEs first export to a country, followed by movement of production facilities abroad so as to avoid transportation costs and import protection, guarantee access to the local market, and generally to compete more effectively with local firms.[3] As discussed in Grosse and Trevino (1996), 'the analysis supports the notion that FDI is used to preserve markets that were previously established by exports'. It is also the case that FDI promotes trade. Eaton and Tamura (1994) indicate that US FDI follows exports, whereas Japanese FDI has a beachhead effect in promoting subsequent Japanese exports. The argument that US FDI abroad serves as a beachhead for US exports has been advanced also in Encarnation (1993) and Graham (1993). Reasons for this include the fact that FDI abroad markets home products and home-made inputs; and MNE retailers are more likely to sell home products. All of this is consistent with much US trade being intra-firm (Hejazi and Safarian, 2001).

The estimation results for the gravity model are provided in Table 4.4. The table has two sets of results, one for exports and the other for imports. Each set has two columns, one for the standard gravity model, and the other that includes FDI as well. The results can be summarized as follows. Both exports and imports are strongly positively related to the product of both GDP and GDP per capita between the United States and the host economy. US trade is also positively related to the adjacency dummy as well as language similarities between countries.

Table 4.4   Gravity model results

	Dependent variable: exports		Dependent variable: imports	
	No FDI	Total FDI	No FDI	Total FDI
Constant	−20.056	−6.3519	−17.240	−4.2213
	(−33.21)	(−8.53)	(−19.55)	(−3.48)
Product of GDPs	0.6060	0.3855	0.6535	0.4441
	(52.22)	(29.40)	(38.57)	(20.81)
Product of per capita GDPs	0.5845	0.2535	0.5532	0.2388
	(30.53)	(12.20)	(19.79)	(7.06)
Exchange rates	−0.0298	−0.0246	−0.0153	−0.0103
	(−8.19)	(−8.04)	(−2.87)	(−2.07)
Distance	−0.6802	−0.7192	−1.1628	−1.1998
	(−15.42)	(−19.41)	(−18.05)	(−19.89)
Adjacency	0.5914	0.2810	0.2273	−0.0676
	(6.35)	(3.55)	(1.67)	(−0.52)
Language	0.4007	0.0039	0.4185	0.0342
	(11.26)	(0.11)	(8.06)	(0.62)
Latin America	0.2403	−0.3105	0.0420	−0.4813
	(4.39)	(−6.09)	(0.52)	(−5.80)
Japan	0.9500	0.8145	1.6865	1.5578
	(9.26)	(9.45)	(11.26)	(11.10)
Europe	**−0.3117**	**−0.5365**	**−0.3392**	**−0.5527**
	(−6.13)	**(−12.31)**	**(−4.57)**	**(−7.79)**
East Asia	0.9264	0.5961	1.6973	1.3835
	(18.71)	(13.68)	(23.49)	(19.51)
Outward FDI		0.3242		0.3080
		(25.10)		(14.65)
Adjusted R^2	0.845	0.891	0.761	0.791

US trade is negatively related to the distance between countries, which is one of the most robust results in empirical international trade. US trade is also found to be negatively related to exchange rates: although a negative relationship is expected for US exports, a positive relationship was expected for US imports. That is, the sign in the gravity model for imports is incorrectly signed.

The estimated coefficients on FDI are positive and highly significant. This adds to the large body of existing evidence that trade and FDI are indeed complementary. That is, as FDI into a country increases, this is followed in future years by more trade with the home. It must be made clear that this result is in no way contradictory to the results which show that, as a result of the NAFTA, trade and FDI move in opposite directions. As a result of an FTA, if the relative cost of one mode of internationalization falls (that is, trade), we expect more of that mode (trade) and less of the others (including FDI). That is, trade and FDI move in opposite directions in reaction to a change in the relative cost of undertaking these channels. The complementary story applies to the impact that increasing one of these modes directly has on other modes. More specifically we find that increasing US FDI into a host economy increases US exports and imports with that same country. A dynamic specification would indicate that such interactions are spread over several years.

The results of most interest, however, are those on the dummy variables. The USA has more exports and imports with Japan than is predicted by the gravity model, and fewer with Europe. These results are robust to alternative specifications as well as to the presence or absence of FDI in the model. There is also more US trade with East Asia than is predicted by the model. An interesting result emerges for Latin America. Although there are more exports with Latin America than are predicted by the gravity model, and just enough imports, once FDI is taken into account as an additional determinant of trade, the Latin America dummies turn negative. That is, in the fully-specified model, there is less US trade in Latin America than is predicted by the gravity model. As in the case of the Europe dummy, the introduction of FDI into the model makes the estimated under-trade between the US and Europe even larger. The reason for this is that FDI is estimated to be a positive determinant of trade. Given the large amounts of US FDI in Europe, once this FDI enters the model the prediction is that there should be even more trade with Europe.

These results are not surprising given the restrictiveness of Japan regarding inward FDI and the relative openness of Europe. More specifically, in the survey of executives across some 50 countries as reported in the World Competitiveness Report, the United Kingdom ranked fourth in terms of being open to foreign investment, Germany ninth, Luxembourg tenth, the Netherlands 11th, Sweden 20th, whereas Japan ranked 41st. In other words, to gain access to the Japanese market, US MNEs are forced to use trade, as FDI is strongly restricted. On the other hand, to gain access to the European market, there are fewer restrictions on FDI and, given the tariffs placed on goods imported into Europe, US MNEs are forced to rely more heavily on FDI to gain access to the European market. This interpretation is certainly consistent with the observation that, while 56.9 per cent of US FDI is in Europe, only 4.8 per cent is in Japan.

The coefficient estimates in Table 4.4 indicate that Europe's trade with the United States is 1.7 times less than it should be according to the model's predictions. Since the dependent variable (trade) is in logs, to get 1.7 the exponential of the estimated value of the Europe dummy variable must be applied. This coefficient is at the heart of the simulations to be undertaken below.

5.   SIMULATIONS

To simulate the impact of an FTA on US trade relations with Europe, assumptions must be made on how such an agreement would affect the amount of US trade with Europe as well as US trade with other regions. These impacts are entered into the model by adjusting the amount of US trade with each region relative to what is predicted. For example, the results presented here indicate that the US trades too little with Europe and too much with East Asia and Japan. An FTA between the USA and Europe would therefore increase the amount of US trade with Europe. The simulations consider the impact of such an agreement depending on how 'deep' the agreement is. As indicated above, there are many dimensions that should be considered in assessing the effects of an FTA. Here the focus is entirely on a one-dimensional measure, on how deep that agreement is, where deep is meant to capture the impact such an agreement has on trade between the members of the FTA.

What complicates the analysis in addition to the depth of the agreement is the impact of such an agreement on trade creation and trade diversion. The impacts of an FTA vis-à-vis trade are classified into trade creation and trade diversion. That is, as a result of an FTA, there is predicted to be an increase in bilateral trade flows among members. There is also expected to be trade diversion away from lower-cost imports from outsiders to higher-cost inside providers who are able to compete against outsiders only because of the preferential access they have to the free trade area. Of course, these effects are offset in a dynamic framework: as growth rates inside the free trade area increase, there is increased demand for imports from all trading partners. Therefore, in addition to making assumptions on the depth of an agreement, further assumptions should also be made on the impact such an agreement would have on non-members.

Although the predicted impacts on trade of an FTA are relatively well understood, this is not the case for FDI. This has to do with the complexity involved in the strategies implemented by MNEs as well as the dependence of these strategies on the nature of the economies and industries involved. The immediate impact of an FTA is to reduce the cost of undertaking trade among members. As a result, MNEs operating inside the area may adjust the way in which they service each member market. To the extent that economies of scale are important, there may be a consolidation of production into fewer locations, with the output then being used to supply the entire free trade area. However where inside that free trade area the increased production takes place is not clear ex ante. Furthermore, to the extent that production can be decomposed vertically, an FTA may increase intraregional FDI within the free trade area as MNEs move to exploit locational advantages of member countries. In reality, it is likely that there are elements of both of the above occurring: increased concentration of some elements of the production process as well as a vertical disintegration of that process across member countries. It can be said, therefore, that an FTA has uncertain ex ante predictions for the impact on FDI among member countries.

An FTA will also affect FDI coming into the area from abroad (that is, from outside the free trade area). Here too the predictions are unclear ex ante. It may be the case that MNEs from countries outside the free trade area did not locate in any one member country because each market individually is too small to justify the fixed costs associated with setting up a production facility, or it may be the case that outside MNEs have set up facilities in each country to gain access to the respective market. Given the size of the European and US economies, the first is unlikely to be relevant, whereas the second is likely quite relevant. As a result of an FTA, to the extent that there is replication within the joining members because MNEs had placed facilities in each member country, the FTA may result in an MNE rationalizing production in such a way as to reduce its total investment inside the free trade area. Where (within the free trade area) they locate of course depends on the locational advantages of each member country.

The simulations presented in the figures below make two or three sets of assumptions suggested by the above discussion. The first set relates to the depth of the agreement, and this is captured by adjusting the Europe dummy in the model to measure the impact an FTA is likely to have on US trade patterns with Europe. The second set of assumptions relates to the likely impact an FTA between Europe and the United States may have on growth rates of economies, as well as on the impact on US FDI.

The third set of assumptions, that is not implemented, relates to trade diversion. This would be implemented by adjusting the other regional dummies in the model, most notably Japan and, to a lesser extent, East Asia and Latin America. These were not implemented here, as will be noted below, because they would simply reinforce the results noted, and hence would not provide additional insights.

Simulations that use elements of the first set of assumptions above are classified as static analyses, as they measure the one-time change in trade shares that result from changing the regional dummy variables in the model. Simulations that include elements of the first two sets of assumptions (and could easily include the third) are classified as dynamic simulations, and represent predictions on the impact such agreements have over a 20-year period. Details of these descriptions are provided below.

Static Simulations

The value of the estimated coefficient on the Europe dummy in the gravity model results, as reported in Table 4.4, was –0.5365 for exports and –0.5527 for imports. In order to interpret this coefficient, one must first take its exponential, which translates into a figure of –1.71 for exports and –1.74 for imports. In other words, US trade with Europe, according to the model, is 1.7 times lower than is predicted by the model.

In the first set of simulations, it is simply assumed that, as a result of an FTA between the United States and Europe, the amount of trade between the two countries moves trade patterns closer to what is predicted by the model. To operationalize this, the estimated model above is used to derive predictions of trade flows between the USA and each of the 52 countries in the sample, and the model is adjusted by making the Europe dummy less negative. As indicated in Table 4.5, the value of the Europe dummy is allowed to increase by increments of 0.10, thus moving trade patterns closer to what the model would predict. The simulations do not go all the way to the point where Europe's trade is equal to what is predicted by the model – there is nothing additional to learn beyond what is reported below. Furthermore, it is unlikely that Europe-U.S. trade would change that dramatically without inducing other FTAs to bring excluded countries into the new larger area.

The static simulations were presented in Figures 4.7a for exports and 4.7b for imports. Along the horizontal axis is the level of trade bias, with the level of the bias falling along the horizontal axis. The vertical axis reports trade shares. The first entry for each country or region at the far left of each figure is the predicted trade share (exports in Figure 4.7a and imports in Figure 4.7b) in 2000. These of course are very similar to the actual trade shares reported in Figure 4.3. As the depth of an FTA between Europe and the United States increases, the extent of the trade bias falls, and Europe's share of US exports and imports increases. Of course, mirroring this is the increasing share of developed country trade shares. Although the predicted trade biases for all other countries and regions are not changing in these static simulations, the trade shares for all non-European countries and

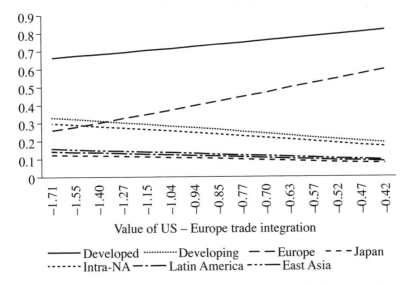

Figure 4.7a   Static simulations: increasing US–Europe trade, export shares

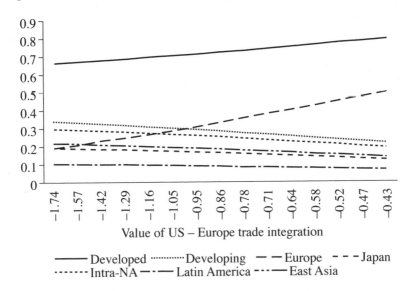

Figure 4.7b   Static simulations: increasing US–Europe trade, import shares

Table 4.5　　Values of Europe dummy in the static simulations

Imports		Exports	
Europe dummy	Level of bias (imports)	Europe dummy	Level of bias (exports)
−0.5527	−1.7379	−0.5365	−1.710 0
−0.4527	−1.5726	−0.4365	−1.5473
−0.3527	−1.4229	−0.3365	−1.4000
−0.2527	−1.2875	−0.2365	−1.2668
−0.1527	−1.1650	−0.1365	−1.1463
−0.0527	−1.0541	−0.0365	−1.0372
0.0473	−0.9538	0.0635	−0.9385
0.1473	−0.8630	0.1635	−0.8492
0.2473	−0.7809	0.2635	−0.7684
0.3473	−0.7066	0.3635	−0.6952
0.4473	−0.6394	0.4635	−0.6291
0.5473	−0.5785	0.5635	−0.5692
0.6473	−0.5235	0.6635	−0.5150
0.7473	−0.4736	0.7635	−0.4660
0.8473	−0.4286	0.8635	−0.4217

regions fall nevertheless. This happens because, as the trade between the USA and Europe increases, the share of total US trade with non-European countries is falling.

There are several additional simulations that could be undertaken in this static framework that would consider trade diversion effects: consideration can be given to the impact that increased trade integration between the USA and Europe could have on trade patterns with Japan, East Asia and Latin America. These are not undertaken here as they would simply reinforce (going in the same direction) the effects noted above. Furthermore the extent of increased trade can be increased more than has been done in Figures 4.7a and 4.7b, but, again, this would simply reinforce the results that have already been documented.

Dynamic Simulations

In this next set of simulations, the extent of the analysis is extended, the horizon being extended to 20 years. Furthermore, in addition to changing the trade bias between the USA and Europe, additional assumptions will be made regarding the impact the trade agreement will likely have on both GDP growth of each country and on the growth in US FDI locating in each country.

The first set of dynamic simulations are given in Table 4.6. It is assumed that each country maintains the compound growth rate that it experienced over the period 1990 to 2000 for the next 20 years. These growth rates apply to both the level of GDP and the amount of US FDI each country received. It is assumed initially for Table 4.6 that the extent of the trade biases estimated between the USA and all countries is exactly as reported in Table 4.4.

The results in Table 4.6 indicated, given the assumptions made, that, in the year 2020, Europe and Japan's trade shares with the United States would fall slightly, Latin America's would be unchanged, but East Asia's would rise dramatically. These results are driven by the superior growth rates in East Asia in terms of both its GDP and its attractiveness to US FDI.

Table 4.6   Dynamic simulations I: estimated trade shares 20 years out

	Developed countries	Developing countries	Exports				
			Europe	Japan	Intra-North American	Latin America	East Asia
2000	0.6671	0.3329	0.2649	0.1289	0.3011	0.1464	0.1602
2020	0.5900	0.4100	0.2531	0.1096	0.2578	0.1485	0.2347
			Imports				
2000	0.6625	0.3375	0.1954	0.1940	0.2983	0.1027	0.2170
2020	0.5633	0.4367	0.1810	0.1608	0.2473	0.1002	0.3187

For the given trade biases estimated above, and using the assumptions noted, the following is expected to occur over the next 20 years. First, Europe's trade shares for both imports and exports are expected to fall by about 1 per cent. Japan's trade shares are expected to fall by about 2 per cent on the export side and 3 per cent on the import side. Intra-North American trade (trade with Canada and Mexico) is also expected to fall, but by 4 per cent. Latin America's shares are not expected to change. On the other hand, East Asia is the region that is expected to pick up these lost trade shares. That is, East Asia's share of US exports is expected to increase by about 7 per cent and import shares by about 10 per cent. These results are driven by the superior growth rates in East Asian GDPs as well as the superior growth of US FDI locating there.

The limitation of the simulations presented in Table 4.6 is the assumption that the trade bias has not changed. Of course, if there was an FTA between the United States and Europe, the extent of their bilateral trade bias would fall (that is, trade between them would increase). These results are given in Figures 4.8a and 4.8b. The first entry on the far left is the trade shares as

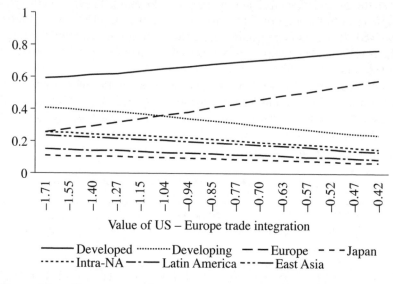

Figure 4.8a   Dynamic simulations: increasing US–Europe trade, export shares

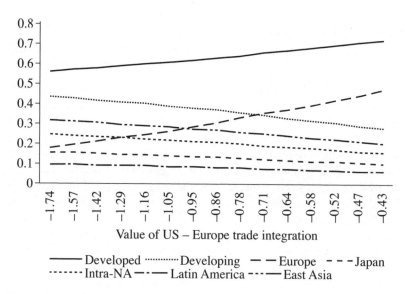

Figure 4.8b   Dynamic simulations: increasing US–Europe trade, import shares

reported in Table 4.6. Once again, given the superior growth in GDPs and US FDI experienced mainly by East Asian countries, this has pushed up the share of US trade developing countries receive.

Nevertheless, as the depth of the agreement between the United States and Europe increases, thus moving to the right in Figure 4.8a and Figure 4.8b, the share of U.S. trade with Europe and hence developed countries increases and that of developing countries including East Asia falls. It should be pointed out that these results are for trade shares: the levels of trade between the USA and other regions is still expected to increase, but not at the same rate as its trade with Europe.

A final set of simulations is implemented where additional assumptions are made on the impact such an agreement would have on the growth rates within the United States and Europe, as well as the likely impact such an FTA would have on the growth in US FDI in Europe. Past experience of FTAs indicates that there is usually an increase in member country GDP growth rates, as well as a slowdown in intraregional FDI patterns. It is therefore assumed that the growth rates within the United States and Europe increase by a full percentage point, and the rate of growth in US FDI into each European country is cut in half. These are reasonable assumptions given the experience of Canada and the United States following their two trade agreements. The first assumption, on GDP growth, works to increase US–European trade, whereas the second, on FDI, works to reduce their bilateral trade. These results are shown in Table 4.7.

Table 4.7   Dynamic simulations II: estimated trade shares 20 years out

| | Exports | | | | | | |
	Developed countries	Developing countries	Europe	Japan	Intra-North American	Latin America	East Asia
2000	0.6671	0.3329	0.2649	0.1289	0.3011	0.1464	0.1602
2020	0.5860	0.4140	0.2457	0.1107	Japan	0.1499	0.2370
	Imports						
2000	0.6625	0.3375	0.1954	0.1940	0.2983	0.1027	0.2170
2020	0.5617	0.4383	0.1780	0.1613	0.2482	0.1006	0.3198

The results for this second set of simulations are remarkably similar to the first set reported in Table 4.6 and in Figures 4.8a and 4.8b. Dynamic Simulations II differs from Dynamic Simulations I in three ways:

1. U.S. GDP growth is higher, which raises exports and imports with all countries
2. GDP growth of the European countries was also higher, which raises U.S. exports and imports with Europe
3. FDI growth in the European countries is lower, which serve to reduce U.S. trade with the European countries

The empirical results indicate that the increased trade induced by higher GDP growth is almost exactly offset by the slowing of US FDI into Europe. If GDP growth is allowed to rise by more than 1 per cent as assumed here and FDI growth was assumed not to be cut in half, the results would show increased trade shares between the United States and Europe. The results are quite sensitive to changes in these assumptions.

Summary

A brief summary of the strategy implemented here is in order. Three sets of simulations were undertaken:

1. static simulation, where the extent of under-trade between the United States and Europe is reduced (that is, the Europe dummy increases in value);
2. dynamic simulations I, where the horizon is 20 years into the future. The basic assumption is that the growth rates experienced in each country's GDP and FDI over the previous ten years were maintained over the next 20 years;
3. dynamic simulations II, where, in addition to the assumptions noted in (2), it was also assumed that US and European GDP growth rates increased and at the same time Europe's attractiveness to US FDI fell.

There are several extensions that can be undertaken for these simulations. As indicated above, the results are sensitive to the assumptions made in (3), namely the impact that an FTA would have on GDP and FDI growth rates. More attention to independently estimating these could be undertaken. Second, there have been no assumptions made here regarding the impact such an FTA could have on trade diversion. That is, as a result of an FTA between the United States and Europe, the amount of over-trade, say, with East Asia or Japan would likely fall. These assumptions were not made here as they would reinforce the results presented. However pursuing both of the suggestions noted here could lead to insightful results.

6. CONCLUSIONS

The overall net benefits associated with increased trade and FDI are well documented. This chapter has reviewed many of these benefits, and hence explains why many governments have pursued liberalization policies with respect to both trade and FDI. Given that a large part of international trade is mediated through the MNE, an assessment of trade policy in general and FTAs in particular cannot be thought of independently of the impact on FDI. That is, consideration for FDI should be embedded in any agreement that considers trade liberalization.

This chapter has also reviewed patterns of US trade and FDI with 52 other countries over the period 1970 to 2000. Several important facts are worth highlighting once again. First, an increasing share of US trade, both exports and imports, is with developing countries. Second, although Canada has a fraction of Europe's GDP share, the United States trades as much with Canada as it does with Europe. Third, and in sharp contrast to the trade side, the United States has about 60 per cent of its FDI in Europe but only 10 per cent in Canada. These differences are directly linked to the role of MNEs and the strategy they pursue inside a free trade area as compared to outside.

There has been much discussion of pursuing an FTA between Europe and the United States. This chapter has measured the impact such an agreement would have on US trade patterns with several regions of the world. As a result of such an agreement, Europe would see its trade shares rise significantly at the expense of East Asia, Japan and Canada.

The rapid growth of the East Asian economies and also the relative attractiveness of those economies to US FDI have resulted in East Asia experiencing a rising share of US trade. The implications of this are seen more in the dynamic simulations than in the static simulations. That is, assuming the growth experience of countries vis-à-vis GDP and US FDI were to continue for the next 20 years, East Asia emerges as a very important trading partner for the United States. Although the introduction of an FTA between the United States and Europe would actually stimulate further trade with East Asia, the *relative* importance of East Asia would fall as a result. The simulations also reduce the trade shares experienced by Canada and Mexico, as the US economy would increase its focus on the freely accessible European market.

There are many dimensions in which an FTA can have an impact on member and non-member countries. This chapter has narrowed the discussion considerably by focusing attention on the impact a potential FTA between the United States and Europe would have on US trade and FDI patterns with Europe, as well as on the rest of the world. The results clearly show that there are enormous trade gains to be had from such an agreement. Furthermore the arguments above also indicate the importance of embedding in an FTA protection for foreign investors, as FDI brings with it many benefits. To the extent that an FTA reduces the amount of intraregional FDI, this may reduce the associated benefits. However, to the extent that the FDI that is lost was tariff-induced, the regional losses may be minimized, although the national losses may be larger.

NOTES

1. An important limitation of a dichotomous split between developed and developing countries as provided in Figure 4.1 is that, over the 30-year period considered, some countries have moved from being developing to developed, or certainly can be considered far more developed today than in 1970. The best examples that come to mind are Korea, Mexico, Ireland, Greece and Portugal. For an analysis that uses continuous measures of development to classify countries, see Hejazi and Safarian (2004b).
2. It should be stated that the operations of Canadian MNEs mirror this strategy; as a result of the FTAs, Canada has reduced the share of its FDI with the United States, opting instead to increase its production of goods and services within Canada and exporting to the United States (Hejazi, 2004a, 2004b; Hejazi and Pauly, 2004, Hejazi and Safarian, 2004a, 2004b).
3. See, for example, the considerable literature on the product life cycle, inspired by Vernon (1966).

BIBLIOGRAPHY

Balasubramanyam, V.N., M. Salisu and D. Sapsford (1996), 'Foreign direct investment and growth in EP and IS Countries', *The Economic Journal*, **106**, 92–105.
Baldwin, J.R. and D. Sabourin (2001), 'Impact of the adoption of advanced information and communication technologies on firm performance in the Canadian manufacturing sector', analytical studies research paper series 11F0019MIE2001174, Analytical Studies Branch, Ottawa: Statistics Canada, accessed at www.statcan.ca/english/research/11F0019MIE/11F0019MIE2001174.pdf
Barrell, Ray and Nigel Pain (1999), 'Domestic institutions, agglomerations and foreign direct investment in Europe', *European Economic Review*, **43**, 925–34.
Bayoumi, Tamim and Gabrielle Lipworth (1997), 'Japanese foreign direct investment and regional trade', IMF Working Paper, 97/103.
Bellak, Christian and John Cantwell (1996), 'Foreign direct investment – how much is it worth? Comment on S.J. Gray and A.M. Rugman', *Transnational Corporations*, **5** (1), 85–97.
Blomström, Magnus and Ari O. Kokko (1994). 'Home country effects of foreign direct investment: Sweden', in S. Globerman (ed.), *Canadian Based Multinationals.*

Blomström, Magnus, Robert E. Lipsey, and Ksenia Kulchycky (1988). 'U.S. and Swedish direct investment and exports', in R.E. Baldwin (ed.) *Trade Policy Issues and Empirical Analysis*, Chicago: University of Chicago Press, pp. 259–97.

Bora, Bijit (2002), *Foreign Direct Investment Research Issues*, London: Routledge.

Borensztein, E., J. De Gregorio and J-W. Lee (1998), 'How does foreign direct investment affect economic growth', *Journal of International Economics*, **45**, 115–35.

Brainard, S. Lael (1997), 'An empirical assessment of the proximity–concentration trade-off between multinational sales and trade', *American Economic Review*, **87** (4), 520–44.

Caves, Richard (1996). *Multinational Enterprise and Economic Analysis*, Cambridge: Cambridge University Press.

Coe, David and Elhanan Helpman (1995), 'International R&D spillovers', *European Economic Review*, May, 859–87.

Collins, William J., Kevin H.O'Rourke and Jeffrey G. Williamson (1997), 'Were trade and factor mobility substitutes in history', NBER working paper 6059.

Deardorff, Alan V. (1995), 'Determinants of bilateral trade: does gravity work in a neoclassical world', NBER working paper 5377.

Dobson, Wendy (2002), *Shaping the Future of the North American Economic Space: A Framework for Action*.

Dunning, John (1993). *Multinational Enterprises and the Global Economy*, Wokingham, England: Addison-Wesley Publishing.

Eaton, Jonathan and Akiko Tamura (1994), 'Bilateralism and regionalism in Japanese and U.S. trade and direct foreign investment patterns', *Journal of the Japanese and International Economics*, **8**, 478–510.

Encarnation, D.J. (1993), 'Beyond Trade: Foreign Investment in the U.S.–Japan and EC–Japan Rivalries', Harvard Business School manuscript.

Ethier, Wilfred (1982), 'National and international returns to scale in the modern theory of international trade', *American Economic Review*, **72**, 389–405.

Feenstra, Robert C., James R. Markusen and Andrew K. Rose (2001), 'Using the gravity equation to differentiate among alternative theories of trade', *Canadian Journal of Economics*, **34** (2), 430–47.

Feinberg, Susan E., Michael P. Keane and Mario F. Bognanno (1998), 'Trade liberalization and delocalization: new evidence from firm-level panel data', *Canadian Journal of Economics*, **31** (4), November, 749–77.

Frankel, J.A., Shang-Jin Wei and Ernesto Stein (1995), 'APEC and regional trading arrangements in the Pacific', in Wendy Dobson and Frank Flatters (eds), *Pacific Trade and Investment: Options for the 1990s*, Kingston, Ontario: John Deutsch Institute.

Globerman, S. (ed.) (1994), *Canadian Based Multinationals*, Industry Canada Research Series, Calgary: University of Calgary Press.

Graham, Edward (1993) 'U.S. outward direct investment and U.S. exports: substitutes or complements – with implications for U.S.–Japan Policy', Institute for International Economics, Washington, DC.

Graham, Edward M. (1994). 'Canadian direct investment abroad and the Canadian economy: some theoretical and empirical implications', in S. Globerman (ed.), *Canadian Based Multinationals*.

Gray, S.J. and A. Rugman (1994), 'Does the United States have a deficit with Japan in foreign direct investment?', *Transnational Corporations*, **3** (2), 127–37.

Grosse, Robert and Len Trevino (1996), 'Foreign direct investment in the United States: an analysis by country of origin', *Journal of International Business Studies*, first quarter.

Grossman, Gene and Kenneth Rogoff (eds) (1995), *Handbook of International Economics*, vol. 3, Amsterdam: North-Holland.

Gunderson, Morley and Savita Verma (1994), 'Labour market implications of outward foreign direct investment', in S. Globerman (ed.), *Canadian Based Multinationals*.

Hejazi, Walid (2001), 'Access to foreign R&D does not undermine domestic R&D efforts', *Policy Options*, October, 43–8.

Hejazi, Walid (2004a), 'The impact of trade agreements on Canada's foreign direct investment performance', prepared for a conference volume to be published by the Department of Foreign Affairs, Government of Canada.

Hejazi, Walid (2004b), 'Canada's FDI experience: how different are services?', in Richard Lipsey and Alice Nakamura (eds), *Service Industries and Knowledge-Based Economy* Calgary: University of Calgary Press.

Hejazi, Walid and Daniel Trefler (1996), 'Explaining Canada's Trade with the Asia–Pacific', in Richard Harris (ed.), *The Asia Pacific Region and the Global Economy: A Canadian Perspective*, The Industry Canada Research Series, University of Calgary Press.

Hejazi, Walid and A.E. Safarian (1999a), 'Trade, foreign direct investment, and R&D spillovers', *Journal of International Business Studies*, **30** (3), third quarter, 491–511.

Hejazi, Walid and A.E. Safarian (1999b), 'Modelling links between Canadian trade and foreign direct investment', Industry Canada Research Publications series, *Perspectives on North American Free Trade*, April.

Hejazi, Walid and A.E. Safarian (2001), 'The complementarity between US FDI stock and trade', *Atlantic Economic Journal*, **29** (4).

Hejazi, Walid and Marc von der Ruhr (2002), 'U.S. firms in world finance', published in Gavin Boyd (ed.), *American Macromanagement*, Cheltenham, UK and Northampton, MA, USA: Edward Elgar.

Hejazi, Walid and Peter Pauly (2002), 'Foreign direct investment and domestic capital formation', Industry Canada working paper series, number 36.

Hejazi, Walid and Peter Pauly (2003), 'Motivations for FDI and domestic capital formation', *Journal of International Business Studies*, **34**, 282–9.

Hejazi, Walid and Peter Pauly (2004), 'Canada's and Mexico's changing FDI positions: what role has the NAFTA played?', in Lorraine Eden and Wendy Dobson (eds), *Governance, Multinationals and Growth*, Cheltenham, UK and Northampton, MA, USA: Edward Elgar.

Hejazi, Walid and A.E. Safarian (2004a), 'Explaining Canada's changing FDI patterns', University of Toronto working paper.

Hejazi, Walid and A.E. Safarian (2004b), 'NAFTA effects and the level of development', University of Toronto working paper, forthcoming in *The Journal of Business Research*.

Hufbauer, G.C. and M. Adler (1968). 'U.S. manufacturing investment and the balance of payments', *Tax Policy Research Study Number 1*, Washington, DC: US Treasury Department.

Journal of Economic Perspectives, entire issues, Summer, 1995; Fall, 1998.

Journal of International Business Studies (1994), vol. 25, no. 4, fourth quarter, 806–8.

Jun, Kwang W. and Harinder Singh (1996), 'The determinants of foreign direct investment in developing countries', *Transnational Corporations*, **5** (2), 67–105.

Lipsey, Robert E. and Merle Yahr Weiss (1981), 'Foreign production and exports in manufacturing industries', *The Review of Economic Statistics*, **63** (4), November, 488–94.

Lipsey, Robert E. and Merle Yahr Weiss (1984), 'Foreign production and exports of individual firms', *The Review of Economics and Statistics*, **66** (2), May, 304–8.

Malnight, Thomas W. (1996), 'The transition from decentralized to network-based MNC structures: an evolutionary perspective', *Journal of International Business Studies*, **27**(1), 43–65.

McFetridge, D.G. (1991a), 'Introduction', *Foreign Investment, Technology and Economic Growth*, The Investment Canada Research Series, Calgary: University of Calgary Press.

McFetridge, D.G. (ed.) (1991b), *Foreign Investment, Technology and Economic Growth*, The Investment Canada Research Series, Calgary: University of Calgary Press.

Mundell, Robert A.(1957), 'International trade and factor mobility', *American Economic Review*, **47**, 321–35.

NBER Reporter, Summer, 1997; Spring, 1998.

Pfaffermayr, M. (1994), 'Foreign direct investment and exports: a time series approach', *Applied Economics*, **26**, 337–51.

Rao, Someshwar, Ashfaq Ahmad and Marc Legault (1996), 'Foreign direct investment and APEC economic integration', Industry Canada working paper series no. 8, February.

Rugman, A.M. (1980), 'Internalization as a general theory of foreign direct investment: a reappraisal of the literature', *Welwirtschaftliches Archives*, **116** (2), 367–79.

Rugman, A.M. (1987), *Outward Bound: Canadian Direct Investment in the United States*, Toronto: C.D. Howe Institute.

Rugman, Alan (1988), 'The multinational enterprise', in Ingo Walter and Tracy Murray (eds), *Handbook of International Management*, New York: Wiley.

Rugman, Alan M. (1990), *Multinationals and Canada–United States Free Trade*, Columbia, South Carolina: University of South Carolina Press.

Rugman, Alan (2000), *The End of Globalization*, New York: Random House.

Safarian, A.E. (1985), 'Foreign direct investment: a survey of Canadian research', The Institute for Research on Public Policy, Montreal.

Safarian, A.E. and Walid Hejazi (2001), 'Canada and foreign direct investment: a study of determinants', University of Toronto Centre for Public Management.

Summers, Robert and Alan Heston (1991), 'The Penn World Tables (Mark 5): an expanded set of international comparisons, 1950–1988', *Quarterly Journal of Economics*, **106**, 327–68.

Swedenborg, B. (1979), 'The Multinational Operations of Swedish Firms: An Analysis of Determinants and Effects', The Industrial Institute for Economic and Social Research, Stockholm.

Tang, Jianmin and Someshwar Rao (2001), 'R&D propensity and productivity performance of foreign-controlled firms in Canada', Industry Canada working paper, no. 33.

Trefler, Daniel (1999), 'Does Canada need a productivity budget', *Policy Options*, July–August, 66–71.

Trefler, Daniel (2004), 'The long and short of the Canada–U.S. Free Trade Agreement', *The American Economic Review*, **94** (4), September, 870–95.

United Nations Conference on Trade and Development (UNCTAD) (1996), *World Investment Report 1996: Investment, Trade and International Policy Arrangements*, New York and Geneva: United Nations.

United Nations Conference on Trade and Development (UNCTAD) (1999), *World Investment Report 1998: FDI and the Challenge of Development*, New York and Geneva: United Nations.

United Nations Conference on Trade and Development (UNCTAD) (2001), *World Investment Report 2001: Promoting Linkages*, New York and Geneva: United Nations.

US Department of Commerce (1995), 'Foreign direct investment in the United States: detail for historical-cost position and related capital and income flows', *Survey of Current Business*, August, 53–78.

van Pottelsberghe De La Potterie, Bruno and Frank Lichtenberg (2001), 'Does foreign direct investment transfer technology across borders?', *The Review of Economics and Statistics*, **83** (3), 490–97.

Vernon, Raymond (1966), 'International investment and international trade in the product cycle', *Quarterly Journal of Economics*, **2**, 190–207.

World Competitiveness Yearbook (1998), Geneva: Institute for Management Development.

World Economy, 2002 July, entire issue.

Zeile, William J. (1997), 'U.S. intrafirm trade in goods', *Survey of Current Business*, February, 23–38.

DATA APPENDIX I   SOURCES AND DESCRIPTION

Trade and FDI Data

US stocks of FDI on a bilateral basis with each of 52 countries were obtained from the US Bureau of Economic Analysis. These data are reported at historical costs. US exports and imports on a bilateral basis with each of 52 countries were obtained from the International Monetary Fund's Direction of Trade Statistics. These data are in current US dollars. To convert these trade data into real terms, export and import deflators were obtained from Citibase.

Intra-firm Trade Data

Intra-firm exports between US parents and their majority-owned foreign affiliates as well as between foreign parents and their affiliates in the USA were obtained from William J. Zeile, 'Intra firm Trade in Goods', *Survey of Current Business*, February 1997.

Gravity Data

GDP data and GDP per capita were obtained from the Penn World Tables. These data have been constructed very carefully to allow for international comparisons (see Summers and Heston, 1991) and are reported in constant 1987 US dollars. Exchange rates were also obtained from the Penn World Tables, and are on a real PPP basis.

Distance variables were kindly provided by Werner Antweiler and were used in Hejazi and Trefler (1996).

Dummy Variables

The language dummy captures whether countries speak the same language. If English is an official language of a country, the dummy takes on a value of one, and zero otherwise. The regional dummies take on a value of one if the country is in the respective region, and zero otherwise. The countries that enter Europe, East Asia and Latin America are listed in Table 4.1.

The Japan dummy takes on a value of one for Japan, and zero otherwise. The adjacency dummy takes on a value of one for Mexico and Canada, and zero otherwise.

DATA APPENDIX II   ISSUES IN CONVERTING FDI STOCK DATA TO REAL VALUES

With the exception of the FDI stocks and foreign sales figures, the data used in this study are in real 1987 constant US dollars. The GDP and GDP per capita data for the 51 countries plus the USA are available from the Penn World Tables on that basis. These data have been constructed very carefully to allow for international comparisons (see Summers and Heston, 1991). US exports and imports are also converted to a constant US dollar basis.

Unlike exports and imports, it is a non-trivial task to convert the FDI stock figures from their present historical cost values to real values. The difficulty in undertaking such a transformation arises because FDI is a stock. Consider the following equation:

$$FDI_t = FDI_{t-1} + \text{retained earnings} + \text{net flows of FDI} + \text{price appreciation/depreciation on } FDI_{t-1}.$$

The level of FDI at any point in time is defined as the level of FDI in the previous period, plus retained earnings, plus net new flows of FDI, plus price appreciation (or less depreciation). The retained earnings and the flows are in current dollars, and are simply added to the stock of FDI from the previous year, which is not in current dollars. The retained earnings and flows form the balance of payments definition of FDI. In addition, however, there is another component which involves revaluation of the FDI stocks. It is this last component which is needed to convert FDI from the historical costs to their market values.

The US Department of Commerce (1995) has published US stock figures on the basis of historical cost, replacement cost and market values, but the country and sectoral data are available only on a historical (book value) basis. There are a variety of private and semi-official estimates of the different valuations for the US and UK stocks of FDI (Bellak and Cantwell, 1996). A straightforward way to adjust stock values is through changes in security prices, as utilized in Gray and Rugman (1994), but this is subject to a number of criticisms, as noted in Bellak and Cantwell (1996). We have decided to use the unadjusted data.

5. The regional dimension of multinational enterprises and antitrust policy

Alan M. Rugman and Alain Verbeke

INTRODUCTION

Rugman and Verbeke (2004), extending the work of Ohmae (1985), have argued that truly global multinational enterprises (MNEs) should be able to achieve a balanced dispersion of their sales across the three legs of the 'triad' of the European Union (EU), North America (NAFTA) and Asia. These are the home regions of most of the world's largest firms in strongly internationalized industries. These regions are also characterized by extensive innovation, sophisticated demand and high purchasing power of buyers. Business cycles do not necessarily converge throughout the triad, thus leading to risk reduction for the MNEs operating globally (Rugman, 1976, 1979). To some extent, the three legs of the triad are also the result of public policy engineering, which has led to institutional arrangements, such as the European Union and the North-American Free Trade Agreement (NAFTA).

A powerful indicator of triad/regional economic activity is the concentration of the world's largest MNEs in the United States, EU and Japan. In 2000, of the world's largest 500 MNEs, 430 were in these core triad regions. In 1996, the figure was 443; in 1991, it was 410 and back in 1981 it was 445. Over the last 20 years the trend has shown a decrease in the proportion of US MNEs, from 242 in 1981 to as few as 157 in 1991, but up to 162 in 1996 and 185 in 2000. The EU number is very consistent, being 141 for the old EEC members in 1981 but up to 155 for the enlarged EU in 1996, and down to 141 again by 2000. These 500 MNEs dominate international business. They account for over 90 per cent of the world's stock of FDI and nearly 50 per cent of world trade (Rugman, 2000). These MNEs are the 'unit of analysis' for research in international business. They are the key vehicles of both FDI and trade.

In this chapter, the strategic market position of the world's 500 largest firms is examined, in terms of sales distribution across the triad. Data are presented on ratios of regional sales for the 380 firms for which data can be obtained. Two companies merged during 2003 and are only counted once in this sample. Of the remaining 379, the vast majority (320) are home-triad based with at least 50 per cent of their sales in their home region of the triad. Of these 320, 58 operate only within their home region, with zero extraregional sales. For those companies which derive less than 50 per cent of their sales outside their home region, 36 are biregional, with at least 20 per cent of their sales in two parts of the triad. For another 14 companies, there are insufficient data to make a categorization. Only nine of the 500 are truly 'global', with at least 20 per cent of their sales in all three parts of the triad, and less than 50 per cent in the home region. This regionalization rather than globalization appears particularly characteristic of the 378 firms from the triad, which need a regional approach to strategy. Only one company in the sample, Petrobras of Brazil, is not headquartered in a triad region.

In our research we distinguish among three types of MNEs: home-triad based MNEs: these are labelled home-region oriented MNEs; MNEs in two parts of the triad: these are labelled 'biregional' MNEs; MNEs in all three parts of the triad: these are labelled 'global' MNEs. It should be noted that MNEs in all three groups are 'international', but not necessarily global. Only the third group of MNEs are actually 'global', but the second group, biregional MNEs, may be regarded as partly global. Clearly the first group of MNES are not global by any definition. For previous discussions, see Rugman and Brain (2003) and Rugman and Verbeke (2004).

COMPARISONS ACROSS THE TRIAD

From the list of the world's largest 500 companies, Table 5.1 reports that there are 378 triad-based firms for which geographic sales data are available: 185 from North America, 118 from Europe and 75 from the Asia–Pacific region. These 378 firms have an average of approximately 71.9 per cent of their total sales in their home region of the triad, with North American firms having the greatest intraregional sales, at 77.2 per cent, followed by Asia–Pacific firms with 74.3 per cent and European at 62.8 per cent.

The 378 firms in the triad can be broken down into three basic classifications:

1. home region-oriented: firms that have at least 50 per cent of their sales in their region of the triad;

2. biregional: firms that have 20 per cent or more of their sales in at least two regions of the triad – including their own – and less than 50 per cent in their own region; or which have over 50 per cent of their sales in a region of the triad other than their own.
3. global: firms that have sales of 20 per cent or more in each of the three regions of the triad but less than 50 per cent in their own triad region.

Table 5.1   The broad triad: average home region sales

Region	Total no. of firms for which some information is available	Average intra regional sales
North America	185	77.2
Europe	118	62.8
Asia–Pacific	75	74.3
Total	378	71.9

Note: Total no. of firms does not include Petrobras, the only company from a country outside the broad triad; average intraregional sales include all 379 firms.

Source: Braintrust Research Group, *The Regional Nature of Global Multinational Activity* (2003) (www.braintrustresearch.com).

As shown in Table 5.2, 319 of the 378 triad-based firms are home region-oriented: 167 in North America; 86 in Europe and 66 in Asia–Pacific. There are three global firms from each of the regions of the triad. Finally, there are 36 biregional firms, with 11 of them being host region-oriented. Tables 5.3, 5.4 and 5.5 report the country breakdown of intraregional sales in each region of the triad. In Table 5.3, the 16 Canadian-based firms have an average of 74.1 per cent of their sales in the North American region. Although there are over ten times as many US firms in the list of the world's largest 500, the US-based firms have almost the same average North American sales, at 77.3 per cent, as the Canadian firms. In other words, the Canadian and US firms are virtually indistinguishable, and they appear to operate on a continental basis.

Table 5.4 reports the intraregional sales of the 118 European firms, averaging 62.8 per cent. The three countries with the highest percentage of intraregional sales and having at least 25 firms are Germany at 68.1 per cent, France at 64.8 per cent, and Britain at 64.5 per cent. The five Dutch firms only average 39.1 per cent and are thus better candidates for globalization. ING and Royal Ahold, which are host region-oriented, and Royal Philips Electronics, a global firm, are examples of interregional expansion. Also

Nokia, from Finland, is a global firm. The other global European firm is Louis Vuitton Moet Hennessy (LVMH) of France.

Table 5.2   The regional nature of global multinational activity

Region	Global	Biregional	Host region oriented	Home region oriented	Insufficient information
North America	3	6	1	167	8
Europe	3	16	8	86	5
Asia–Pacific	3	3	2	66	1
Total	9	25	11	319	14

Note: Total no. of firms does not include Petrobras, the only company from a country outside the broad triad.

Source: Braintrust Research Group, *The Regional Nature of Global Multinational Activity* (2003) (www.braintrustresearch.com).

Table 5.3   The country distribution of North American MNEs and their intraregional sales

Country	No. of firms	Average revenues (US$bn)	Average intra regional sales (%)
Canada	16	13.5	74.1
United States	169	30.3	77.3
North America	185	28.8	77.2

Source: Braintrust Research Group, *The Regional Nature of Global Multinational Activity* (2003) (www.braintrustresearch.com).

Table 5.5 reports the intraregional sales of the 75 firms from Asia–Pacific. The 66 Japanese firms have average home region sales of 74.7 per cent. The five Australian firms average 71.4 per cent. The Singapore firm, Flextronics, only has 22.4 per cent of its sales in the region and is classified as a global firm. Some of the Japanese firms, like Toyota Motor, Honda Motor and Nissan Motor, are biregional with North America. Sony is a global firm and so is Canon.

Table 5.4   The country distribution of European MNEs and their intraregional sales

Country	No. of firms	Average revenues (US$bn)	Average intra regional sales (%)
Belgium	2	18.8	58.4
Britain	27	25.3	64.5
Denmark	1	10.9	94.3
Finland	2	20.0	55.1
France	26	27.2	64.8
Germany	29	37.3	68.1
Italy	5	38.7	83.4
Luxembourg	1	13.0	95.0
Netherlands	5	42.1	39.1
Norway	2	21.6	83.0
Spain	2	29.1	50.3
Sweden	5	16.4	54.3
Switzerland	8	34.7	49.6
Bi-national	3	73.9	47.9
Europe	118	31.0	62.8

Note: The following companies are headquartered in more than one country: Fortis (Belgium/Neth), Unilever (Brit/Neth) and Royal Dutch/Shell Group (Brit/Neth).

Source: Braintrust Research Group, *The Regional Nature of Global Multinational Activity* (2003) (www.braintrustresearch.com).

Table 5.5   The country distribution of Asia–Pacific MNEs and their intraregional sales

Country	No. of firms	Average revenues (US$bn)	Average intra regional sales (%)
Australia	5	13.6	71.4
Japan	66	28.9	74.7
Singapore	1	13.1	22.4
South Korea	2	26.3	71.2
Taiwan	1	11.6	100.0
Asia–Pacific	75	27.4	74.3

Source: Braintrust Research Group, *The Regional Nature of Global Multinational Activity* (2003) (www.braintrustresearch.com).

Table 5.6 reports the intraregional sales of the triad firms by major sector. There are 179 manufacturing and 200 service firms. The average intraregional sales for manufacturing firms are 61.9 per cent and for services 81.7 per cent. Services are more localized and home region-based than manufacturing. North American banks average 85.5 per cent intraregional sales, merchandisers 95.1 per cent, telecommunications and utilities 90.8 per cent and transportation services 85.3 per cent. Asia–Pacific services are also heavily localized, while European firms tend to be somewhat less intraregional.

Table 5.6   The triad, by industry

Industry category	North America: intraregional No.	sales	Europe: intraregional No.	sales	Asia–Pacific: intraregional No.	sales	World average intraregional sales
Manufacturing							
1 Aerospace and Defence	9	71.0	2	42.7	0	na	66.3
2 Chemicals and Pharmaceuticals	10	64.4	7	37.6	1	86.9	56.5
3 Computer, Office & Electronics	17	51.4	6	49.4	13	64.8	56.2
4 Construction, Building Materials and Glass	—	na	5	60.6	6	89.2	73.5
5 Energy, Petroleum & Refining	20	72.4	7	53.8	3	89.1	66.0
6 Food, Drug & Tobacco	8	65.0	5	36.4	1	90.5	55.0
7 Motor Vehicle and Parts	10	72.1	8	54.4	11	52.7	60.6
8 Natural Resource Manufacturing	7	80.8	6	71.8	4	77.2	77.6
9 Other Manufacturing	6	55.3	4	56.5	2	72.8	58.8
Services							
1 Banks	11	85.5	23	75.4	6	77.8	78.3
2 Entertainment, Printing & Publishing	3	84.8	3	67.2	3	57.7	73.1
3 Merchandisers	36	95.1	15	75.5	12	84.0	87.9
4 Other Financial Services	16	76.4	8	62.9	3	99.2	71.9
5 Telecommunications & Utilities	10	90.8	11	82.8	6	92.5	87.6
6 Transportation Services	6	85.3	4	73.9	3	92.9	83.7
7 Other Services	16	79.9	4	51.5	1	95.0	75.8

Source: Braintrust Research Group, *The Regional Nature of Global Multinational Activity* (2003) (www.braintrustresearch.com).

Table 5.7 reports the top ten firms from each region of the triad. The North American firms have sales of over $62 billion and average intraregional sales of 69 per cent and are mostly home region-based. The European firms have sales of over \$66.5 billion and average 42.1 per cent intraregional sales. The top ten European firms include six biregionals: BP, DaimlerChrysler, ING Group, Volkswagen, Siemens and Deutsche Bank. With missing data, Shell cannot be classified as global, although it probably is. The Asian firms' sales are all over \$55 billion. There are two biregional firms: Toyota and Honda. In addition, Sony is global. The rest are home region-based.

Table 5.7   The top 10 companies in each region of the triad

Rank	500 Rank	Company	Revenues in bn US\$	F/T sales	% intra regional	North America % of total	Europe % of total	Asia– Pacific % of total
North America								
1	1	Wal-Mart Stores	219.8	16.3	94.1	94.1	4.8	0.4
2	2	Exxon Mobile	191.6	69.6	37.5	37.5	8.9	10.4
3	3	General Motors	177.3	25.5	81.1	81.1	14.6	na
4	5	Ford Motor	162.4	33.3	66.7	66.7	21.9	na
5	9	General Electric	125.9	40.9	59.1	59.1	19.0	9.1
6	19	Intl. Business Machines	85.9	64.8	43.5	43.5	28.0	20.0
7	24	Philip Morris	72.9	42.1	57.9	57.9	25.8	na
8	26	Verizon Communications	67.2	3.8	96.2	96.2	na	na
9	29	U.S. Postal Service (q)	65.8	3.0	97.0	97.0	na	na
10	34	American International Group	62.4	na	59.0	59.0	na	na
		Average	123.1		69.0			
Europe								
1	4	BP	174.2	80.4	36.3	48.1	36.3	na
2	7	DaimlerChrysler	136.9	na	29.9	60.1	29.9	na
3	8	Royal Dutch/Shell Group	135.2	na	46.1	15.6	46.1	na
4	15	Total Fina Elf	94.3	na	55.6	8.4	55.6	na
5	18	Allianz	85.9	69.4	78.0	17.6	78.0	4.4
6	20	ING Group	83.0	77.3	35.1	51.4	35.1	3.4
7	21	Volkswagen	79.3	72.3	68.2	20.1	68.2	5.3
8	22	Siemens	77.4	78.0	52.0	30.0	52.0	13.0
9	27	Deutsche Bank	66.8	69.0	63.1	29.3	63.1	6.5
10	28	E.ON	66.5	43.4	80.1	9.4	80.1	na
		Average	100.0		42.1			
Asia–Pacific								
1	10	Toyota Motor	120.8	50.8	49.2	36.6	7.7	49.2
2	12	Mitsubishi	105.8	13.2	86.8	5.4	1.7	86.8
3	13	Mitsui	101.2	34.0	78.9	7.4	11.1	78.9
4	17	Itochu	91.2	19.1	91.2	5.5	1.7	91.2
5	23	Sumitomo	77.1	12.7	87.3	4.8	na	87.3
6	25	Marubeni	71.8	28.2	74.5	11.6	na	74.5
7	32	Hitachi	63.9	31.0	80.0	11.0	7.0	80.0
8	37	Sony	60.6	67.2	32.8	29.8	20.2	32.8
9	41	Honda Motor	58.9	73.1	26.9	53.9	8.1	26.9
10	45	Matsushita Electric Industrial	55.0	35.1	64.9	12.4	6.9	64.9
		Average	80.6		57.6			

Source: Braintrust Research Group, *The Regional Nature of Global Multinational Activity Enterprises* (2003) (www.braintrustresearch.com).

Finally, Table 5.8 reports specifically the aggregated sales penetration of MNEs from one triad region in the two other triad regions. It extends the data of Table 5.1. European firms have an average of 22.3 per cent of their sales in North America and 3.9 per cent in Asia, as compared to 62.8 per cent in their home region. North American firms have less than 9 per cent in Europe and 3 per cent in Asia, while their home region represents 77.2 per cent. Finally Asian firms have 74.3 per cent in Asia, 14 per cent in North America and 5.4 per cent in Europe.

Given the observed, comparatively weak position of MNEs in host regions, the question arises whether this situation could be influenced and improved through interregional public policy. More specifically, if we assume that institutional distance among triad regions contributes to the observed weak market position of MNEs in host regions, in line with Ghemawat (2001, 2003), can interregional cooperation alleviate this distance or will it likely further exacerbate it? In the next section, we briefly highlight the possible importance of interregional public policy cooperation for MNE competitiveness. We then apply this framework to antitrust policy.

Table 5.8　　Average sales by triad region

	No. of firms	Total sales	Average sales	NA %	Europe %	Asia %	% accounted by data
North America	185	5 333.8	28.8	77.2	8.7	3.0	88.9
Europe	118	3 674.5	31.1	22.3	62.8	3.9	89.0
Asia	75	2 053.2	27.4	14.0	5.4	74.3	93.7

Notes:
There is a lack of consistency to the data. A company might only list data for the UK in Europe; a US firm may not report sales in Canada and Mexico in its intra-regional sales; foreign companies may only list the United States for North America.
The total number of firms excludes non-triad Petrobras and only counts LVMH/Dior once.
Average sales are in $m, total sales are in $m.

Source: Adapted from Braintrust Research Group, *The Regional Nature of Global Multinational Activity* (2003).

THE REGIONALIZATION OF MNE–PUBLIC POLICY LINKAGES

In Rugman and Verbeke (1998), we developed a comprehensive framework to analyse the interactions between MNEs and public policy, building upon a large body of conceptual and empirical work, especially Boddewyn

(1988), Boddewyn and Brewer (1994), Caves (1996), Brewer and Young (1998), Dunning (1997), Vernon (1971) and Rugman (1996). We will now reconsider five components of that framework in order to capture the regional dimension in MNE strategy and public policy linkages.

First, we discussed the consistency and conflicts between MNE goals and the public policy goals of home and host countries. We argued that some consistency now exists between MNEs' goals and the goals of home and host countries, especially if MNEs are recognized as sources of knowledge transfer and arbitragers of country-level 'inter-stage growth', that is, MNEs can contribute to the structural improvement of developing countries and emerging economies. To the extent that MNEs develop triad-based strategies rather than solely single nation-oriented strategies (Rugman and Verbeke, 2004), the regional dimension becomes important. Such a regional dimension implies that MNEs need to pay attention, where relevant, to regional policies, rather than only to national policies. Specifically, for example, if policy choices on one side of the Atlantic diverge from the choices made on the other side, MNEs may find themselves in a difficult situation. This may occur in the context of a proposed merger, approved by one regulator but rejected by the other. MNEs should also consider the added complexity of a regulator in one region taking into account the effects of MNE strategic behaviour on actors in another region. This issue is discussed in some depth in the next section, with an application to competition law.

Second, we argued that a higher symmetry between inward and outward foreign direct investment (FDI), that is, the presence of substantial volumes of both FDI types in a single nation, would likely lead national governments to eliminate discriminatory regulations against foreign MNEs and to pursue policies of national treatment. However, we did not discuss at that stage the possibility that the entry mode decision might constitute a critical determinant of government attitudes. Specifically, mergers and acquisitions, as well as a variety of cooperative arrangements involving MNEs from another triad region, may be viewed much less favourably than greenfield investments. The problem is that non-greenfield, inward FDI may be viewed as an instrument to increase market power and economic control held by foreign economic actors, without contributing anything worthwhile from the host region's perspective. Hence, especially in a triad context, the impact of entry mode choice on public policy should be carefully analysed.

Third, and related to the previous point, we argued that symmetry in inward and outward FDI would lead to a 'government preference for a supranational approach' to MNE regulation, whereby we focused especially on the role of the World Trade Organization (WTO) to remove remaining trade and investment barriers. However, since the publication of a recent paper (Rugman and Boyd, 2001), the WTO has had to face numerous challenges. Those include sharp criticism from a very vocal, and increasingly better organized, anti-globalization movement, as well as increased tensions among a number of key actors in the WTO, especially the United States and the European Union (Rugman and Verbeke, 2003). As a result, it has now become unlikely that the WTO will achieve any progress towards deeper multilateral integration in the near future. In contrast, the last few years have seen increasing attention devoted to widening and deepening regional agreements and interregional cooperation. It is therefore important to study regional policies, as they represent an alternative approach to trade and investment in an era of trade and investment protection and regulation.

Fourth, we suggested that many MNEs are characterized by an increasing geographic dispersion of their firm-specific advantages (FSAs). Such FSA dispersion largely results from two elements. First, many MNEs are now capable of developing location-bound FSAs in host countries, including FSAs in government relations, that permit benefits of national responsiveness. Second, dispersed FSAs also imply that subsidiaries are capable of developing new non-location-bound knowledge in host countries, leading to benefits of scale, scope and exploitation of national differences. However, if the world is to be viewed primarily as a limited set of regions, rather than as a much larger number of countries, should MNEs try to 'upgrade' their location-bound FSAs toward region-boundedness rather than merely nation-boundedness? In addition, the comparatively poor market performance of MNEs in host regions could itself be interpreted as a limit of these firms' non-location-bound FSAs. At the customer end, those FSAs appear to lack global deployability; in many cases their successful use is restricted to the home region, rather than to the triad as a whole. This is especially true for all knowledge that has an institutional dimension, for example knowledge embedded in regional clusters and FSAs in government relations.

Finally, we discussed the danger of shelter-based behaviour, building upon our earlier work on business–government relations (Rugman and Verbeke, 1990). We argued that government policy is often abused by firms seeking home country protection from more efficient foreign rivals. A major problem arises when the shelter-seeking economic actors themselves rationalize their behaviour as a reasonable response to alleged market imperfections created by foreign rivals, and argue that they are merely seeking to re-establish a level playing field. If region-based institutions become more important as regulators of economic behaviour, can these institutions be responsive to shelter-seeking behaviour by home-region firms, thereby discriminating against foreign rivals?

In the next sections, we shall explore the regional complexities discussed above through an application of a growing area of regulation critical to the world's largest MNEs, namely antitrust regulation. We will focus our analysis on managerial implications for MNEs, rather than on technical details of the prevailing regulatory regime.

TRANSATLANTIC COOPERATION IN ANTITRUST POLICY

If an MNE is particularly successful internationally, as in the case of Microsoft, this may lead to a dominant position in the industry in more than one leg of the triad. Alternatively a lower level of international sales may force MNEs to seek alternative routes to penetrate host triad regions. Strategic asset-seeking FDI has contributed to a wave of cross-border merger (and acquisition) activity, as well as strategic alliances in the triad, sometimes involving firms of only one country, but with widespread international ramifications. Well-known cases involving top 500 firms, include, Daimler Benz–Chrysler, BP–Amoco, Ford–Volvo Cars, General Motors–Saab Automobile, Ciba Geigy–Santos, General Electric–Honeywell and Hewlett-Packard–Compaq.

Antitrust regulation, in both the USA and the EU, aims to curb both the immediate and future anti-competitive effects resulting from large-scale mergers, and agreements leading to oligopolistic dominance and abuse of a dominant position. Immediate anti-competitive effects are alleged to result from market share dominance, and related pricing impacts. Anti-competitive effects are alleged to occur as a result of a reduction in the speed and scope of innovation, resulting from weaker competition in industry (for example, fewer new product launches and elimination of substitutes). The regulatory problem, from a regional perspective, is threefold.

First, antitrust decisions in one region of the triad, and involving large MNEs, may affect competition in another region (for example, the blocking of mergers involving US firms by the European Commission). Second, the nature of the effects may differ substantially in the various regions. In other words, the existence of large MNEs operating across borders poses new challenges to the definition of what constitutes the relevant market, which may incur both anti-competitive and inefficiency effects of merger and acquisition activity. These include scale economies, scope economies in areas such as standard setting and product compatibility, and positive network externalities. Third, as trade protectionism and discrimination against greenfield investment become increasingly difficult to implement, given the large number of international agreements in these areas, inefficient incumbents with weak FSAs may well revert to anti-trust as a tool to obtain shelter, as suggested by some empirical evidence for the United States (Shugart *et al.*, 1995).

> Anti-trust, rather than being solely driven by consumer welfare considerations, is at the service of domestic firms adversely affected by imports. If trade stimulates anti-trust, particularly targeted at foreign firms, the potential for direct conflict of laws and lobbying interests across borders can only grow as economic globalization progresses. (Evenett *et al.*, 2000, p. 15)

The appropriate venue to eliminate the possibility of antitrust being used as a tool to serve protectionist purposes would be the WTO, but it has not agreed on a multilateral policy. Indeed, much more progress has been made in bilateral cooperation, at least between the EU and the US:

> The much cited Van Miert report of 1995 provided the foundation for the EU's response to the growing challenges posed by international cases for competition policy enforcement. Based on this report, the European Commission has taken a two-pronged approach: attempting to advance proposals on competition policy within the WTO and enhancing bilateral cooperation. Unlike progress at the WTO, bilateral cooperation has rapidly expanded and deepened. (Ibid., p. 18)

In the triad context, bilateral agreements have been signed by the EU with the US in 1991 and 1998, and with Canada in 1999. In the EU, competition policy is addressed by the European Commission, Directorate General (DG) Competition, previously DGIV. The Commission's review pre-empts reviews at the level of member states if it has a community dimension.

Two sets of criteria are used to determine whether a merger has an EU dimension. The first set is defined as follows: (a) combined worldwide revenues of at least 5 billion euro; (b) two firms have revenues in the EU of at least 250 million euro per firm; and (c) not all firms involved have more than two-thirds of their total EU sales in a single EU country. The second set includes the following: (a) combined worldwide revenues of at least 2.5 billion euro; (b) combined revenues of more than 100 million euro in each of three member states; (c) two firms have revenues of 25 million euro per firm, in at least three of those member states; and (d) two firms have revenues in the EU of at least 100 million euro per firm. The notification process requires extensive information disclosure, including definition of the relevant market, description of current market position and the expected impact of the proposed transaction on that position. After notification, the Commission needs to decide within one month whether it will initiate, in a second phase, a four-month investigation. Such investigation may lead the Commission to oppose the transaction or to authorize it, subject to commitments by the parties involved to divestments aimed at restoring effective competition. The Commission decision can then be appealed to the European Court of Justice.

In the United States, the antitrust regulations are implemented by the Federal Trade Commission (FTC) and the Antitrust Division of the Department of Justice. The threshold is much lower, namely only $15 million in assets or voting securities. In addition, any state attorney-general may challenge FTC and Department of Justice decisions.

What are the effects on MNEs from interregional cooperation between two such distinct regimes? The answer is that, in recent years, significant convergence has been achieved on a number of substantive and procedural matters (Rugman, 2001; Boyd and Rugman, 2003). These are especially important for large MNEs engaged in merger activities with cross-border implications, as shown in Figure 5.1, which addresses the effects of interregional cooperation on MNEs. The horizontal axis measures the substantive convergence towards common, efficiency-based objectives by the regulatory agencies involved. This commonality can be weak or strong. On the vertical axis, the procedural convergence of the cooperation is measured. This convergence can again be weak or strong. Procedural convergence can be achieved by formal regulatory adaptation or, more informally, through 'learning by doing'.

From the MNE's perspective, the ideal case is quadrant 3: a strong, substantive efficiency focus by regulators, and strong procedural convergence. Such an approach is the key to reducing transaction costs associated with

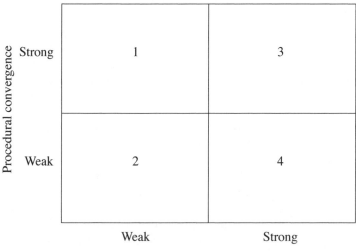

Figure 5.1   Effects of interregional cooperation on MNEs

international operations for MNEs. A sole efficiency focus prevents shelter-based behaviour, either by regulators or by business, a perspective we have advocated in our earlier work (Rugman and Verbeke, 1990, 1991). The worst-case scenario is quadrant 2: lack of a common efficiency focus, and absence of procedural convergence over time. Here, regional cooperation is used mainly as a communication tool across borders, but ultimately with little value added. Quadrant 1 has strong procedural convergence, but it is not effective, as there is weak substantive convergence. Quadrant 4, although reflecting a common efficiency focus agreement on substantive convergence, is associated with a lack of procedural convergence, for example as regards timing of procedures, the role of competitors in the process, possibilities of appealing decisions of regulatory agencies and so on.

As we shall explain in the next section, the transatlantic cooperation on antitrust has unfortunately been a quadrant 1 phenomenon, with a relative lack of substantive convergence and a joint efficiency focus, given the broader policy goals taken into account by the European Union. The progress made towards procedural convergence has been informal rather than formal. Recent changes at the level of the European Commission may well signal a future move towards quadrant 3, with more attention devoted to efficiency-based, antitrust implementation, and therefore more substantive convergence with transatlantic policies (see next section).

WEAK CONVERGENCE IN TRANSATLANTIC COOPERATION

Antitrust, if not guided solely by efficiency considerations and following 'less than best practice' procedures, has conventionally been perceived as an unnatural market imperfection by many MNEs, Rugman and Verbeke (1990). Although many MNEs would generally prefer an across-the-board reduction in regulation on this matter, most realize the societal importance of antitrust. Transatlantic cooperation among antitrust agencies may substantially reduce transaction costs for MNEs, to the extent that it implies a move towards quadrant 3 in Figure 5.1. The MNEs would benefit from a single agency administering anti-trust law, addressing transatlantic cases, as compared with the present situation of multiple agencies being involved. Given the substantive and procedural differences that remain between the US and the EU, especially in the minds of the regulators involved, a monopolistic government agency would do more harm than good.

The present system permits a discussion among agencies about non-efficiency related parameters drawn into merger evaluations, and about agency discretion in the interpretation of findings. For example, in spite of important divergences on substantive matters, the EU has adopted the FTC's approach to market definition, as 'the smallest product and geographic market in which a hypothetical monopolist could impose a "small but significant and non-transitory increase in price"', (Evenett *et al.*, 2000, p. 20). This means the de facto adoption of a 'best practice' standing, since it increases the attention devoted to efficiency considerations.

However, important substantive differences remain. Here we should note that, during the 1980s, the US changed its focus from alleged distortions caused by monopolistic behaviour towards taking into account broader efficiency considerations (that is, all effects on consumer welfare that are specific to the merger and can be readily identified and measured). In contrast, the EU still focuses on the potential abuse of dominant position in the market, and has somewhat lagged in making the transition towards recognizing the importance of efficiency effects, especially regarding dynamic efficiencies. These accrue when merged firms, especially MNEs, have complementary FSAs that accelerate or improve the quality of innovation. However the concept of FSA itself embodies an element of proprietary knowledge and is therefore an isolating mechanism against unfettered competition, which would destroy the incentives for future innovation. In addition, in many cases an element of monopoly and the associated short-term rents will attract new entry into the market, thereby eliminating long-term rents, an observation which has regularly been confirmed by empirical data on the financial performance of the world's largest MNEs (Rugman, 2000).

The 1991 EU/US agreement on competition policy includes notification of enforcement activities important to the partner; exchange of information; cooperation and coordination in enforcement; and positive comity, meaning that the requesting party can ask the other party to initiate appropriate enforcement activity when anti-competitive behaviour on the latter's territory is adversely affecting the interests of the former. Notification, as well as cooperation and coordination, applies to mergers. The 1998 agreement further specifies how positive comity should be implemented, especially regarding resource commitments. Although each party remains fully sovereign to determine the extent to which it will consider the other party's request, the agreements have created a context for transatlantic cooperation.

The effect on MNE transaction costs can be illustrated by the following quotation, reflecting the views of some EU officials:

> for the Commission, an Agreement on the use of positive comity was essentially a means to restrict the extraterritorial use of anti-trust legislation by the United States ... The application of positive comity not only represents a commitment to cooperate rather than seeking to apply anti-trust law extraterritorially, it also

reduces the possibility of conflicting decisions made by different competition authorities. (Devuyst, 1998, p. 467), cited by Janow (2000, p. 37)

In other words, given the largely political nature of past extraterritorial application of US law, the transatlantic antitrust agreements have also had some impact on efficiency, by providing an incentive to the United States to remain on an efficiency-based course in cases that reach beyond national borders. This is an indication of some movement towards quadrant 3, though quadrant 1 rather than 3 still appears the most accurate description of antitrust cooperation at present.

Janow (2000) concluded, on the basis of several cases involving large MNEs, that multi-jurisdictional merger control through 'soft harmonization', that is, the addition of some transatlantic cooperation routines to complement the respective US and EU procedures, has had five types of effects, signalling a further move towards quadrant 3. First, mainly on the procedural front, she observes a deepening, broadening and regularization of transatlantic cooperation. This includes agency interactions on relevant product and geographic markets, timing of respective procedures, potential effects and potential remedies, as illustrated by the 1994 Shell–Montedison case, a merger between the world's largest polypropylene producers, whereby extensive transatlantic discussion took place on the respective intellectual property rights systems and contract law.

Second, cooperation appeared particularly effective when the firms involved waived their rights to confidentiality in the transatlantic exchange of information, as shown by two cases involving only US firms, WorldCom–MCI and Halliburton–Dresser. In both cases, the mergers were approved subject to divestiture requirements.

Third, and this relates more to substantive issues, transatlantic cooperation does not always result in identical judgments by agencies on both sides of the Atlantic, as illustrated by the Ciba-Geigy merger with Sandoz to form Novartis. This merger, involving two Swiss pharmaceutical companies, was judged by the EU to have no anti-competitive effects warranting specific antitrust remedies. In contrast, the US agencies focused on the 'highly concentrated gene therapy market', where they expected anti-competitive effects to occur, and therefore 'required the merged firm to license certain gene therapy patent rights and other technology to the rival firm Rhône-Poulenc'. Even in that case, the reduction of transaction costs for MNEs is clear, as compared to a situation without transatlantic cooperation. The impact on transaction costs is illustrated by the following view, expressed by an FTC official:

even if the transaction needs to be addressed somewhat differently on both sides of the Atlantic because of differing market conditions and competitive realities, we reach solutions involving divestitures and licensing that neither conflict nor force firms to choose between complying with US or EC law. (Valentine, 1998, cited by Janow, 2000, p. 44)

Fourth, in rare cases, major conflicts inspired by nationalistic/regional interests do occur, and cannot be avoided by transatlantic cooperation, such as in the case of the proposed merger between Boeing and McDonnel Douglas in the area of large civil aircraft. This case involved the merger of two companies lacking any assets in Europe, but playing a key role in the global market for large civil aircraft. This merger was approved by the US, but in a first stage rejected by the EU, and almost led to a trade war. In the end the EU cleared the merger, subject to a number of conditions regarding ending alleged, anti-competitive vertical restraints. Irrespective of triad-based, political elements, the US agencies were willing to accept the defence that McDonnel Douglas would, because of its weak FSAs, ultimately be incapable of competing with either Boeing or Airbus in the market for large civil aircraft, and might even be forced to leave the market. Hence, the efficiencies anticipated by the merging parties were judged sufficiently high to counterbalance the expected increase in market power that would accrue to the merged entity. Here, it should be noted that the Commission has now accepted the concept of the 'failing firm' defence, thus indicating the presence of transatlantic learning over time. Interestingly, from a triad perspective, Japan changed its laws soon after this case in order to permit the review of offshore mergers.

Fifth, building upon game-theoretical insights, Janow (2000, p. 45) argues that institutionalized, repeat interactions among agencies on both sides of the Atlantic are likely to lead to a virtuous cycle of convergence, in spite of continuing, and sometimes escalating, trade disputes. An interesting difference between trade disputes and antitrust regulation is that, in the former, the firms involved themselves have conflicting objectives (consider US-based complaints on agricultural subsidies in Europe). In the latter, the directly affected firms hope to receive a merger clearance (or more generally a clearance from competition law remedies) on both sides of the Atlantic, and therefore have strong incentives to facilitate agency convergence towards clearance, rather than towards divergence in judgment. Yet, in Europe, substantial regulatory attention is devoted to the views of competitors, which almost systematically injects a non-efficiency component in the proceedings, at the expense of a sole focus on efficiency criteria (see also below).

It can be concluded that the institutional context described above should provide for more advanced procedural harmonization that could lead to further reductions in transaction costs faced by MNEs. Such procedural harmonization could include the standardization of information requirements at different stages of the investigation. The EU has excessive information requirements during the first stage (when it is still unclear whether serious competition issues are in play), and the US during the second stage. In addition, there is a need for increased transparency in the EU towards merger review guidelines. The investigating agency in the EU has much more discretion in this area than its US counterpart.

On the issue of substantive harmonization, less formal progress can be expected, as the European Commission has so far refused to adopt the US standard for blocking a merger, that is, a substantial lessening of competition. Instead the EU is focused on the strengthening of a company's dominant position in a market. However, within the dominant position framework, the US-based approach, such as taking into account cost savings achieved, can still be included in the analysis without much difficulty. Given the higher discretion prevailing in Europe, adopting stronger substantive convergence without equivalent procedural convergence could, however, be detrimental to large MNEs, as suggested by a competition lawyer:

> The last thing we want is to give the Commission more discretion ... They are already pushing the boundaries of the current tests with theories of doubtful pedigree. It is worrying to think what they would do with a broader instrument. (*Financial Times*, 11 December 2001)

Janow (2000, p. 52–3) argues that far-reaching substantive harmonization (this may include the thresholds adopted for review and the precise criteria used to determine whether antitrust relief is warranted), is only a distant vision. In the ideal case, the agencies on both sides of the Atlantic (or one coordinating agency) would agree to 'accept the mantle of parens patriae for world competition', investigating the entire spectrum of anti-competitive and efficiency effects. Given the weak market position across the triad and the rest of the world of even the largest MNEs, as we documented in the early sections of this chapter, such a substantive approach would likely lead to a sharp reduction in transaction costs for those firms. Substantive harmonization would likely lead to the recognition, in most cases, that no dominant position or abuse is likely on a global scale. Unfortunately such harmonization, solely based on efficiency considerations, would require fundamental changes of several beliefs strongly held in the EU where there is

- A greater distrust of bigness, which has its origins in concerns about the potentially negative influence that large concentrations of economic power can have on democratic institutions

- Less thorough internalization of the consumer welfare model, under which the sole focus is on whether a merger is likely to restrict output or increase price
- A distrust of synergies due to concerns about unemployment
- A greater willingness to manipulate the industrial structure, which may have its roots in greater state economic involvement in Europe
- A tendency to equate preserving effective competition with preserving competitors. (Venit and Kolasky, 2000, pp. 85–6)

The EU attaches much more importance than the US to the views of competitors affected by merger activity. Specifically these competitors may challenge the merging firms, during the oral hearings, after the merging firms have defended themselves against the Commission's objections. In addition, this is then followed by

> a very important body of non-public opinion (member states experts and representatives of other services of the Commission) magnify[ing] the role of competitors far beyond anything in the US system. (Ibid., p. 88)

Especially if the proposed merger includes US-based companies, the role of competitors illustrates the concern expressed in the previous section on the danger of shelter-based strategies against firms from another triad region. For example, in the case of the $5.5 billion takeover bid by US cruise group Carnival for the UK-company P&O Princess, their rival, US-based Royal Caribbean, lobbied against Carnival's bid (*Financial Times*, 17 July 2002).

Given the size and the strategic impacts of many transactions reviewed by antitrust agencies, the relatively higher uncertainty facing MNEs in the EU as compared to the US, has important implications:

> The risks are greater than in the US. [The EU is] less predictable. Therefore you need to be sure, if all goes wrong, that's a result you can live with. If you believe the reputation of your company would be irreparably damaged by being seen to lose then you would be taking a huge risk. Many CEOs are under question and pressure. For them this could destroy their careers. (*Financial Times*, 24 May 2002)

Although only 18 mergers had been blocked by the Commission out of 2100 files examined between 1990 and the end of 2002, the discretion held by the Commission has often been perceived as leading to inefficiencies:

> Even when mergers have been approved ... the mere threat of veto has stacked the odds in favour of EU enforcers, enabling them to bully businesses into making concessions that were not always justifiable. (*Financial Times*, 28 October 2002)

RECENT DEVELOPMENTS IN TRANSATLANTIC CORPORATION

In 2002, the non-efficiency focus of the European Commission (at least relative to US agencies) led to three Commission decisions being overruled by the European Court of Justice for inadequate analysis of the mergers' expected effects. This reversal affected the Commission's decision to block the mergers of travel firms Airtours (currently called My Travel) and First Choice, electronics firms Schneider and Legrand, and packaging firms Tetra Laval and Sidel. These were court decisions of great political importance, as they created an incentive to reduce prevalent bureaucratic discretion in the EU as compared to the US where courts systematically discipline the review of mergers:

> The US government cannot block a deal, it has to go to court. That has a disciplining effect on the approval process … If an official in the US looks [at a situation] and thinks he will lose in court, he will not proceed. A Brussels official may have private reservations but still approve a junior official's recommendation to block a transaction. (*Financial Times*, 24 May, 2002)

The above court rulings undoubtedly contributed to EU competition commissioner Mario Monti's proposal in March 2003 to disband the 'Merger Task Force', a set of approximately 80 elite bureaucrats, mostly lawyers and approximately a dozen economists, accused of 'being arrogant and jumping too quickly to conclusions on complicated issues', (*Financial Times*, 30 March 2003). They were 'nicknamed the "ayatollahs" for their aggressive tactics and unerring self-belief', (*Financial Times*, 28 October 2002). The Merger Task Force's unofficial logo had been 'a sheriff's star with a piranha inside' (ibid.).

The gradual integration of the former task force officials into various other, sector-based, antitrust units was announced on 30 April (*Irish Times*, 1 May 2003). A smaller task force will remain for coordination purposes, but most of the preparatory work and decision making will be performed in units with industry expertise on the sectors in which the investigated firms are active. The post Merger Task Force era does not necessarily imply a much softer stance of the Commission on merger deals, or on wider antitrust investigations.

One of the most important cases being scrutinized at the time of writing (September 2003) is the *Microsoft* case. The European Commission has found, in its preliminary investigation, that Microsoft has leveraged its dominant position from the PC into low-end servers, and that tying its Windows Media Player (a tool to play video and music on a PC) to the

Windows operating system reduces competition and innovation, and negatively affects consumer choice.

Low-end servers provide core services to PCs in corporate networks. The problem is that Microsoft has consistently refused to disclose interface information, which would permit interoperability between competitors' servers and Window PCs and servers. This has led to artificial incentives to users in favour of Microsoft server products. In addition Microsoft is believed to have engaged in an abusive licensing scheme for Windows 2000, forcing customers to select an all-inclusive Microsoft solution, detrimental to consumers' freedom of choice. As regards the bundling of Windows Media Player to Windows, this has artificially skewed the preferences of content owners, content providers and software developers in favour of Microsoft.

The US proceedings against Microsoft were primarily of a different nature. In the US, the focus was on the abuse of its PC operating system dominance to weaken Netscape's Navigator Internet browser and Sun's Java system. Approximately 25 per cent of Microsoft's sales occur in Europe and, if the company is found guilty of violating antitrust laws, fines could be as high as 10 per cent on global revenue (*Washington Post*, 8 February 2003).

The outcome of the Microsoft case will likely be indicative for the potential of further antitrust convergence between the EU and the USA in the years to come. The 2001 blocking of the General Electric–Honeywell merger by the EU, after it had been cleared in the US, and which is still under appeal with the European Court of Justice, has cast a shadow over significant further transatlantic convergence. One important reason is that the Commission used 'portfolio effect theory' as one of the foundations for its judgment. Portfolio effect theory builds upon the assumption that 'companies with a wide range of brands can harm competition by imposing their will on suppliers and distributors' (*Financial Times*, 4 April 2003). In the case of General Electric–Honeywell, the merger would have combined GE's strong position in aircraft engines with Honeywell's strong position in avionics and non-avionics (weather turbulence detection systems, collision avoidance and flight management systems, black boxes). In addition GE had strengths in financing (GE Capital) and leasing (GECAS being the world's largest purchaser of aircraft, larger than any airline (Commission, 3 July 2001).

On the more general substantive front, the 2002 Commission Notice 'on the appraisal of horizontal mergers', provides useful guidance as to how the Commission reaches decisions and suggests a significant move towards more transparent, efficiency-based analysis of proposed mergers, to come into force in 2004, and undoubtedly inspired by a decade of transatlantic cooperation (Commission, 11 December 2002).

Finally it should be noted that the Commission publishes a yearly report which addresses the application of transatlantic antitrust cooperation between the EU, on the one hand, and the US and Canada, on the other. Transatlantic cooperation in antitrust between the EU and Canada is a relatively new phenomenon, resulting from the EU/Canada Summit in June 1999. The transatlantic interactions described in the report, especially with the US, appear manifold and intensive:

> The increase of cooperation ... with respect to the combating of global cartels is noteworthy ... The Commission, [Department of Justice] and FTC are taking increasingly convergent approaches to the identification and implementation of remedies, and to post-merger remedy compliance monitoring. The Commission [Department of Justice] and FTC also continued to maintain an ongoing dialogue on general competition policy/enforcement of common concern. (Commission, 17 September 2002, p. 5)

CONCLUSIONS

In this chapter, we have developed a regional lens to evaluate the interactions between MNEs and the antitrust aspect of public policy. The world's 500 largest MNEs operate mainly in their home regions of the broad 'triad' of the EU, North America (NAFTA) and Asia. Published company data indicate that these MNEs have the large majority of their sales in their home region of the triad. Few firms have a market position in host regions comparable to that earned in the home region. This observation suggests that MNEs face substantial difficulties, at least at the customer end, in becoming global, in the sense of achieving a more balanced distribution of sales across the triad regions. One of the key challenges is undoubtedly the greater 'distance' of host regions, from a geographic, economic, cultural and institutional perspective.

The chapter has addressed the issue of institutional distance, and investigated the extent to which interregional public policy cooperation can contribute (or be detrimental) to expansion in a host region and globally. We have focused our analysis on the recent transatlantic cooperation between the United States and Europe, in the area of antitrust policy. This analysis leads to a paradoxical conclusion.

It is apparent that antitrust is a policy domain worrisome for large MNEs, especially if discretion exists at the level of public agencies administering these policies, as such policies can prevent the implementation of competitive strategies in the realm of mergers and cooperative business practices. Hence, prima facie, MNEs should be concerned about transatlantic cooperation among regulatory agencies, especially if these agencies take into account the effects of strategic behaviour in one region of the triad on consumer and producer welfare in another region. However, in practice, the recent transatlantic cooperation between the United States and Europe has led to some convergence of procedural approaches, thereby improving the quality of the information used by policy makers on both sides of the Atlantic to make more grounded decisions. Increased transatlantic convergence, though mainly through learning rather than formal harmonization, may somewhat reduce transaction costs for the affected MNEs in all regions where they operate, thereby decreasing the institutional distance between regions.

It now appears critical for any large MNE to develop region-based FSAs, especially in dealing with EU regulation, as suggested by the following excerpt from a recent *Financial Times* article:

> corporate counsels' ignorance is dangerous for a company and its shareholders. If the legal adviser does not tell his chief financial officer that it pays to be the first to confess a cartel to Brussels, the company could end up with a massive fine (just ask Roche, BASF and Nintendo). And if the company does not know how to stop a rival from derailing a merger by whispering nasty things in the Commission's ear, shareholders could miss out on potentially-large benefits (just ask General Electric and Honeywell). (*Financial Times*, 4 April 2003)

REFERENCES

Boddewyn, Jean J. (1988), 'Political aspects of MNE theory', *Journal of International Business Studies*, **19**, 341–63.

Boddewyn, Jean J. and T.L. Brewer (1994), 'International business political behaviour: new theoretical direction', *Academy of Management Review*, **19** (1), 119–43.

Boyd, Gavin and Alan M. Rugman (2003), 'Corporate alliances and competition policies', in John H. Dunning and Gavin Boyd (eds), *Alliance Capitalism and Corporate Management*, Cheltenham, UK and Northampton, MA, USA: Edward Elgar, pp. 154–70.

Brewer, T.L. and S. Young (1998), *Multinational Investment Rules and Multinational Enterprise*, Oxford: Oxford University Press.

Caves, Richard E. (1996), *Multinational Enterprise and Economic Analysis*, 2nd edn, Cambridge: Cambridge University Press.

Commission Decision of 3 July 2001, declaring a concentration to be incompatible with the common market and the EEA Agreement. Case No COMP/M.2220 – General Electric/Honeywell.

Commission Notice of 11 December 2002, on the appraisal of horizontal mergers under the Council Regulation on the control of concentrations between undertakings.

Commission Report of 17 September 2002, to the Council and the European Parliament on the application of the agreements between the European

Communities and the Government of the United States of America and the Government of Canada regarding the application of their competition laws. 1 January 2001 to 31 December 2001.

Devuyst, Youri (1998), 'The international dimension of the EC's antitrust policy: extending the level playing field', *European Foreign Affairs Review*, **3**, 467.

Dunning, John H. (ed.) (1997), *Governments, Globalization and International Business*, Oxford: Oxford University Press.

Evenett, Simon J., A. Lehman and B. Steil (eds), (2000), *Antitrust Goes Global*, London: Royal Institute of International Affairs and New York: Brookings Institution.

Financial Times, 11 December 2001.

Financial Times, 24 May 2002.

Financial Times, 17 July 2002.

Financial Times, 28 October 2002.

Financial Times, 30 March 2003.

Financial Times, 4 April 2003.

Ghemawat. P. (2001), 'Distance still matters: "the hard reality of global expansion"', *Harvard Business Review*, **79** (8), 137–47.

Ghemawat, P. (2003), 'Semiglobalization and international business strategy', *Journal of International Business Studies*, **34** (2), 138–52.

Irish Times, 1 May 2003.

Janow, Minet E. (2000), 'Transatlantic cooperation on competition policy', in Simon J. Evenett, Alexander Lehman and Benn Steil (eds), *Antitrust Goes Global,* London: Royal Institute of International Affairs/New York: Brookings Institution, pp. 29–56.

Ohmae, K. (1985), *Triad Power: The Coming Shape of Global Competition*, New York: The Free Press.

Rugman, Alan M. (1976), 'Risk reduction by international diversification', *Journal of International Business Studies*, **7** (3), 75–80.

Rugman, Alan M. (1979), *International Diversification and the Multinational Enterprise*, Lexington: D.C. Heath.

Rugman, Alan M. (1991), 'Environmental change and global competitive strategy in Europe', in Alan M. Rugman and Alain Verbeke (eds), *Research in Global Strategic Management*, vol. 2, *Global Competition and the European Community*, Greenwood, CT and JAI Press, pp. 3–28.

Rugman, Alan M. (1996), *Multinational Enterprises and Trade Policy: Volume 2 of the Selected Scientific Papers of Alan M. Rugman*, Cheltenham, UK and Brookfield, USA: Edward Elgar.

Rugman, Alan M. (1998), 'Multinational enterprise and public policy', *Journal of International Business Studies*, **29** (1), 115–36.

Rugman, Alan M. (2000), *The End of Civilization*, London: Random House.

Rugman, Alan M. (2001), The impact of globalization on Canadian competition policy, in David W. Conklin (ed.), *Canadian Competition Policy: Preparing for the Future*, Toronto: Pearson Education Canada/Richard Ivey School of Business, pp. 30–44.

Rugman, Alan M. (2003), 'The World Trade Organization, multinational enterprise and the civil society', in Michele Fratianni, Paolo Savona and John J. Kirton (eds), *Sustaining Global Growth and Development: G7 and IMF Governance*, Aldershot, UK: Ashgate, pp. 81–98.

Rugman, Alan M. (2004), 'Regional and global strategies of multinational enterprises', *Journal of International Business Studies*, **35** (1) 3–18.

Rugman, Alan M. and Gavin Boyd (2001), *The World Trade Organization in the New Global Economy*, Cheltenham, UK and Northampton, MA, USA: Edward Elgar.

Rugman, Alan M. and Cecilia Brain (2003), 'Multinational enterprises are regional, not global', *The Multinational Business Review*, **11** (1), 3–12.

Rugman, Alan M. and Alain Verbeke (1990), *Global Corporate Strategy and Trade Policy*, London: Routledge.

Shugart, William F., Jon D. Silverman and Robert D. Tollison (1995), 'Antitrust enforcement and foreign competition', in Fred S. McChesney and William F. Shugart, (eds), *The Causes and Consequences of Antitrust: The Public-choice Perspective*, Chicago: University of Chicago Press.

Valentine, Debra A. (1998), 'Building a cooperative framework for oversight in mergers: The answer to extraterritorial issues in merger review', *George Mason Law Review*, **6**, 525.

Venit, James S. and William J. Kolasky (2000), 'Substantive convergence and procedural dissonance in merger review', in Simon J. Evenett, Alexander Lehman and Benn Steil (eds), *Antitrust Goes Global*, London: Royal Institute of International Affairs/New York: Brookings Institution, pp. 79–97

Vernon, Raymond (1971), *Sovereignty at Bay: The Multinational Spread of US Enterprises*, New York: Basic Books.

Washington Post, 8 February 2003.

6. Interregional integration: collective management tasks

Gavin Boyd

Atlantic structural interdependencies, because of their magnitude and imbalances, set urgent requirements for sound collective management. The deepening integration in which these interdependencies are increasing between North America and the European Union results from the independent and generally competing operations of North American and European transnational enterprises, and these are not forming a coordinated pattern of dynamic efficiencies. Market failures as well as productive functions are assuming cross-border dimensions, and are interacting with government efficiencies and failures. Policy-level and corporate efforts are needed to promote extensive entrepreneurial complementarities, to orient financial sectors more towards productive funding aligned with such complementarities and to improve macromanagement. These imperatives have to be affirmed with reference to very serious problems in the interactions between financial sectors and the real economies, concentration trends increasing Atlantic structural imbalances, the USA's high debt levels and current account deficits and the persistence of slow growth and high unemployment in the European Union.

Interregional policy cooperation has to engage with issues of policy interdependence, as well as structural interdependence, and the need to promote entrepreneurial complementarities, for the development of a more coordinated Atlantic market economy, has to be recognized as an advance in policy learning. Such learning has been seen to be necessary in the fiscal and monetary areas, as well as in trade relations, on the basis of understandings about the potential benefits from interregional market openness. Advances towards market integration on such a vast scale have been felt to promise efficiencies in production specializations, with progress towards competitive equilibrium; and a policy responsibility to promote production complementarities has not been thought of as a solution for deficiencies in the operation of market forces.

Explicit subsidies for industries are in principle to be avoided, in the USA and the EU, to allow full scope for market forces, although observance of this liberal principle is certainly not comprehensive, and is qualified by tacit concerns with enhancing structural competitiveness. Competition policies are considered necessary, to ensure market efficiencies, but collaborative implementation of these policies by the USA and the EU is difficult, because of European views about the international market strengths of large US enterprises. On each side of the Atlantic differing perspectives relating to implicit structural policy rivalries and to competition policy objectives have tended to qualify understandings about transregional market efficiencies and, in this context, questions about policy initiatives to facilitate coordinations of entrepreneurial choices have not attracted attention. Research on contrasts between coordinated and liberal market economies, however, has indicated areas of policy learning of significance for structural competitiveness, in contexts of structural interdependence made complex by transnational enterprises. Further policy learning attuned to international public goods issues has clearly been possible, but has been hindered by attachments to concepts of efficiencies driven by market forces operating across borders.

The context for Atlantic policy learning has meanwhile been made more complex by strong speculative and manipulative propensities in financial sectors, especially in the USA, which have destabilizing potential. Misallocations of investment for often high-risk rent seeking, evading regulatory discipline, have indicated capacities to drive stock prices to unsustainable levels and, in recession, have continued with virtual limitations on productive funding for recovery. Non-financial enterprises, moreover, have been attracted by opportunities for speculation in financial markets. Furthermore, strong oligopolistic trends in world financial markets, in which US investment enterprises have been very prominent, have indicated vital issues for the EU as well as for the USA.

THEORY

The effects of economic integration on growth have been studied with a focus on the European Union, with interest in the structural effects of expanded scope for production specializations, the funding of regionally rationalized production by capital markets, the degrees of policy convergence induced by macromanagement rivalries and concerns with regional macromanagement, and overall progress in the evolution of Europeanized knowledge-intensive political economies.[1] Research on the USA has mainly sought to assess the effects of deepening external economic involvement on the national political economy, with its macromanagement problems, and the most challenging structural and policy interdependencies demanding attention have been those with the European Union.[2] In Atlantic relations the USA's higher degrees of political and economic integration, and more advanced industrialization, have been examined as sources of bargaining advantages and as achievements relevant for European policy learning, but exceptional US policy problems have been identified as dangers threatening stability, and entailing vulnerabilities for the European Union.[3]

Issues of systemic development in the transregional Atlantic economy now demand close attention, for policy planning and corporate planning, because of the magnitude of the structural linkages that are being shaped by corporate expansion, with imbalances affecting dynamic and allocative efficiencies, and with misallocations of investment in speculative financial operations affecting the real economies.[4] Concentration trends are associated with the corporate expansion, and in these trends US transnational enterprises are prominent.[5] Analytical perspectives are being obliged to respond to declines in economic sovereignty, and failures in the exercise of such sovereignty, which have consequences for Atlantic relations and for the world economy.[6] With the increasing structural significance of transnational manufacturing, resource-based and non-financial service enterprises and the expanding scale of financial sector interactions with real economies, questions about the systemic effects of market forces are assuming larger dimensions.[7] Questions about the efficacy of political competition in the USA and the EU, for the generation of constructive new forms of statecraft through policy learning, also demand recognition. Political competition driving fiscal expansion with dysfunctional effects is a serious macromanagement problem, more serious in the USA than in the EU that is in conjunction with the stronger speculative propensity in the US financial sectors.[8]

General expectations of efficiencies in equilibrium resulting from intercorporate competition, shown to be unwarranted by insights in behavioural macroeconomics (Stiglitz, 2002), have special relevance for study of the deepening integration in Atlantic relations, that is, when combined with research in behavioural finance (Shiller, 2003) on investment misallocations and the funding of industry. The significance of increasing concentration trends, moreover, has to be recognized in this context, while the entire perspective has to be expanded to take account of the interaction of policy failures with problems in the linkages between financial sectors and the real economies.[9]

A major conclusion to be drawn is that, for improved macromanagement in Atlantic relations, with recoveries of economic sovereignty, very active cooperation between policy levels and corporate decision makers will be necessary. The objective will have to be a coordinated interregional market economy aligned with imperatives for comprehensive efficiencies and social justice.[10] These imperatives can be stressed with reference to all the regulatory and motivational problems associated with the numerous cases of large-scale high-risk corporate fraud in the USA since the ending of its speculative boom after the 1990s.[11] All these cases have had serious implications for Europe as well as for the USA because of a general weakening of regulatory discipline, associated with losses of economic sovereignty, and because what might be called 'market discipline' has had lagged effects, but also because heightened uncertainties in world financial markets have increased compulsions to hedge against risks, and also to engage in speculative risk taking that endangers the interests of passive investors, without immediate detection.[12]

Problems of advanced political development in the USA and in the major members of the EU have diverse effects on their policy orientations, and these interact with changes in their systems of corporate and intercorporate governance. Contests for office involve rivalries for support across class and ideological cleavages, and groups in power strive to retain allegiances while endeavouring to strengthen structural competitiveness, in response to challenges in world markets, and while meeting the expectations of key interest groups. The USA's intensely individualistic culture, the institutional weaknesses of its main political parties and its fragmented pattern of corporate associations hinder coherent interest representation and leadership efforts to build policy consensus: hence much trading of political favours complicates attempts to enhance structural competitiveness, and causes alternations in domestic policy biases. Cultural and political as well as economic diversity in the EU causes more serious problems of governance, hindering cooperation that might increase structural competitiveness. Weaker development of financial markets, however, has limited vulnerabilities to destabilizing speculation, while this problem has remained intractable in the USA because of dysfunctional pluralism.[13] Despite the difficulties of collective governance in the European Union, moreover, its monetary structure is a source of significant fiscal discipline.[14]

Theorizing about trends and issues in US and European political evolution of significance for Atlantic economic cooperation can draw some guidance from institutional economics (Pollack and Shaffer, 2001), but this area of the discipline has remained focused on national economies. Wider-ranging analysis, examining contrasts between coordinated and liberal market economies (Hall and Soskice, 2001) has combined institutional economics with research on cultural factors, but has not taken up questions of convergence and divergence in the EU that have become especially significant because of pressures for change in systems of corporate governance.[15] These pressures have been related to the internationalization of financial markets and the expansion of production operations by transnational enterprises.

Atlantic economic cooperation has been viewed primarily as a bilateral process, with little attention being given to the potential value of shared institutions for consultations and negotiations. The main areas in which cooperation is seen to be imperative, in theoretical literature and in established policy orientations, are monetary, fiscal and trade policies, but prospects for productive collaboration in line with shared interests have been considered unfavourable because of trends in US and European political dynamics, imbalances in structural interdependence and changes in bargaining strengths. The rationale for achieving monetary stability under a single European authority has been extended into understandings about imperatives for monetary cooperation with the USA, especially because of the potential for volatility in financial markets that could severely affect the real economies.[16] Capacities for Atlantic monetary collaboration, however, have been adversely affected by problems in US fiscal and trade policies and by the difficulties of recovery from recession. Theorizing about policy linkages in this context has had to take account of the effects of high-volume speculation on the interactions between financial sectors and the real economies in conjunction with the consequences of strong fiscal expansion.[17]

For the development of theory that can contribute to policy learning on each side of the Atlantic, a key requirement that has received little attention is the functional imperative of entrepreneurial coordination for balanced dynamic growth in the transregional economy. This tends to be obscured in perspectives dominated by interest in the efficiencies expected to result from competitive pressures in an integrating transregional market.

Interregional Market Forces and Market Failures

The areas of theory significant for policy learning in the Atlantic context of interregional integration relate especially to market functions. These functions have been studied mainly in national economies, with interest in allocative efficiencies. Dynamic efficiencies, resulting from entrepreneurial innovations activating further entrepreneurial innovations and increasing with degrees of coordination that expand complementarities, increase allocative efficiencies, subject to critical balances between competition and cooperation.[18] The economics of information, of technology sharing and development, and of technology-based production interdependencies, assume greater importance as advances are made in applications of frontier research, causing economies to become more knowledge-intensive, with more substantial intangible assets, including especially relational assets.[19]

Much research interest, however, has focused on allocative efficiencies, while dynamic efficiencies have been viewed mainly as outcomes of competition rather than cooperation.[20]

Allocative efficiencies are reduced by increases in oligopoly and monopoly power, resulting from intensities of competition relative to levels of cooperation, and reflecting the influence of cultures and regulatory endeavours. Dynamic efficiencies are affected, especially because entry barriers are raised to hinder potential new firms, and because information flows are made more restrictive. Both dynamic and allocative efficiencies, meanwhile, are affected by speculative market manipulations, as misallocations of investment to these have destabilizing effects while limiting the funding of productive activity.[21] As market processes become more international the relational ties between firms that can restrain competition and sustain cooperation in national economies may become weaker, while failing to expand across borders. With the interregional expansion of financial markets, moreover, relational intercorporate ties also tend to become weaker between the enterprises leading concentration trends in these markets, while the speculative propensities of the managements tend to become stronger, relative to their orientations towards productive funding. The international rent seeking can make rapid gains while exploiting and increasing volatility, and taking advantage of international regulatory weaknesses.[22]

In the deepening Atlantic integration, market linking expands opportunities for increases in dynamic efficiencies. Overall growth, however, depends more on extensive coordinations of production, for orderly development of the interdependent real economies. Coordination failures result in excess capacity (steel and automobiles), capacity deficiencies and inadequate information flows, and increase the scope for speculative exploitation of sectoral disruptions, while heightening risks for new entrepreneurs. Low levels of trust persist, and the general uncertainties tend to impose caution on productive funding, yet invite much speculation because of the prospects for volatility.[23] Recovery from a post-boom recession, as has been evident in the recent history of the USA, can be difficult because of the vast losses of wealth, underinvestment and excessive consumption during the boom, declines in investor confidence and the attractions of speculative opportunities elsewhere in the world economy.[24]

Externalities, related to the growth of transregional oligopoly power and to speculative exploitations of volatility, include deindustrialization and unemployment, associated with the formation of international production systems, with patterns of vertical specialization extending outside the Atlantic system. The deindustrialization and unemployment, in Europe and the USA demand urgent attention as failures in dynamic efficiencies. As capital is mobile while labour is not, the costs of adjustment, when not met adequately, fall more on labour. The overall costs, in terms of failures in growth, tend to increase, in conjunction with the disruptive effects of the speculative propensities in financial sectors.[25] Moreover there are transregional asymmetries, because of the greater entrepreneurial significance of the American corporate presence in Europe, compared with that of the weaker European presence in the USA.[26]

The regional and interregional market failures are offset by allocative and dynamic efficiencies, but with diminishing effects, as concentration trends continue in financial sectors and real economies, with related negative externalities, and as rent-seeking misallocations of investment remain large, compared with productive funding. In the EU, market integration and monetary integration facilitate increases in allocative and dynamic efficiencies, but strong oligopoly power persists in retailing, while productive investment is limited by capital outflows, especially in search of higher yields in the USA.[27] The dynamic efficiencies, inferior to those in the USA, reflect the costs of delays in regional market integration and monetary union, due to slow policy learning. In the USA, dynamic efficiencies are sustained by a strong entrepreneurial culture, which also drives allocative efficiencies, but, as noted, with fluctuations attributable primarily to the effects of speculation on stock and property prices, and with the negative consequences of increases in oligopoly power.

In the integrating transatlantic market the effects of allocative and dynamic efficiencies and failures move principally from the USA to Europe. This happens because of the dimensions of US corporate involvement in the global economy as well as in the interregional pattern, and because of the competitive leads of US transnational enterprises, gained while European firms have been rather confined to their home market.[28] Competition policy in the EU is intended to facilitate the establishment of globally competitive firms through mergers and acquisitions, but EU enterprises seeking to expand tend to align themselves with US corporations rather than other European firms.[29]

GOVERNMENT EFFICIENCIES AND FAILURES

Policy efficiencies and failures in the Atlantic interact with interregional market efficiencies and failures. The most extensive consequences are that US policy deficiencies affect the mix of cross-border market processes; the principal failures are heavy fiscal expansion, neglect of unsustainable current account deficits and toleration of strong speculative propensities in the financial sector. The heavy fiscal expansion substantially increases domestic demand, in excess of domestic output, drawing high-volume imports that add to the very large current account deficits. These tend to be offset by investment inflows, but those decline in a post-boom recession. The promotion of recovery after the ending of the 1990s boom has been an objective of the fiscal expansion, but the effects on domestic output have been limited by corporate emphasis on foreign production, low investor confidence and the interests of financial enterprises in global speculative opportunities.[30] The principal market failures, affecting especially the interactions between the financial sectors and the real economies, have been the speculative misallocations of investment, activating booms and declines, to the detriment of productive funding, with persistently high uncertainties and information deficiencies. Imperatives for trust and goodwill in the culture of the political economy have not been met. Politically, then, this has had consequences in the assertion of interests contributing to policy processes, thus making regulatory improvements more difficult.[31]

The combination of high fiscal deficits, unsustainable current account deficits and speculative investment misallocations raises questions about institutional development and institutional economics, as well as behavioural finance. Weakening market discipline has been evident in the interactions of the financial sector and the real economy, while weakening of regulatory discipline has also been apparent in that context.[32] Problems of building policy consensus aligned with the common good are serious because of the intense pluralism generated by an individualistic culture. Intercorporate competition, extending especially into the Atlantic economy, makes difficult the formation of institutions for economic governance.[33] The very difficult public goods problems, then, are general increases in risks, for households, firms and communities (Shiller, 2003), dramatized by the heavy losses of wealth at the end of the 1990s boom and by the numerous high-profile cases of corporate fraud.

A transregional effect is that the EU experiences increases in the vulnerabilities of interdependence. European macromanagement has benefited from more prudent fiscal policies and from stronger financial sector orientations towards productive funding, while slower development of an equity culture has resulted in smaller losses of monetary sovereignty. Such losses in the USA entailed difficulties in restraining the irrational speculation of the 1990s boom.[34]

European fiscal prudence has been maintained, on the whole, on the basis of policy learning and accountabilities under the European Monetary Union, a significant institutional achievement, despite contrasting national policy orientations, styles and capabilities, with tensions in the central political links between Germany and France.[35] The French political economy lacks deliberative and coordinating mechanisms like those in Germany, and industrially has lower status. Neither administration identifies with the common regional interest to the extent of working for a Union structural policy: domestic political linkages motivate concerns with enhancing structural competitiveness. There is qualified endorsement of the European Commission's endeavours to promote market-driven regional growth through a common competition policy and measures for financial market unification, but the concerns with structural competitiveness have higher priority and restrict interest in bilateral structural policy cooperation.[36]

Very demanding regional coordination requirements, in conditions of imbalanced structural interdependence with the USA, are the key challenges for the EU. Policy-level efficiencies and failures are evolving in a mix which does not engage sufficiently with problems of slow growth and high unemployment. Coordination deficiencies allow the continuation of outward investment flows to the USA as a potentially higher growth area, and growing speculative pursuits of high returns in world financial markets. A weakening of solidarity and of relational cooperation in the German system of corporate and intercorporate governance is one of the most serious consequences of these trends.[37] Regional assertions of common corporate interests, directed mainly at the European Commission, are not driving effective engagement with the Union-level coordination deficiencies, and for this may be even less potent, with the admission of East and Central European members in 2004, because of the increased complexities of collective decision making.[38] The Commission's responsibilities for regional interest aggregation and policy initiation have been put into effect with much emphasis on regulatory directives, seen as appropriate for growth based on increases in the scope for market forces. In the increasingly competitive regional market, however, growth is tending to become more dependent on the entrepreneurial dynamism of the US corporate presence, while European firms linked with that presence evolve mainly as subordinate partners.[39] EU-level regulatory initiatives cannot respond directly, and meanwhile the regulatory orientation and the complexities of decision making associated with it divert attention from the region's structural problems.

Transatlantic Interactions

While the effects of interactions of Atlantic market efficiencies and failures are transmitted mainly towards the European Union, owing to asymmetries in competitiveness, there is a similar causality at the policy level, but primarily as a consequence of US macromanagement failures. Very challenging imperatives for policy learning thus have to be confronted by the EU. In prospect is the next generation of unsustainable asset appreciations in the USA and of speculation-induced financial crises in industrializing countries, as recipients of investment flows from the USA and the EU.[40] Thus far the EU has been rather sheltered from crises in emerging markets, but is becoming more exposed in this regard because of its speculative outflows. The policy-learning challenges for the USA are very demanding and the EU has vital interests in encouraging highly constructive US responses, despite disadvantages in status and bargaining strengths.

Corporate learning can benefit from, and contribute to, the policy learning. The European corporate networks for consultative exchanges with the European Commission have very significant potential, especially because of the leadership of the European Roundtable of Industrialists.[41] A challenge can be seen to provide knowledge-intensive inputs into EU policy making that will result in more effective engagement with regional macromanagement issues and with problems of transatlantic interdependence. Vigorous quests for collaboration by US corporate groups would be warranted *by* the magnitude of the interests threatened in the mix of interregional market processes and policy deficiencies.

The importance of European potentials for policy learning and corporate learning can be stressed because of the acute dangers threatening on account of US macromanagement problems. Those problems can generate pressures in the USA for the imposition of adjustment costs on Europe and, meanwhile, it must be reiterated, are causing increases in the EU's vulnerabilities. The challenges for US policy learning and corporate learning are formidable, but encouragement can be drawn from the extensive political coordination that has developed between major corporations in Europe (Coen, 1998).

If interregional policy interactions become more knowledge-intensive, shared responsibilities for the provision of Atlantic public goods and motivations based on transnational accountabilities can become more significant than the use of bargaining strengths on behalf of politically prominent interest groups, and the demands of such groups can become more enlightened. These beneficial results will be made more probable if strong corporate associations in Europe and the USA work vigorously to aid learning at the policy level and to promote general increases in structural harmony through extensive entrepreneurial coordination. Fundamental considerations here are that politically prominent interest groups in the USA and in Europe impart inward-looking bias to policy making, in conflict with functional requirements for managing structural interdependencies on the basis of shared interests, and that the fortunes of productive enterprises, providing increases in growth for real economies, depend on substantial funding by financial sectors.[42] A coordinated transatlantic economy, with dynamic efficiencies, will be feasible with policy learning and corporate learning on scales matching the degrees of cross-border market integration. The formation of strong Atlantic corporate associations, with stable comprehensive aggregations of interests, understood in socially responsible perspectives, could contribute very actively to functional continuity in European and US economic policies.

Supplementary considerations are that a liberal transatlantic market economy, while increasingly imbalanced, will be under stress. The adverse trends in oligopoly power and in financial sector orientations will tend to make coordination achievements more difficult, especially in the USA, while reducing potentials for policy learning and corporate learning, as well as those for institutional development. Rivalries for advantages in structural competitiveness can be expected to increase in such a context, but with results limited by losses of economic sovereignty as transnational enterprises extend their operations.

Altogether the logic of regional market integration has been profoundly changed since the establishment of the EU and the USA's entry into deepening integration through transnational production at levels higher than arm's length exports. Regionally based European economic growth has not been sufficient for balanced involvement in the world economy, while asymmetric linkages with the USA have increased.[43] US internal market integration well ahead of the EU's has enabled national firms to gain domestic strengths for the support of large-scale foreign production, with emphasis on penetration of the European Union.[44] Interregional economic linkages without substantial governance set imperatives for more than regulatory cooperation, because of transnational market failures, as well as the effects on these of policy failures.

MACROMANAGEMENT IMPERATIVES

Transregional interdependencies set clear requirements for Atlantic economic cooperation, but this tends to be seen as a bargaining rather than a learning and community-building process, with little recognition of the value of common institutions and with perspectives dominated by concepts of the efficiencies of market forces but qualified by concerns with structural competitiveness. Bargaining is motivated by pressures to meet domestic assertions of interests through inducing foreign collaboration with promises of beneficial exchange, notably by increases in market openness but also by monetary adjustments, for expected effects on demand and for exchange rate stability. At arm's length, and instrumental rather than integrative, the bargaining tends to become adversarial, because of efforts to extract concessions, especially on trade issues that have domestic political prominence. The main intent is to secure hard and precise agreements, yet with flexible commitments subject to further bargaining.[45]

Corporate demands are active in the domestic assertions of interests, but are articulated in the USA through a fragmented pattern of associations, and for major US transnational enterprises there are incentives to seek consideration from numerous foreign governments, outside as well as within the Atlantic pattern.[46] Strategic planning, moreover, demands focus on specific trends in diverse external markets served through international production systems. European firms, less involved in transnational operations, and more attentive to home market concerns, in a context of regional competitive inferiority, tend to assert more protectionist interests in the dynamics of their Union's external economic policies.[47]

Potentials for structural policy cooperation tend to be obscured by the bargaining orientations and the concepts of market efficiencies. This has to be emphasized despite the diverse indirect and direct subsidies for industry in the EU and the USA and despite frictions in attempts at Atlantic competition policy cooperation. For the Europeans, a liberal orientation in US antitrust enforcement has major structural implications, and any possibilities for structural policy collaboration with the USA have to be seen in terms of bargaining asymmetries and inferior competitiveness.[48]

Policy learning and corporate learning focused on structural issues have become imperative because of vast problems of efficiency and social justice in the liberal transatlantic market economy that is being shaped by independent corporate operations. Risks affecting the welfare of great numbers of people are increasing because of internationalized market failures and government failures. The combined effects of perverse interactions between financial sectors and real economies, of concentration trends and of fiscal mismanagement, demand attention in advance of prospective unsustainable speculative booms. Their transnational disruptions are likely to be on scales much more extensive than the adaptive capacities of governments resorting to macroeconomic expansion. Rationales like that for the 'Greenspan put' are unfounded.[49] The political incentives to promote a speculative boom, for recovery from recession, however, are very potent, and accordingly corrective policy learning is extremely urgent. The destructive effects of collapsing speculative booms are becoming greater as transnational economic linkages expand, as speculative propensities in financial sectors increase relative to productive funding and as levels of government debt also reduce productive funding while adding to the incentives of transnational enterprises to expand foreign production.[50]

Policy learning and corporate learning therefore must be comprehensive, recognizing the functional logic of very active cooperation between governments and industry across the interregional economy, and the importance of institutionalizing this cooperation under a common structure, for continuity in the development of technocratic expertise and coordinated corporate planning. The rationale for this institutional innovation will not find ready political acceptance, but will have to be pressed in initiatives to promote the interactive learning.

For higher, more stable and more balanced growth, the main priorities will have to be concerted fiscal discipline, financial sector reform and the sponsorship of entrepreneurial complementarities. Two themes in the logic of fiscal prudence are the restriction of public spending to essential services and infrastructure development, and the maintenance of low tax levels, with the lightening of welfare burdens through structural measures.[51] Financial sector reorientations towards more productive funding will require remedial pressure through associations of producer enterprises, large reductions of government borrowing and tightened regulation of trade in financial assets.[52] The promotion of coordinated entrepreneurship, as an especially significant innovation, will have to have a rationale stressing growth potentials and the costs of industrial fragmentation[53] and of destructive entrepreneurship (Foss and Foss, 2002).

High principled motivation, at policy levels and in corporate associations, will be essential for all the consultative learning and the generation of collegial commitments to macromanagement tasks. All the interdependencies multiplying in knowledge-intensive market economies increase the significance of moral development, trust, relational assets and social capital. The numerous cases of large-scale corporate fraud in the USA have indicated a contrary trend in social evolution, which has no doubt had undetected effects in political circles, but it is clear that the trend must be reversed, through renewals of dedication to authentic values.[54]

Mutual accountability for fiscal discipline has become essential between the USA and the European Union, but cannot be dependent on discretionary efforts by administrations under changing domestic pressures. Continuing independent assessments, forecasts and recommendations by a common Atlantic institution are needed, in line with the operational logic of the European Monetary Union, based on understandings of macroeconomic interdependence, and of requirements to balance national representations of interests with sensitivities to those of partners in trade and cross-border production.[55] The European monetary authority, despite decisional problems (Hallett et al., 2001) has to cope with the Union's vulnerabilities, and cannot become dependent on discretionary US macroeconomic cooperation.

Financial sector reform for the Atlantic region, according with the growth objectives of collaborative fiscal discipline, will also have to be promoted with strong resolve and sustained through well established institutions. This, however, will not have to be primarily a regulatory process. Regulatory functions are extremely important, and concern the interests of vast numbers of passive and uninformed investors as well as the stakeholders of innumerable firms vulnerable to the collapses of speculative booms.

These interests, however, require fundamental changes in the operations of financial enterprises, towards stable productive funding of coordinated entrepreneurial ventures. The proper roles of financial enterprises in knowledge-intensive economies have to be defined in terms of these functions, and fulfilment of those roles will have to be ensured on a basis of accountability to strong associations of producer enterprises and to structural policy authorities as well as regulators. Speculative market manipulation for the exploitation of volatility will have to be severely discouraged in part through preferential official dealings with more reputable financial enterprises. The rather permissive trend in US antitrust policy which has allowed strong concentrations of power in financial sectors, and which has serious implications for the EU, will have to be changed.[56]

There are urgent imperatives for European initiatives. European political culture shows strong concern for public goods and social justice, as has been evident in welfare state policies, and in forms of cooperation between governments and corporations. The vulnerabilities to economic fluctuations in the USA are associated with losses of sovereignty and with inferior structural competitiveness. There are perceptions that the USA's problems of governance visible in its current account deficits and high debt levels could be made more manageable by greater external accountability.[57] Economic advice to policy levels in Europe, moreover, is directed very much to permanent bureaucracies less disturbed by political rivalries and more involved in cross border collaborative deliberations.[58]

The promotion of Atlantic entrepreneurial complementarities would be aided by productive financial sector reorientations. Here also institutionalized collaborative reform is clearly necessary for functional continuity that will not be subject to shifts in administrative discretion. Vital contributions will be needed from peak corporate associations, and their development will have to be assisted by shifts to stakeholder corporate and intercorporate governance.[59] The public good to be striven for is orderly evolution of the interregional market economy through extensive entrepreneurial coordination, sustained by relational ties and responsive to US and European technocratic assessments of potentials for structural harmony. The formation of transregional industry groups, open to new entrants, and active in consultations with national structural policy authorities as well as with an Atlantic structural policy institution, would be a key innovation for sponsorship of the entrepreneurial complementarities.

MACROECONOMIC COOPERATION

Coordinated Atlantic fiscal discipline, with continuity ensured by institutional arrangements, would provide a favourable context for the development of entrepreneurial complementarities, subject to progress in financial sector reform. Substantial reductions in government spending, while facilitating more productive investment, would be conducive to increases in domestically based growth, especially in the USA, where tax burdens add to corporate incentives to produce abroad, thus increasing the problems of achieving external balance. Of immediate policy level and corporate concern, however, are issues of interdependent monetary management. Surveillance by the International Monetary Fund sustains elite awareness of these issues, with appropriate warnings about conflicting pressures on the US currency, but a tradition of fully independent monetary management is well established in the USA, despite much recognition that false signals to investors contributed to the speculative boom in the 1990s.[60] Management of the European Monetary Union is more rationally deliberative, and endeavours to remain so while reacting to the uncertainties in foreign exchange markets. Losses of monetary sovereignty due to the growth of securities industries have been less than in the USA, and perspectives are influenced by expectations of greater regionally based growth after enlargement, but it is necessary to reckon with increasingly difficult problems in the Atlantic relationship because of the cumulative effects of foreign exchange volatility.[61]

The uncertainties in currency markets extend well outside the Atlantic area, because of large East Asian holdings of dollars, and trade-motivated interventions, but the main challenges for Europe are in relations with the USA, and the highest American priority has to be the interdependence with the EU. Union acceptance of the logic of institutionalizing monetary cooperation in a new Atlantic consultative organization would be slow but fairly probable, and this may well motivate efforts on each side to encourage European initiatives.[62] There is very substantial European expertise that could assist interactive policy learning and there is potential bargaining leverage related to European holdings of excess dollar reserves. The learning capability, moreover, is based in part on lessons from the attainment of considerable fiscal discipline under the European Monetary Union through institutionalized mutual accountabilities, after national failures to control the expansionary effects of political competition.[63] The collective fiscal restraint has been considered responsible for slower growth, but it has been clear that the real economies could benefit from higher productive investment, despite financial flows attracted to the USA during its boom. The policy learning that has now become urgent for the EU concerns the imperative for a common structural policy, focused on the promotion of entrepreneurial complementarities for coordinated regional growth.[64]

European advice in Atlantic monetary consultations will have to stress very forcefully the increasingly urgent requirements for fiscal prudence in the USA, referring to linkages with trade policy and the regulation of financial markets, and to issues of exchange rate stability, price stability and the coordination of reaction functions. The key European interests are to restrain fiscal laxity in the USA in so far as that increases its external imbalance, through strong internal demand, thus contributing to exchange rate volatility; and to encourage monetary tightening in the USA, to the extent that this can moderate the speculative propensities of its financial sector. European monetary management has emphasized tightening to ensure unemployment at levels considered necessary for price stability, as if unemployment were not a problem of market failure, to be dealt with through structural policy, and as if price levels were not attributable in a large measure to oligopolistic retailing, and to incomplete integration in the Union market. The negative growth effects have caused the Union's status to remain inferior in US perspectives, but European concerns about the destabilizing consequences of US fiscal expansion have remained valid.[65]

Recession in the USA, and problems of recovery caused by strong financial sector speculative orientations, encouraged by opportunities to exploit monetary loosening as well as volatility in currency and stock markets, have serious implications for European exports. Motivations for constructive engagement, then, are strong, and there are structural costs to be considered, not only because of export problems, but because an important consequence of the USA's domestic difficulties is that they increase the incentives for US transnational enterprises to expand in Europe, despite its growth problems, and in part because of those problems.[66] This has been noted, but it must be added that an indirect effect is to make European monetary and fiscal policies gradually less significant for growth and price stability. What the EU can learn, in intensive monetary policy interactions with the USA, is a difficult lesson about funding industrial growth through bank financing less conservative than that in Europe, but with relational intercorporate cross-holdings, and with restraint on the development of potentially destabilizing trade in securities and on the evolution of an equity culture. The Japanese model of coordination with an entrepreneurial culture is relevant, despite failures in policy-level direction of the banking sector.[67]

FINANCIAL SECTOR REFORM

Efficiencies in international financial markets can be considered possible to the extent that there is priority funding for firms demonstrating high profitability, in countries with superior growth levels. Expectations of such efficiencies can refer to capital flight from developing areas to industrialized states, and to flows of investment from Europe to the USA. Large-scale use of opportunities for high profits through speculative trading in financial assets, however, can affect the anticipated efficiencies of benefit to real economies. This necessitates repeated references to problems of Atlantic financial sector interdependence that have vital significance for monetary policies

US regulatory efforts to prevent large-scale corporate fraud have had to enhance investor protection in areas of complex high-volume risk taking where financial statements are opaque and where official surveillance is quite limited. In these areas, moreover, political will to support regulatory tightening tends to be lacking, especially in sections of financial communities with interests in hedge funds.[68] The basic problem of strong rent-seeking propensities in financial sectors, especially in the USA, while greatly complicating Atlantic monetary relations, is an increasingly serious challenge in the larger context of Atlantic economic relations. Imperatives for collaborative authoritative engagement are quite evident, because of the magnitude of the public goods issues. Mutual recognition arrangements have been proposed for closer links between US and EU stock exchanges (Steil, 2003). Increases in European capital flows to the USA, stronger development of an equity culture in Europe, and more potent US pressures for European cooperation with the external reach of US regulatory endeavours would be probable, together with higher volume financing for US firms in Europe.[69] Scope for the speculative bidding up of stocks would be widened, especially for US financial enterprises, and their prominence in Atlantic concentration trends would rise. In Atlantic interactions, a common European negotiating strategy would be difficult to manage, but would be necessary.

Asymmetries in bargaining strengths, in conjunction with problems of vulnerability, indicate the importance, for Europe, of striving to increase US policy learning on issues of trade in financial assets and on the desirability of a common institution that would work with one for macroeconomic policy coordination, and that would have very active consultative links with peak corporate associations, constituted on an Atlantic basis. The European Central Bank could well be the lead organization for policy learning engagement, with US authorities and financial groups. The slow pace of the Union's own policy-learning processes is a serious problem, but it must be reiterated that the issues are urgent. It must also be added that Atlantic monetary and financial interdependencies will become larger, with greater asymmetries, while 'dollarization' continues in Latin America, in advance of progress toward hemispheric trade and investment liberalization.[70]

A special European concern will have to be the danger that recovery from the 2001/3 recession in the USA, although hindered by speculative financial sector orientations, may lead into a boom in which those orientations will be more active. Hence this possibility has to be stressed, especially because, during the 1990s boom in the USA, unfounded investor optimism reached high levels and influenced the outlook of regulators; asset appreciations thus went extremely high before the inevitable recession, which became severe and destructive. Literature on European financial markets since monetary integration has referred to the positive effects of that integration on financial sector development in the Union, but has rather avoided the potential for further speculative asset appreciations in the USA that would draw high-volume investment from Europe and increase funding for US corporate expansion in Europe.[71]

ENTREPRENEURIAL COORDINATION

Production complementarities of major systemic significance could be promoted for dynamic structural balance through Atlantic combinations of policy learning and corporate learning. These would have to be made possible by intensive conference activity, bringing together technocrats and industry representatives, principally in medium and high technology manufacturing sectors. A special purpose, initially, could be the promotion of collaboration that would reduce the European lag in semiconductor development. The rationale for sponsoring coordinated entrepreneurship could emphasize the need to overcome the effects of delays in policy learning and corporate learning that have entailed the neglect of potentials for the orderly expansion of production interdependencies, within and across sectors, in the transatlantic context. Because of this neglect, diverging and conflicting corporate interests have been pursued, information failures have tended to persist, investment allocations have been less productive and overall balances between competition and cooperation have been tilted unfavourably, while relational assets have not increased. Concentration trends have been strong, and there have been increasing needs for collaborative engagement with negative externalities, including problems of deindustrialization, unemployment and social exclusion.[72]

Within the EU delays in complete market integration have contributed to delays in cross-border corporate learning, thus limiting potentials for regionally rationalized production specializations, with increased employment. Rivalries between member governments implementing their own structural policies, moreover, have tended to perpetuate degrees of market separation, with resultant limitations on the contributions of investment to the development of industrial capacity. European corporate and technocratic capabilities for constructive involvement in transatlantic entrepreneurial consultations do not encourage optimism, but may well increase with intensive dialogue. The USA's strong entrepreneurial culture, operative with the advantages of long-standing domestic market integration, has made possible comprehensive technological leads over Europe's industries. These leads have been especially apparent in information and communication technologies.[73] A highly significant potential can be seen for entrepreneurial coordination that would ensure strong infusions of these technologies into the EU. General increases in productivity across most sectors could follow, and could help the regional rationalization of production specializations. European policy-level and corporate cooperation could be forthcoming because of the rapid and extensive improvements to be anticipated in productivity, but consensus for the collaboration could be hindered by the Union's decisional problems and by hopes of significant results from the Union technology enhancement programmes.[74]

A different logic of entrepreneurial coordination would be significant in aerospace, where the achievements of the Airbus consortium have resulted in advances in applied frontier technology comparable with those in the USA. More or less equal rivalry in world markets may be considered to be generating balanced efficiencies that would weaken the rationale for consultations about potential complementarities. The context for possible entrepreneurial cooperation will be changed, however, as the EU acquires stronger bargaining power with the admission of East and Central European states. This bargaining strength could be used to secure changes in air transportation arrangements that would restrict operations by US carriers within the Union, in line with US restrictions on European carriers between points in the USA.[75]

Entrepreneurial coordination potentials in automobile sectors relate to another kind of structural interdependence. Relative balance in these medium technology sectors indicates scope for symmetrical complementarities between US and European firms, and these demand attention because of general overcapacity, the scale of operations and the prominence of the European sectors in national structural policies. The excess capacity in Atlantic automobile industries is related to excess steel capacity, and this also warrants consideration in consultations on transatlantic entrepreneurial coordination.

Medium and low technology sectors as well as resource-based industries in Europe, which have remained relatively large in the overall structural pattern while the diffusion of innovations from science-based sectors has lagged, would be transformed by Atlantic entrepreneurial coordination for accelerated European absorption of US information and communication technologies. This has to be reiterated with recognition of structural imperatives to make these sectors more open to and more supportive of science-based industries that will have to grow in relative size.[76] The rationale for entrepreneurial cooperation focused on information and communication technology transfers could very appropriately be given much emphasis in US governmental and corporate communications. These could increase understanding of the limitations of the Union's rather self-reliant technology development projects.[77]

In the medium technology Atlantic sectors transportation has the highest profile. Evolving with much cross investment, its challenge of excess capacity can be met with coordinations of production specializations, with expansions into outside markets, including Latin America, where the prospect of hemispheric trade liberalization raises questions about the treatment of incoming European direct investment. High order requirements for structural harmony between the USA and the EU will have to motivate relational interactions, with US goodwill signifying support for complementary European industrial development. This will require reorientations of corporate and policy-level outlooks towards more knowledge-intensive understandings of dynamic market efficiencies and of broad social justice issues, drawing inspiration, it must be stressed, from insights in behavioural macroeconomics.[78] The multiple functions of forecasting and advising that could be performed by an Atlantic consultative organization can thus be seen to have great significance.

POLICY LINKAGES AND CORPORATE LINKAGES

A comprehensive philosophy is needed for Atlantic macromanagement. Increasing imbalances and risks, with more serious policy failures and market failures, are tending to evoke US and European responses emphasizing self-reliant efforts to enhance macromanagement as a competitive endeavour, for advantageous shifts in the spread of gains from interregional commerce. The common interest is typically seen in terms of market-driven production achievements, facilitated by liberal economic policies. Learning potentials for policy makers and corporate managements are recognized, but receive less attention than the scope for bargaining to increase openness to trade and direct investment, and to restrict government subsidies for industry. On the European side inferior structural competitiveness motivates much of the emphasis on self-reliance, while in the USA the remedies for Europe's economic problems are frequently seen to be quests for higher performance obligated by US challenges.

Self-reliant macromanagement endeavours on each side of the Atlantic are assisted by knowledge-intensive business services operating internationally.[79] These are private ventures facilitating the development and transmission of knowledge of value for corporate managements and policy makers, that is for the systemic evolution of learning economies through continuing innovations. The international operations of knowledge-intensive business services constitute transnational systems, extending well beyond the Atlantic context, but more active in it than elsewhere in the world economy. Global credit reporting firms are major actors in these systems.[80] The diverse communications of knowledge, about the performance of interdependent real economies and financial sectors, and about entire ranges of administrative measures, serve the competitive but also the alliance strategies of vast numbers of firms. There are no concerted efforts to encourage intercorporate collaboration, but such efforts could certainly be encouraged by corporate and policy-level initiatives. Atlantic conferences for entrepreneurial coordination would extend the functional logic of corporate efforts to enhance production capabilities (Cohendet *et al.*, 1999; Maskell and Malmberg, 1999)

Increasing corporate and policy-level understanding of technology-based production interdependencies, and of related potentials for innovative complementarities, is aided by the autonomous development of international knowledge-intensive business services, but these accord high priorities to the support of planning by large transnational enterprises. Knowledge, moreover, can be presented with diverse biases to different firms, for example on the basis of auditing work. The technocratic involvement that has been suggested for Atlantic conferences on entrepreneurial complementarities could help to correct biases imparted by knowledge-intensive business service enterprises, while in effect assisting especially smaller firms disadvantaged by the priority attention given to large multinationals by business service companies. Here public goods have identified, with awareness that market forces do not tend to provide, business service activities that will unambiguously contribute to the development of coordinated entrepreneurship aligned with common interests.[81] In the larger context, moreover, there are regulatory issues related to the quality of knowledge-intensive business services, and particularly to the types of information they may provide about the finances of firms active in, or seeking, corporate alliances.[82]

Market-led generation and transmission of knowledge is absorbed at policy levels in perspectives influenced by domestic political exchange concerns and by understandings of functional imperatives derived from economic theory. Basic problems in the USA and the EU are that the costs of political exchange biases tend to increase quests for more efficient political trading while relativizing understandings about economic dynamics. The primary consequence of competitive political trading is fiscal expansion, with institutional weakening that allows policy making to become less knowledge-intensive in terms of public goods requirements. Dysfunctional policy linkages thus become serious as deepening Atlantic integration continues with expanding transnational production, trade and financial flows. Monetary policy tasks are affected through changes in internal and external balance, and in overall growth because of reduced productive investment. As the US experience illustrates, moreover, this tends to happen while speculative propensities in the financial sector increase relative to productive funding of significance for the real economy. The declining sovereignty in the area of financial policy then brings into prominence a larger problem, a multiplication of efforts by producer enterprises to secure greater international as well as domestic market strengths through intensified competition rather than cooperation: the risks and costs of policy failures make the culture of the political economy less conducive to the growth of trust and relational cooperation, despite increases in technology-based production interdependencies between firms.

Reconsideration of the interacting effects of macroeconomic policy failures and of speculative financial sector propensities on production functions serving real interdependent economies raises questions about potential for coordinated corporate responses, that is through learning that might reverse the non-cooperative trend. For US and European producer enterprises the logic of forming domestic and, more importantly, international alliances becomes very persuasive; that is, to expand market strengths with greater security and with entrepreneurial synergies. Incentives to devote energies to interest representation in home and host country policy processes can motivate intercorporate cooperation, across as well as within alliances, but large-scale political collaboration to introduce broad public goods concerns into national policies does not develop. This is a fundamental problem of interdependent political development in knowledge-intensive economies. A key public goods imperative, then, is a combination of advances in political development with international corporate cooperation aligned with the requirements for dynamic as well as allocative market efficiencies that are being set for the Atlantic economy by transnational production and trade.

OPTIMAL POLICIES

Abstract modelling to indicate optimum policies for industrialized states has generally neglected the significance of large-scale complex structural interdependencies, while focusing on the dynamics *of* corporate competition in industrialized states evolving as liberal market economies. Potentials for non-market cooperation between firms are not recognized, and the increasing internationalization of market efficiencies and failures is not taken into account. Unemployment, as a problem that is more and more a matter of transnational market failure, related to the production strategies of international firms, is treated only as a national policy issue, to be dealt with through fiscal and monetary measures guided by estimates of the effects of employment changes on inflation and overall growth. Also ignored are the effects of balances between speculative and productive funding in the interactions of financial sectors on the real economy; that is, while financial markets become further internationalized and the structural linkages between real economies become larger.

Fiscal and monetary reaction to increases and declines in economic activity that may appear logical in relatively closed economies, linked with others only through trade controlled through official arrangements for market openness, can become dysfunctional because of structural interdependencies and losses of economic sovereignty. Fiscal expansion and monetary loosening to increase non-inflationary growth causes stronger internal demand but encourages stronger outflows of investment into speculation in world financial markets. Sequences in economic activity caused by speculative asset appreciations and declines moreover contribute to corporate incentives to spread production abroad, rather than at home, so as to reduce overall risks while seizing opportunities in foreign markets. This has to be reiterated because of the cognitive limitations of the abstract modelling.[83]

The concept of competitive pressures driving allocative efficiencies towards equilibrium has to be changed as these efficiencies assume international dimensions, with elements of market failure associated with cross-border oligopoly power, the externalities of production relocations and disruptions, and information deficiencies attributable to marketing strategies, the use of entry barriers and the restriction of communications in alliances, industry groups and associations. Changes in dynamic efficiencies alter and are altered by changes in allocative efficiencies but tend to be considered responsive to policy shifts only through the overall effects of those shifts on demand and supply. Potentials for direct policy effects on efficiencies through the promotion of entrepreneurial complementarities are not seen, and the multiple uncertainties affecting major investment decisions are not recognized (Richardson, 2002.)

Potentials for the clearing of markets change as transactions are internationalized. Market clearing, to the extent that it happens and is projected, activates increases in supply, and this dynamic efficiency contributes to further growth, but oligopoly power can be used to limit supply, so as to increase profits. Market discipline does not restrain the growth of oligopoly power, and accordingly a policy responsibility is recognized, but of necessity it has to be more and more international, and if it is to be guided by economic theory this will have to generate a multi-government consensus. What might be considered an optimal policy mix for one national administration will depend on its understanding of the operations of its own economy as this experiences deeper integration with others, and on its assessments of macromanagement processes in those others. Assumptions about rational expectations guiding the choices of economic agents and of policy makers have to be viewed critically in this large and expanding context, especially because of the proliferation of uncertainties affecting entrepreneurial choices and consumer behaviour. The problems of irrational investor behaviour have to be seen in this context; that is, in conjunction with the interests of financial enterprises in predicting, causing and exploiting volatility.[84]

Corrective perspectives have to be provided by behavioural finance and behavioural macroeconomics, especially for the understanding of motivational issues that affect possibilities for resolving coordination problems. Moral hazard, adverse selection and opportunism are familiar terms identifying difficulties in projections about rational expectations. The imperatives for systemic development in knowledge-intensive market economies, however, require focus on the resolution of entrepreneurial coordination problems through relational cooperation. An optimal policy mix can thus be considered to have, as a vital component, affirmations of principles and values conducive to relational cooperation, with the building of relational assets between enterprises, and between enterprises and governments. Policies designed to influence individual and corporate behaviour only through the use of economic incentives ignore the potential efficiencies of higher motivations (Stewart, 1993).

Altogether theoretical advances for policy guidance and corporate planning in the deepening Atlantic integration are needed for enlightened understanding of imperatives for relational knowledge-intensive coordination, between firms and between firms and governments. An optimal policy will be broadly coordinated interdependent macromanagement, with emphasis on structural partnering through dedicated consultative interaction between policy levels and corporate managements, sustaining patterns of complementary entrepreneurship, with civic friendships extending across borders. With the partnering, fiscal prudence would be maintained through assertions of aggregated corporate interests and these would help to induce policy-level focus on advisory tasks assisting entrepreneurial coordination. The resulting synergies would in turn induce emphasis on productive funding by the financial sectors.

The most urgent concerted policy objective for the Atlantic will have to be reorientation of US financial sector operations towards stable productive funding, with strong restraint on speculative market manipulation to push up stock prices. The European interest in this necessary market reform is a matter of acute complex vulnerability: large-scale investment drain to the USA during its booms and the transmission of following recessions. This double vulnerability increases as deepening integration continues in the Atlantic, and as an equity culture develops in the EU, setting related imperatives for more constructive financial sector development in the service of European industries. For the USA, the reform imperative is becoming more urgent because opportunities for speculation in world financial markets are tending to attract more interest than the scope for productive funding at home: larger and more rapid returns can be anticipated, with greater spreading of risks. In the larger calculations influencing the strategies of financial enterprises, moreover, major risks that have to be reckoned with concern the exchange rate effects of heavy current account deficits and very high levels of government debt. The gravity of this problem has to be given great stress because the knowledge-intensive political economy is not generating solutions. The severe macromanagement deficiency is causing firms to emphasize independent quests for international market strengths and improved security through expansion of their international production systems.

TRANSATLANTIC COLLABORATION

The expansion of structural linkages between European countries in their economic union is obligating institutional development for regional collective management, with consultative corporate participation, more or less in line with the functional logic of the German model, despite the strains which are weakening its cohesion. This logic, although understood with national attachments and loyalties, has relevance for the deepening integration which is transforming relations with North America and which will become more significant as deepening integration continues in the Americas. European institutional advances for collective management reflect traditions of corporate–government cooperation, in national contexts that hinder replication of that collaboration at the Union level, and that effect potentials for further institutional development at the regional level. Uncertainties about potentials for coordination thus incline corporate managements towards independent pursuits of market opportunities, influenced especially by the attractions of alliances with US enterprises, because of their competitive strengths.

Change in the European configuration is likely to be distinguished by more active independent forms of corporate expansion, with weak Union-level potentials for promoting entrepreneurial coordination, owing to changing problems of consensus at that level because of the dynamics of interest representation and policy making in member governments. Altogether the Union political economy will tend to become more liberal, with coordination problems negatively affecting growth potentials. An optimal policy mix would have to engage directly with structural tasks, building on the experience of the aerospace consortium, but political and corporate will for this would be difficult to generate.

The liberal US political economy, more affected by independent corporate pursuits of market opportunities, on a much larger international scale, with prospects of continuing gains in Europe, but threatened by destabilizing speculation, has extremely difficult macromanagement problems. Institutional development in response to these is not in prospect. This has very serious implications for the structural linkages through which the transatlantic economy is being shaped. Imperatives for an optimal policy mix with a strong structural thrust are more urgent than those in Europe, but are given even less attention in the politics of agency-type democracy. A prominent feature of the overall pattern is the policy deficiency which neglects the destabilizing potential of international rent seeking by financial enterprises. As the US sector is becoming very prominent in global concentration trends, the implications for stability in the world economy are becoming more serious. At the same time surveillance tasks in world financial markets are becoming more difficult for regulators, because of the use of highly sophisticated methods of spreading risks, and weak cooperation by European and other governments.

A rationale for the formation of well-institutionalized Atlantic elite networks is thus becoming more persuasive. Atlantic social capital has to be built at this level, to help develop and sustain relational cooperation in corporate and political networks and alliances. The influence of individualistic cultures hinders continuity in such systems of cooperation, and this is a challenge which must be overcome through moral efforts. The requirements are to ensure that, in Keynesian terms, speculation will not prevail over enterprise, and that enterprise will be fully productive through widening strategic coordination, with more pervasive rational expectations as a basis for corporate planning and policy planning: all this in the transatlantic context of deepening integration where structural linkages are being shaped without sufficient harmony, and with dangers of increasing imbalances and instability. Advances in frontier technology in this context increase the significance of capacities for relational adaptation, to avoid and overcome discontinuities in productive capacities extending across sectors that are difficult to forecast. Imperatives to reduce substantially the uncertainties caused increasingly by speculation are becoming more urgent, while technology-based production interdependencies are becoming more extensive.

The implications for interdependent knowledge-intensive Atlantic policy management are very demanding. Consultative interaction with industry groups and corporate networks, alliances and associations has to become highly innovative and constructive, to facilitate strategic coordination with increasing entrepreneurial dynamism and with openness to learning from that dynamism. The international public good that becomes more and more necessary as transnational producer enterprises extend their operations is the orderly development of the structural interdependencies which they are shaping, with stability in the entire pattern. Such stability has to be provided by relational entrepreneurial cooperation; it is threatened by the rent seeking speculation of financial enterprises – the danger that speculation will prevail over entrepreneurship. Here there is a dual challenge for productive enterprises serving real economies and for the policy levels dealing with all areas of Atlantic macromanagement.

NOTES

1. See Sebnem Kalemli-Ozcan, Bent E.Sorensen and Qved Yosha, 'Economic Integration, Industrial Specialization and the Asymmetry of Macroeconomic Fluctuations', in Elhanan Helpman and Efraim Sadka (eds) *Economic Policy in the International Economy*, Cambridge: Cambridge University Press, 2003, ch. 5, and Luc Soete, 'The New Economy: a European Perspective', in Daniele Archibugi and Bengt-Ake Lundvall (eds), *The Globalizing Learning Economy*, Oxford: Oxford University Press, 2001, ch. 1.
2. See Horst Siebert (ed.), *Economic Policy Issues of the New Economy*, Berlin: Springer, 2002.
3. See Pier Carlo Padoan, Paul A. Brenton and Gavin Boyd (eds) *The Structural Foundations of International Finance*, Cheltenham, UK and Northampton, MA, USA: Edward Elgar, 2003.
4. See Alan M. Rugman and Gavin Boyd (eds), *Alliance Capitalism for the New American Economy*, Cheltenham, UK and Northampton, MA, USA: Edward Elgar, 2003.
5. See Thomas L. Brewer and Gavin Boyd (eds) *Globalizing America*, Cheltenham, UK and Northampton, MA, USA: Edward Elgar, 2000.
6. The declines are associated especially with interactions between internationalized financial markets and real economies. See David T. Llewellyn, 'Financial intermediaries in the New Economy: will banks lose their traditional role?', in Siebert, cited in note 2, pp. 215–49.
7. See Horst Siebert, *The World Economy*, London: Routledge, 1999; Horst Siebert (ed.), *The World's New Financial Landscape: Challenges for Economic Policy*, Berlin: Springer, 2001; Wendy Dobson and Gary Clyde Hufbauer, *World Capital Markets*, Washington, DC: Institute for International Economics, 2001; and Jean Tirole, *Financial Crises and the International Monetary System*, Princeton: Princeton University Press 2002.
8. See references to this propensity in *The Structural Foundations of International Finance*, cited in note 3.
9. See ibid., references to these linkages.
10. On the concept of a coordinated market economy, see Peter A. Hall and David Soskice (eds), *Varieties of Capitalism*, Oxford, Oxford University Press, 2001, esp. ch. 1.
11. See extensive discussions in Peter K. Cornelius and Bruce Kogut (eds), *Corporate Governance and Capital Flows in a Global Economy*, Oxford: Oxford University Press, 2003, esp. chs 2, 3, 16 and 17.
12. The speculative trend has been given much attention in issues of the *Financial Times* (London). See for example Gary Silverman, Ed Crooks and Vincent Boland, 'The hint for yield hots up: investors and pension funds plunge deeper into illiquid and riskier assets', *Financial Times*, 22 July 22, 2003.

13. On the development of an equity culture in Europe, see Luigi Guiso, Michael Haliassos and Tullio Jappelli, 'Household stockholding in Europe: where do we stand and where do we go?', *Economic Policy*, **36**, April 2003, 123–70.

14. See symposium on European Monetary Union, *Oxford Review of Economic Policy*, **19** (1), Spring 2003.

15. See Erik Berglof and Mike Burkart, 'European takeover regulation', *Economic Policy*, **36**, April 2003, 171–214.

16. See Stephen G. Cecchetti and Roisin O'Sullivan, 'The European Central Bank and the Federal Reserve', *Oxford Review of Economic Policy*, **19** (1), Spring 2003, 30–43; Pier Carlo Padoan (ed.), *Monetary Union, Employment and Growth*, Cheltenham, UK and Northampton, MA, USA: Edward Elgar, 2001.

17. See *73rd Annual Report*, Bank of International Settlements, 2003, Basle.

18. On market efficiencies, see Tyler Cowen and Eric Crampton (eds), *Market Failure or Success*, Cheltenham, UK and Northampton, MA, USA: Edward Elgar, 2003, part 1; Peter Howitt, 'Expectations and uncertainty in contemporary Keynesian models', in G.C. Harcourt and P.A. Riach (eds) *A Second Edition of the General Theory*, vol. 1, London: Routledge, ch. 15.

19. On relational assets, see John H. Dunning 'Relational assets, networks and international business activity', in John H. Dunning and Gavin Boyd (eds), *Alliance Capitalism and Corporate Management*, Cheltenham, UK and Northampton, MA, USA: Edward Elgar, 2003, ch. 1.

20. On the significance of cooperation, see Hall and Soskice, cited in note 10.

21. See references in *The Structural Foundations of International Finance*, cited in note 8.

22. On volatility in financial markets, see Claudia M. Buch and Christian Pierdzioch, 'The growth and volatility of international capital flows: reconciling the evidence', *The World's New Financial Landscape: Challenges for Economic Policy*, pp. 3–54.

23. Ibid.

24. A major problem is that monetary loosening to aid recovery enables US firms to borrow at low rates and invest abroad for higher returns, especially to exploit volatility, while restricting credit in the home economy. See 'US lenders treat more cautiously in downturn', *Financial Times*, 18 May 2001.

25. On the costs of the US recession, see references in *The Structural Foundations of International Finance*, cited in note 8.

26. See references to cross-investment in *Alliance Capitalism for the New American Economy*, cited in note 4.

27. On oligopoly power in retailing, see Paul Dobson and Michael Waterson, 'Retailer power: recent developments and policy implications', *Economic Policy*, **28**, April 1999, 135–66. See also effects of regulatory factors in Giuseppe Nicoletti and Stefano Scarpetta, 'Regulation, productivity and growth: OECD evidence', *Economic Policy*, **36**, April 2003, 9–72.

28. See references in *Alliance Capitalism for the New American Economy*, cited in note 4.

29. See comments in Thomas L. Brewer, Paul A. Brenton and Gavin Boyd (eds), *Globalizing Europe*, Cheltenham, Edward Elgar, 2002.

30. Investor confidence has been affected by the slow recovery and by corporate scandals; see *Corporate Governance and Capital Flows in a Global Economy*, cited in note 11, chs 3, 16, 17 and 18.

31. See Andrew Hill, 'Skeptics say Sarbanes–Oxley will create litigation chaos', and Joel S. Demski, 'Corporate conflicts of interest', *The Journal of Economic Perspectives*, **17** (2), Spring 2003, 51–72.

32. On the larger context, see Frederic L. Pryor, *The Future of US Capitalism*, New York: Cambridge University Press, 2002; Kenneth W. Dam, *The Rules of the Global Game*, Chicago: University of Chicago Press, 2001. On behavioural finance, see Robert J. Shiller, 'From efficient markets theory to behavioural finance', *The Journal of Economic Perspectives*, **17** (1), Winter 2003, 83–104.

33. The representation of corporate interests is fragmented. See references in *Alliance Capitalism for the New American Economy*, cited in note 4, and comments on social capital in Pryor, cited in note 32.

34. See references in *The Structural Foundations of International Finance*, cited in note 8.
35. See symposium on EMU, *Oxford Review of Economic Policy*, cited in note 4.
36. See contrasts between France and Germany in *Varieties of Capitalism*, cited in note 10, and references to France and Germany in Justin Greenwood and Henry Jacek (eds) *Organized Business and the New Global Order*, New York, St Martin's Press, 2000.
37. See Reinhard Heinisch, 'Coping with economic integration: corporatist strategies in Germany and Austria in the 1990s', *West European Politics*, **23** (3), July 2000, 67–96; Richard Deeg and Susanne Lutz, 'Internationalization and financial federalism', *Comparative Political Studies*, **33** (3), April 2000, 374–405.
38. See Alec Stone Sweet, Wayne Sandholtz and Neil Fligstein (eds), *The Institutionalization of Europe*, New York: Oxford University Press, 2001.
39. The US direct investment position in Europe at the end of 2002 was $796 913 million on a historical cost basis, an increase of 11 per cent on the previous year. The significance of this direct investment position has to be assessed with reference to Europe's growth problems, discussed in Luc Soete, cited note 7 and in Nicoletti and Scapetta, cited note 43. See also Maria Joao (ed.), *The New Knowledge Economy in Europe*, Cheltenham, UK, and Northampton, MA, USA: Edward Elgar 2002, and Peter Johnson (ed.) *Industries in Europe*, Cheltenham, UK, and Northampton, MA, USA: Edward Elgar, 2003.
40. See *Economic Policy in the International Economy*, cited, part 1; Robert J. Shiller, *Irrational Exuberance*, Princeton: Princeton University Press, 2000.
41. See Greenwood, 'Organized business and the European Union' in Greenwood and Jacek, cited, ch. 5.
42. On bias in the USA, see Dam, cited, and on both the USA and Europe see William D. Coleman and Eric Montpetit, 'Multi-tiered systems and the organization of business interests', in *Organized Business and the New Global Order*, cited, 160–76.
43. European direct investment in the USA comprises groups with separate home country identities, mostly reflecting home country economic weaknesses illustrated in Nicoletti and Scapetta, cited.
44. Europe is the main destination of US direct investment: see *Survey of Current Business*, **83** (7), July 2003. A major trend is the development of integrated production systems, noted in *World Investment Report 2000*, Geneva: United Nations Commission on Trade and Development.
45. See symposium on Legalization in World Politics, *International Organization* **54** (3), Summer 2000.
46. On issues in relations with host governments, see *World Investment Report 2000*, cited in note 44.
47. On EU trade policies see Paul A. Brenton, 'The changing nature and determinants of EU trade policies' in Thomas L. Brewer, Paul A. Brenton and Gavin Boyd (eds), *Globalizing Europe*, Cheltenham, UK and Northampton, MA, USA: Edward Elgar, 2002, ch. 8.
48. See references to antitrust policy in *Alliance Capitalism and Corporate Management*, cited in note 19.
49. See discussions of unfounded investor optimism in *The Structural Foundations of International Finance*, cited in note 8; also Shiller (2003).
50. These incentives include reduced tax exposure. See Dani Rodrik, *Has Globalization Gone too far?*, Washington, DC: Institute for International Economics, 1997.
51. Unemployment has to be regarded as a consequence of failures in entrepreneurial coordination aligned with public goods requirements. See discussion of Pasinetti's work in Mathew Forstater 'Full employment policies must consider effective demand and technological change: a prime point of Pasinetti's political economy', in Paul Davidson (ed.), *A Post Keynesian Perspective on 21st Century Economic Problems*, Cheltenham, UK and Northampton, MA, USA: Edward Elgar, 2002, ch. 10.
52. See discussions in *The Structural Foundations of International Finance*, cited in note 8.
53. Further analysis of the dynamics of a coordinated market economy, examined in Hall and Soskice, cited, is therefore needed.
54. On the problems in political circles see Dam, cited.
55. This is an extension of the logic sustaining the European Commission's role in aggregating interests and promoting consensus for cooperation between member governments in the European Union. See *The Institutionalization of Europe*, cited.

56. On the concentration trends see *World Capital Markets,* cited.
57. See, for example, John Plender, 'America, land of the not-so-free market', *Financial Times,* 25 July 2003.
58. The significance of deliberative functions, notably in Germany, is stressed in Hall and Soskice, cited. See also references to political trading in Dam, cited.
59. See Margaret M. Blair, 'Shareholder value, corporate governance, and corporate performance', in *Corporate Governance and Capital Flows in a Global Economy,* cited.
60. US monetary policy is discretionary. See John T. Woolley, 'The politics of monetary policy: a critical review', *Journal of Public Policy,* **14** (1), Jan.–March 1994, 57–85; and references to monetary policy in *The Structural Foundations of International Finance,* cited in note 3.
61. East Asian interventions in foreign exchange markets to slow dollar depreciation are factors in this context, as well as downward pressures caused by the USA's very large current account deficits and fiscal deficits. On issues in Atlantic monetary cooperation, see *73rd Annual Report,* Bank of International Settlements, cited.
62. See discussions of the rationale for cooperation in *The Structural Foundations of International Finance,* cited in note 3.
63. See symposium on EMU, *Oxford Review of Economic Policy,* cited in note 14.
64. This conclusion is drawn from studies indicating the emphasis that several member governments give to their own industrial policies, and the limitations of the Union's technology enhancement policies. See references to Germany and France in *Varieties of Capitalism,* cited, and chapters on Germany, France and the United Kingdom in Benn Steil, David G. Victor and Richard R. Nelson (eds) *Technological Innovation and Economic Performance,* Princeton: Princeton University Press, 2002. The evolution of differing systems of corporate governance indicates that a common structural policy would be difficult to introduce, although necessary for the Union as a whole; see Antoine Rebérioux, 'European style corporate governance at the crossroads', *Journal of Common Market Studies,* **40** (1), March, 2002, 111–34.
65. Increases in the US deficits have made the European concerns more justified. See references to fiscal deficits in *73rd Annual Report,* Bank of International Settlements, cited.
66. See trends in US foreign direct investment, *Survey of Current Business,* cited.
67. The problems in Japan's banking sector, examined in a symposium on Japan in *The World Economy,* **26** (3), March 2003, have not invalidated the logic of relational intercorporate cooperation in Japanese industry groups.
68. Hill, cited, and Demski, cited.
69. These projections are based on trends in international financial markets. See *The World's New Financial Landscape: Challenges for Economic Policy,* cited.
70. On 'dollarization' in Latin America see Sidney Weintraub, Alan M. Rugman and Gavin Boyd (eds) *Free Trade in the Americas: Economic and Political Issues for Governments and Firms,* Cheltenham, Edward Elgar, 2004, ch. 8.
71. See symposium on EMU, *Oxford Review of Economic Policy,* cited.
72. Technological progress, meanwhile, has made entrepreneurial cooperation more necessary for overall growth. See Nicolai Foss and Volker Mahnke (eds), *Competence, Governance and Entrepreneurship,* Oxford: Oxford University Press, 2000.
73. Luc Soete, cited.
74. These hopes have to be cautious because of the degrees to which member governments focus on their own industrial policies. See references in *Technological Innovation and Economic Performance,* cited.
75. In the background is a recent history of EU opposition to mergers between US aerospace companies that would increase their world market strengths, to the disadvantage of the Airbus consortium. See Bernard M. Hoekman and Michel M. Kostecki, *The Political Economy of the World Trading System,* 2nd edn, Oxford: Oxford University Press, 2001, p. 430.
76. See contrasts in structural profiles in Nicoletti and Scarpetta, cited.
77. On this self-reliant orientation, see *The New Knowledge Economy in Europe,* cited.
78. See Joseph E. Stiglitz, 'Information and the change in the paradigm in economics', *American Economic Review,* **92** (3), June 2002, 460–501.

79. See Birgitte Andersen, Jeremy Howells, Richard Hull, Ian Miles and Joanne Roberts (eds), *Knowledge and Innovation in the New Service Economy*, Cheltenham, UK and Northampton, MA, USA: Edward Elgar, 2000.
80. See references to Europe and the USA, in Margaret J. Miller (ed.), *Credit Reporting Systems and the International Economy*, Cambridge: MIT Press, 2003.
81. Tullio Japelli and Marco Pagano, ibid., ch. 2, indicate that in Europe credit reporting agencies operate mainly on a national basis, with differences in the quality of services; Jarl G.Kallberg and Gregory F. Udell ibid., ch. 5, examine private business information exchange in the USA, which is dominated by one large firm. There are no references to problems in the auditing industry which have been publicized because of corporate scandals as reviewed by Demski, cited.
82. See *Knowledge and Innovation in the New Service Economy*, cited.
83. An example is Jean-Pascal Benassy, *The Macroeconomics of Imperfect Competition and Non-clearing Markets*, Cambridge: MIT Press, 2002, which discusses market processes and policies in national economies that are assumed to be functioning without structural interdependencies resulting from transnational production.
84. See *The Structural Foundations of International Finance*, cited in note 8.

REFERENCES

Coen, D. (1998), 'The European business interest and the nation state: large scale lobbying in the European Union and member states', *Journal of Public Policy*, **18** (1), Jan.–April, 75–100.

Cohendet, P., F. Kern, B. Mehmanpazir and F. Munier (1999), 'Knowledge coordination, competence creation, and integrated networks in globalized firms', *Cambridge Journal of Economics*, **23** (2), March, 225–41

Foss, K. and N.J. Foss (2002), 'Economic organization and the trade offs between productive and destructive entrepreneurship', in N.J. Foss and P.G. Klein (eds), *Entrepreneurship and the Firm*, Cheltenham, UK and Northampton, MA, USA: Edward Elgar, ch. 6.

Hall, P.A. and D. Soskice (eds) (2001), *Varieties of Capitalism*, Oxford: Oxford University Press.

Hallett, A. Hughes, P. Mooslechner and M. Schuerz (eds) (2001), *Challenges for Economic Policy Coordination within European Monetary Union*, Dordrecht: Kluwer.

Maskell, P. and A. Malmberg (1999), 'Localized learning and industrial competitiveness', *Cambridge Journal of Economics*, **23** (2), March, 167–85.

Pollack, M.A. and G.C. Shaffer (2001) (eds), *Transatlantic Governance in the Global Economy*, Lanham: Rowman and Littlefield.

Richardson, G.B. (2002), 'Innovation, equilibrium and welfare', in S.C. Dow and J. Hillard (eds), *Post Keynesian Econometrics, Microeconomics and the Theory of the Firm*, Cheltenham, Edward Elgar, ch. 2.

Shiller, R.J. (2003), 'From efficient markets theory, to behavioural finance', *The Journal of Economic Perspectives*, **17** (1), Winter, 83–104.

Steil, B. (2003), *Building a Transatlantic Securities Market*, New York: Council on Foreign Relations.

Stewart, J. (1993), 'Rational choice theory, public policy and the liberal state', *Policy Sciences*, **26** (4), 317–30.

Stiglitz, J.E. (2002), 'Information and the change in the paradigm in economics', *American Economic Review*, **92** (3), 460–501.

7. Concerting entrepreneurship: an international public good

Peter J. Boettke and Christopher J. Coyne

There is little contention that entrepreneurship is the driver of economic growth (Leff, 1979; Kasper and Streit, 1998; Kirzner, 1985; Boettke and Coyne, 2003).[*] Globalization – specifically, ever-expanding technologies and avenues into economic markets throughout the world – characterize today's economic environment in which the entrepreneur must act. This ever-growing interdependence is illustrated by the relationship between the United States (USA) and the European Union (EU).

The relationship between the USA and the EU can be described as cooperative, but cautious. The cooperative element is clearly illustrated by the growth of the trading relationship between them, as summarized in Tables 7.1a and 7.1b.

Table 7.1a   US–EU trade from 1991 to 2001 (billions of US dollars)

	Total trade	US exports to EU	EU exports to USA	US trade deficit with EU
1991	201.9	108.5	93.4	15.2
1992	209.0	107.7	101.3	6.5
1993	207.1	101.5	105.6	(4.1)
1994	227.3	107.8	119.5	(11.7)
1995	255.6	123.7	131.9	(8.2)
1996	270.6	127.7	142.9	(15.2)
1997	298.3	140.8	157.5	(16.7)
1998	325.4	149.0	176.4	(27.3)
1999	347.0	151.8	195.2	(43.4)
2000	385.1	165.1	220.0	(55.0)
2001	378.8	158.8	220.0	(61.3)

Note: US International Trade Administration, data available at http://www.ita.doc.gov/td/industry/otea/usfth/tabcon.html. Note that Austria, Finland and Sweden joined the EU in January 1995, but are included in all years in the table. Figures in parentheses indicate a negative balance.

Table 7.1b   US–EU trade, main products in 2001 (Euro mm and %)

EU Imports Products	Value	EU Exports US share of EU total, by products	Value	US share of EU total, by products	Balance
Chemical products	28 407	36.7	38 781	27.3	10 374
Transport. Materials	32 317	29.7	52 448	32.1	20 131
Machinery	74 556	27.3	65 283	21.9	(9 273)
Agricultural products	9 260	11.2	10 743	17.4	1 483
Textiles and clothing	1 870	2.6	5 861	13.9	3 991
Energy	2 229	1.5	8 922	37.3	6 693

Source: http://europa.eu.int/comm/trade/bilateral/data.htm.

As Table 7.1a illustrates, total trade between the USA and the EU increased year after year in the 1990s. In 2001, the USA was the top trading partner with the EU in terms of total trade.[1] Table 7.1b highlights this relationship in terms of the major products traded between the two. To further highlight the importance of the relationship between the EU and the USA, consider foreign direct investment by both the EU and the USA.

Table 7.2   US–EU foreign direct investment position on a historical cost basis, 1999–2002 (millions of dollars)

	US FDI in the EU	EU FDI in the USA
1999	564.0	582.0
2000	609.7	814.0
2001	632.8	861.3
2002	670.0	862.6

Note: Source of foreign direct investment data, *Survey of Current Business*, July 2003, available at http://www.bea.doc.gov/bea/ARTICLES/2003/07July/0703DirectInvest.pdf.

As Table 7.2 indicates, both US foreign direct investment in the EU and EU foreign direct investment in the USA have steadily increased since 1999. Moreover, it is estimated that 4.9 million US jobs of which EU-owned firms directly provide 3.8 million, are supported by EU investment in the USA.[2] As the data above indicate, the transatlantic relationship is continually strengthening. As the two economies become more and more intertwined, a firm understanding of the connection between entrepreneurship and the economic, political and social environments becomes critical.

Understanding entrepreneurship within these contexts is no simple task. As will be discussed below, entrepreneurship can manifest itself in a multitude of ways and settings. To illuminate this, consider the case of the firm which is critical to the success of the transatlantic relationship. As Loasby (2002) contends, the firm ultimately exists because knowledge is incomplete, fragmented and often difficult to express in a usable form. Given the realization that the entrepreneur and firm are critical to the learning process, it must be recognized that a complete understanding of the learning process and the incentives that influence this process is largely undeveloped (Garrouste, 2002). Incentives that influence the continually evolving learning process, both within and between firms, stem from the structure of the firm itself as well as the political and social environment in which the firm's agents must act. Of the utmost importance is the realization that competition between firms coexists with great potential for increased efficiency via cooperation and coordination of entrepreneurial activities (Dunning and Boyd, 2003). Such collaborations between firms can be viewed as an international public good. Furthermore because the learning process is integrated into the wider economic and political system, policies in other areas (education, labour laws and so on) may have a significant impact on the learning process itself (Archibugi *et al.*, 1999; Lundvall, 1999). Understanding this learning process requires a broader understanding of the effects of policies undertaken and their impact on entrepreneurship in the transatlantic relationship.

The cautious element of the relationship between the USA and the EU arises because increased trade, although presenting many opportunities for all parties involved, has also raised many political, social and economic issues (Fischer, 2000, p. 128). These issues are not new as they mirror in some fashion many of the tensions that have been present since the beginning of the US–EU relationship. The relevant issues include, but are not limited to, different laws and regulations in the different regions, the fear of monopoly and collusion, changes to 'ways of life' and 'unequal distributions' when borders are opened, and changes in standard of living.

In this chapter, we address many of the aforementioned issues. We begin with a general consideration of the notion of entrepreneurship. This theoretical rendering is critical since it provides the foundation for analysing the impact of various political, social and economic considerations on entrepreneurship. After setting forth an understanding of entrepreneurship, we consider entrepreneurship as a public good. We then turn to a discussion of destructive competition: the idea that entrepreneurship is destructive to jobs, progress and the established way of life. Also considered is the role of the entrepreneur in establishing trust in areas where social capital may be deficient. Finally we will discuss the role of government in the transatlantic relationship.

At the basis of our analysis are two methodological frameworks which we employ to better understand the dynamic relationship between the EU and the USA. The first approach, *market process theory*, emphasizes the market as a continuous process which requires one to recognize that temporality, incomplete knowledge and hence error and uncertainty are fundamental categories of all economic action.[3] Given the presence of uncertainty, entrepreneurs (and all economic agents) must always speculate to some degree on what the future will bring. As time passes and new data become available via entrepreneurial discovery, past uncertainty is removed and new uncertainty is introduced.

The second methodological approach is a *comparative institutional approach* which recognizes that the institutions in which entrepreneurs must act differ between geographic locations.[4] Furthermore, not only are these institutions distinct, but they are grounded in the historical occurrences of a particular region. Examples include, but are not limited to, differences in laws, social protection from the state, government policies, tendencies towards cooperation versus competition and corporate governance (Hall and Soskice, 2001). Throughout this chapter, emphasis will be placed on the similarities and differences between the institutional structure in the USA and the EU and the impact on entrepreneurship. In this sense, this chapter can be seen as an extension and complement to the varieties of capitalism approach set forth by Hall and Soskice. The varieties of capitalism framework attempts to analyse institutional similarities and differences in order to better understand such things as economic and political capabilities, complementarities strategies and challenges (ibid., pp. 1–2).

THE NOTION OF ENTREPRENEURSHIP

Entrepreneurship has received much attention in the literature. Instead of recapping this extensive discussion here, we offer a brief overview of the notion of entrepreneurship. Doing so will provide a solid foundation for the analysis that follows in the rest of the chapter.

We must first note that entrepreneurship does not describe a distinct group of individuals. Rather, following Mises (1949, pp. 252–3) and Kirzner (1973), entrepreneurship is an omnipresent aspect of human action. Economic decision makers do not simply react to given data and allocate their scarce means to realize given ends. The entrepreneurial element in human action entails the discovery of new data and information, discovering anew each day not only the appropriate means, but also the ends that are to be pursued (Kirzner, 1973, pp. 30–87). Moreover, the ability to spot changes in information is not limited to a selective group of agents – all agents possess the capacity to do so. Every economic actor makes an estimate of the uncertain situation of his forthcoming action. This is not to deny that some agents are more alert to opportunities, but rather to assert that all agents have the ability to be alert.

The entrepreneur has been characterized as an innovator (Schumpeter, 1950, 1961), an arbitrageur (Kirzner, 1973), one who bets on ideas (Brenner, 1985; Mokyr, 1990) and as a forecaster and capitalist (Rothbard, 1962). It is reasonable to conclude that each of these elements plays a role in the notion of the entrepreneur. No matter what the notion of entrepreneurship, one can envision the entrepreneurial process as consisting of three distinct moments:

1. *serendipity*: this involves the initial recognition of the idea. The entrepreneur need not actively and continually search for new ideas. Instead, the entrepreneur who is alert to an unrecognized opportunity for profit can be said to discover that opportunity;
2. *search*: after the entrepreneur recognizes the idea in the previous stage, he engages in active search to gain more knowledge about the idea as well as its feasibility;
3. *seizure*: after recognizing a potential idea and deeming the idea feasible via active search, the entrepreneur bets on or seizes the profit opportunity through action.

The entrepreneur (in discovering previously unexploited profit opportunities, consciously organizing business affairs and actively capturing profits) pushes the economy at any point in time from an economically (and technologically) inefficient production point towards an economically (and technologically) efficient point. Moreover, in discovering new technology and new production processes which use resources in a more efficient manner, the entrepreneurial process shifts the entire production possibility frontier (PPF) outward (Kirzner, 1985). The tendency towards the efficient allocation of resources given a fixed stock of technical knowledge, coupled with the shift of the PPF, represents the essence of economic growth: an increase in real output due to increases in real productivity.

Given that entrepreneurs are always among us, it is critical to distinguish between productive and unproductive entrepreneurship (Baumol, 1990, 2002). Although often overlooked, it is the allocation of entrepreneurial activities that is of the utmost importance. Productive entrepreneurship is characterized by entrepreneurial actions which are transformative; that is, catalysts of economic progress. Entrepreneurship aimed at productive ends either moves the economy towards the production possibilities frontier or shifts the PPF outward. In stark contrast, unproductive entrepreneurship is characterized by rent seeking, the evasion of laws and regulations and organized crime, actions which do not spur economic progress. Consequently these activities do not produce anything per se, but rather involve transfers of the current stock of resources. Unproductive entrepreneurship does not increase efficiency but rather increases deadweight losses through resources expended in securing transfers.

Whether or not entrepreneurial talent will be expended in a productive or unproductive direction is a function of the institutional environment within which individuals operate. The most fundamental notion of entrepreneurship we have discussed is the alertness an individual demonstrates in pursuing opportunities to better their current condition. It is within the human capacity to be alert to those opportunities that drive economic progress, but we must recognize that the institutional context within which individuals act will determine what opportunities it is in their interest to be alert to. An institutional environment that rewards productive entrepreneurial activity through the lure of pure profit will entice actors to be alert to such opportunities. On the other hand, an environment that rewards unproductive entrepreneurial activity through the reward of rents via predation will entice actors to expend effort in predatory behaviour. To realize the wealth-creating benefits of entrepreneurship, an institutional environment which wards off predation and rewards actors who satisfy consumer demands with profits must be securely established.

In other words, if we want the entrepreneurial moments of serendipity, search and seizure to be moments in a process of wealth creation, we must also institute rules of the game (and their enforcement) which make the payoff for productive activities higher relative to the payoff for unproductive activities. Such rules include security in private property and the freedom of contract. Absent the security of property and contract, gains from exchange will not be exploited and the entrepreneurial roles of ensuring efficient resource use and spurring innovation will be thwarted. The 'spirit of entrepreneurship' will not be eradicated but will be shifted towards unproductive ends.

Admittedly measuring or quantifying entrepreneurship is a difficult task. Various proxies have been used, including self-employment rates, business start-ups and ownership rates (Audretsch, 2002). However none of these perfectly captures the essence of entrepreneurship. The difficulty in measuring entrepreneurship stems from the fact that, by its very nature, it is a heterogeneous activity which can take on many shapes and forms. Attempting to apply a homogenous quantification is bound to lead to problems of misrepresentation and mischaracterization. This poses a problem, then, for those trying to develop policies based on past or current quantities of entrepreneurship.

However there is a solution to this problem, focusing on the institutional mix which unlocks the entrepreneurial aspect of human action, as described above. That is, the question that should drive policy is this: what institutional structure best allows an individual to undertake productive activities in the form of innovation, arbitrage, betting on ideas and so on? The ability of individuals to act entrepreneurially, as well as the direction of their activities towards productive or unproductive ends, is directly affected by the institutional mix (political, economic and cultural) they act within. The institutional structures will encourage or discourage the general direction of entrepreneurial activities.

Of course, this also raises the critical issue of differing institutional structures in different regions and how those differences affect the opening of borders to entrepreneurship.[5] There are both costs and benefits to the gradual integration of national markets. On the one hand, there are increased opportunities for trade, transnational production and the potential for efficiency gains via coordinated entrepreneurial efforts. However, on the other hand, the gradual integration of national markets leads to changes in competitive dynamics resulting from concentration trends.

The insights addressed above also have an impact on the potential for the standard competitive equilibrium framework that has been employed to understand these issues. The potential for such a framework must be considered in the context of national markets becoming more open and intertwined with other national markets. As entrepreneurship, trade and transnational production increase, an interdependent economic system is formed. As these dynamic changes have occurred, the market efficiencies and failures, as identified in the standard equilibrium model, have changed. As a result, the theoretical framework must be revised to incorporate these realizations.

ENTREPRENEURSHIP AS AN INTERNATIONAL PUBLIC GOOD

Having established what the notion of entrepreneurship entails, we now turn to a discussion of entrepreneurship as an international public good and the potential for market failure in providing this good. To begin with, it is necessary to clarify the theoretical meanings of '*market failure*' and '*public goods*'.

Standard economic theory begins with the foundational assumptions of full and complete information, zero transaction costs and given prices which are beyond the manipulation of any one or group of individuals. Given this framework, economic theory dictates that individuals will exchange goods and services until all mutually beneficial exchanges are exhausted. This is a situation of Pareto optimality: any further exchange or redistribution would make some better off but would also reduce utility for others. In short, given these assumptions, the market is capable of reaching an efficient outcome.[6]

The formal proofs of economic theory demonstrate that, under conditions of general competitive equilibrium, the economic system will simultaneously achieve (a) production efficiency – all cost technologies are employed, (b) exchange efficiency – all mutually beneficial exchanges from trade are realized; (c) product-mix efficiency – agents receive the bundle of products they are willing to pay for. Following from these simultaneous efficiencies are the two fundamental welfare theorems: an economy in general equilibrium is Pareto efficient, and any Pareto efficient distribution of resources desired can be achieved via the market mechanism.

Economists compare the market with the standard of the two welfare theorems when determining the presence or absence of a market failure. If a market does not meet this optimum, it is then considered a failure. Simply put, economists use the term 'market failure' to describe those situations where voluntary exchanges fail to obtain the efficient outcome. A good that produces a negative externality is an example of a market failure.[7]

To understand the notion of public goods, consider a good that produces a positive externality. Further assume that (a) consumption of the good by one individual does not reduce the amount available for other consumers. That is, there is non-rival consumption; and (b) it is not technically possible to prohibit free-riders. If these two criteria are met, the good is then characterized as a public good. The most common example of this is national defence. The sense of security derived from a programme of national defence does not reduce the defence available to others. Once the service is produced, other citizens cannot be prohibited from enjoying the sense of protection. The issue then turns to the incentive structure present for agents to produce the optimal or efficient level of public goods. Standard theory dictates that the incentive will be lacking because non-payers cannot be excluded. While the production of the public good will not be non-existent, output will fall far short of the optimal level owing to the existence of free-riders. Even when the market does produce the public good, it is argued, it will not produce the socially optimal or efficient amount. The standard solution to this market failure is for government production of the good to make up for the shortfall. Having provided this theoretical framework, we can consider entrepreneurship in terms of public goods and market failure theory.

Entrepreneurship cannot be considered a pure public good. Returning to the public good criteria established above, there are aspects that are both rival and excludable. However there are significant benefits in terms of spillover that are non-rival and non-excludable. The public characteristics of entrepreneurship could be viewed as similar to the discussion of Sanford Grossman and Joseph Stiglitz (1980) regarding the public characteristics of information. But this would be to miss essential features of the entrepreneur's role in coordinating market exchange. Grossman and Stiglitz argued that efficient conveyance of information would be underproduced in a competitive economy because, once private information is revealed in a market transaction, it becomes public information. Thus private actors will reveal less information than would be publicly optimal to achieve an efficient equilibrium.

Grossman and Stiglitz are led to this conclusion precisely because they fail to recognize the entrepreneurial element in the market process. The Walrasian system to which they are reacting presupposes a pre-reconciliation of all plans prior to exchange activity and, in so doing, all excess supply and excess demands are corrected. This theoretical perspective overstates the role played within the market economy by equilibrium prices and underestimates the role that disequilibrium prices play in generating market adjustments by economic actors.[8] In short, prices serve a role precisely when reconciliation of plans must be worked out through exchange activity. Furthermore, assuming the individual private agent, given his current stock of information and knowledge, is indeed supplying information at the private optimal level, there is no way for any external party to calculate the optimal social stock and hence to claim that it is over- or undersupplied. To do so would require complete and perfect knowledge that one cannot possibly possess. What must be realized is that the continual disequilibrium that characterizes the market is the very thing that provides the incentive for entrepreneurs to obtain and exploit new information leading to continual market adjustments.

Given this rendering of the public good aspects of entrepreneurship, the key question is whether entrepreneurship will be undersupplied in view of these public good characteristics. Let us first consider the benefits of entrepreneurial activities and then, within that context, consider whether entrepreneurship is indeed undersupplied. As discussed above, the entrepreneur is continually alert to new profit opportunities, whether they are through arbitrage or through innovation. Thereby he raises the general standard of living for those around him as well. This occurs on several levels. By constantly introducing new goods and services to the market, the entrepreneur does not benefit only the buyer who is directly involved in the exchange. Consider, for example, the introduction of the computer. With the advent of personal computers and widespread access to the Internet in many households, new buyers and sellers, who were previously unaware of each other, were connected. In short, new markets were opened. By drastically lowering barriers to search, information and communication, the computer and Internet increased the number of buyers available to sellers and sellers available to buyers. From the comfort of their homes, consumers could order products for direct delivery from sellers located hundreds or thousands of miles away. The benefits of the initial transaction extended far beyond those involved in the initial transaction – the developer and subsequent buyer and seller of the computer. Entrepreneurs in addition to the initial entrepreneur who created and sold the computer were able to introduce their products and services via the Internet.

The public benefits related to the computer do not end here. The advent of the personal computer and the Internet also drastically lowered the cost of communication, both within geographic borders and beyond. The introduction of new technology expands the opportunity sets of individual agents, allowing them either to undertake new activities or to accomplish already existing activities faster than before. The result is that economic agents can dedicate their time and efforts to different activities where those who were not involved in the initial entrepreneurial act can and do benefit. For example, individuals can now do all their holiday and food shopping over the Internet at any time that is convenient, saving time involved in travelling, walking around stores, standing in queues and so on.

The same reasoning applies to firms who can now communicate with each other with and clients over the Internet, providing a plethora of new goods and services to an ever-expanding, worldwide market. Moreover technology increases the opportunities for partnerships between firms, allowing them to exploit new cooperative comparative advantages. In short the initial entrepreneurial act creates significant spillover effects. The potential for collaboration between firms and entrepreneurs is a significant international public good. Firms have an incentive to share relational assets and become more oriented towards innovative forms of complementary entrepreneurship. Furthermore, entrepreneurial coordination can overcome the problem of deindustrialization associated with international entrepreneurship (Dunning and Boyd, 2003).

We have now highlighted how the introduction of a good or service by an entrepreneur opens new markets by introducing buyers and sellers who may not have been previously aware of the exchange opportunity. But the activity of one entrepreneur also benefits other entrepreneurs in another fashion: the dispersion of knowledge throughout the market.

Market process theory informs us that entrepreneurs have varying degrees of knowledge and uncertainty. Each entrepreneur observes the world through a different lens and, hence, views opportunity, uncertainty, risk and so on differently than others. The particular knowledge of one entrepreneur is not the same as that held by others. Additionally, where one entrepreneur is more certain regarding an opportunity and outcome, others may not be. One can see then how the market process is continually progressing with the discovery of new knowledge and the removal of uncertainty. As one entrepreneur acts according to his stock of knowledge and uncertainty, others observe his activities and incorporate them into their stock of knowledge. Entrepreneurial activity spills over for all to observe and act on as well. The market process forges ahead as entrepreneurs in the current period build on the innovations and knowledge discovered by those in previous periods. The result is that the arrow of economic progress continuously moves forward.

A certain narrow reading of economic theory might suggest that, since the individual entrepreneur does not capture or internalize all the benefits from his activity, entrepreneurial activities will be undersupplied. But it must be realized that this does not mean that most of the benefits are not internalized. In fact, as we hope the preceding paragraphs have suggested, our historical experience with markets defies what narrow economic theory might dictate. Entrepreneurs capture profits by exercising the knowledge they have of 'time and place' and revealing the information they are in possession of through their actions in the marketplace. It is true that, once entrepreneurs introduce a good to the market, others outside the exchange will benefit. It is true also that, once entrepreneurs reveal information, it is in a fundamental sense now publicly available and free to others. However, as long as the private benefits are large enough, even if all the benefits are not internalized, we will still get the efficient level of entrepreneurship.

In fact, despite the public good characteristics, there is a strong incentive to be the first to market. At least in the short run, the first to market will earn supernormal returns. Only after others enter the market will those profits be eroded. In other words, entrepreneurial profits earned exclusively by the first to enter the market constitute the full internalization of that entrepreneurial act. Profits fall as more entrepreneurs act on the public information and enter the market. If we think sequentially, each subsequent entrepreneur internalizes the full benefit of having appeared in the market when he does: after some entrepreneurs but before others. Simply put, the lure of that pure profit from that initial recognition of the opportunity is enough to bring forth action and generate a series of market adjustments to better satisfy the demands of consumers. To continue with our example of the computer, its introduction created many new entrepreneurial opportunities:

new hardware, software, and so on. The fact that all these future profit opportunities were not captured by the initial entrepreneur did not prevent the introduction of the computer.

It is our contention that the spillover aspects of entrepreneurship will not cause an underproduction of entrepreneurial activities. Rather it is because these spillovers generate pecuniary benefits to those who are alert to the opportunities to realize gains from exchange that market economies realize, not only the degree of efficiency that they exhibit, but also the continual pressure to innovate (Baumol, 2002). In the context of the transatlantic relationship, there are many opportunities for concerting entrepreneurship. These collaborations have the potential to create significant positive spillover effects, benefiting both economies. This of course assumes that the institutional structure is such that the relative payoff for productive activities is greater than that for unproductive opportunities, so that cooperative potentialities can be exploited in an efficiency-enhancing manner.

CREATIVE DESTRUCTION: THE IMPACT OF ENTREPRENEURSHIP ON *MÉTIS*

We now turn to a discussion on the notion of destructive competition, the idea that increased levels of entrepreneurship lead to disruptive and growth-retarding effects at home. It is often argued that globalization leads to the destruction of a region's 'way of life': jobs, industries, culture and the rest. We frame this issue in the context of *métis* to gain analytical traction. *Métis*, a concept passed down from the ancient Greeks, is characterized by local knowledge resulting from practical experience. It is one's way of life or knowledge of 'how to get things done'. It includes such things as skills, culture, norms and conventions, which are shaped by the experiences of the individual. This concept applies both to interactions between people and the physical environment (such as learning to ride a bike) and to the interactions between people (such as interpreting the gestures and actions of others). The notion of *métis* is tacit, in that it is not one that can be written down neatly as a systematic set of instructions, but rather is gained only through experience and practice.

In terms of a concrete example, think of *métis* as the set of informal practices and expectations that allow ethnic groups to construct successful trade networks. For instance, orthodox Jews dominate the diamond trade in New York City (and many other locales), using a complex set of signals, cues and bonding mechanisms to lower the cost of trading. The trade would not function nearly as well if we simply dropped random traders into the same setting; that difference can be ascribed to *métis*. This locus of informal rules is self-enforcing in that an overwhelming majority of traders are better off by sticking to the established rules which work to facilitate coordination.

Firms, too, have a distinct *métis*, as highlighted by the recent attention that industrial clusters have received. In these clusters, the sharing of both tacit and codified knowledge by facilities within close proximity opens up many possibilities for complementary entrepreneurial ventures.[9] As firms become more and more linked, the unique pre-relationship *métis* evolves and adapts to include the experiences of the cooperative relationship.[10] Intercorporate trust therefore becomes central as it facilitates the interaction and exchange of knowledge between firms. For instance, the building of international production systems by transnational enterprises has extensive effects in terms of knowledge sharing between firms and entrepreneurs.[11] *Métis* can be seen as an informal, common knowledge that allows individuals and firms to coordinate on a specific equilibrium offering high returns (Hall and Soskice, 2001, p. 13). The link with entrepreneurship as a public good should be highlighted. As entrepreneurs interact in different regions, there is significant spillover in terms of *métis* for others to observe and incorporate into their activities.[12] To illuminate this point, consider that US firms in Europe have been adapting well to opportunities for representation in the EU's business associations.

Given this understanding of *métis*, we can link it to one of the most widespread criticisms of globalization: the claim that it destroys the way of life of certain groups of individuals. By introducing American products in Europe, an American entrepreneur destroys part of the European *métis* and replaces it with American *métis*. The effects of increased entrepreneurship are even more destructive, it is argued. Not only is *métis* affected, but so too are jobs and industries in the country that is importing the products of the foreign entrepreneur. Furthermore, critics often choose some distribution (based on trade surplus, deficit and so on) at some point in time and discuss the 'distributions of globalization'. More specifically they are concerned with the potential for an 'unequal distribution' due to globalization.

It is our contention that it is wrong to view changes in *métis* as destructive to the progress or 'way of life' of a geographic area. *Métis* is not a static concept that was created at some specific point and remains in that permanent state forever. Rather one must view the path of *métis* as a process that is continually changing. Over time, it is both created and destroyed.

Additionally, changes in *métis* are not necessarily due primarily to entrepreneurship. As people move between and/or introduce new products or services to regions, they bring with them a unique *métis* based on their personal experiences that influences and changes the existing *métis*. It is critical to remember that the current 'way of life' that critics of globalization are so quick to defend was not always in its current form. Rather the current 'way of life' evolved over time, destroying some *métis* while creating new ones and, through this process, arrived at its current state. This is the only way that man can progress. As Cowen convincingly argues, globalization allows for both increased homogeneity and heterogeneity of culture (*métis*). While some parts of the market become more alike, others become more different (Cowen, 2002, p. 16). In this regard, it is important to note that the EU, absent any relationship with the USA, has a continually changing *métis* as new members are accepted into the union.

The understanding of *métis* set forth here offers key insights into the potential problems of differing institutional structures in different geographic regions. For instance, Hall and Soskice (2001, pp. 8–21) distinguish between 'liberal market economies', where firms coordinate their activities via competitive market arrangements, and 'coordinated market activities' where firms depend more on non-market relationships, such as networking and strategic collaboration, to build competencies.[13] The means of coordination within these two distinct spheres can be viewed as *métis* that has developed within these unique economies and institutional structures.

Anyone who views these differing institutional structures as being in permanent conflict falls into the fallacy of viewing *métis* as a static stock of knowledge. Rather applying the view of *métis* as a continually changing process forces one to realize that the current stock of *métis* has developed over time and will continue to develop as entrepreneurs from these different regions interact. There is no reason to assume that, over time, entrepreneurs (without interference preventing them from doing so) will fail to integrate aspects of the different institutional structures into their stock of *métis*, forming a completely new and distinct one. The key question then becomes determining the best way to form new *métis*. Should the government take an active role or should it focus on providing institutions which allow participants to interact and converge over time on a new and unique *métis*? By its very nature, *métis* cannot be planned by external parties. Emphasis should therefore be placed on developing an environment where parties with differing *métis* can interact productively, with the result being a new and unique *métis*.

It cannot be disputed that an opening of borders to international entrepreneurship has a distinct economic effect. It is true that jobs in the foreign country may be both created and lost. Companies and entire industries may be replaced. This, however, is an unavoidable result of economic progress. Those who lose their jobs because of a foreign entrepreneur are free to reallocate their labour towards other ends, which are more highly valued by society.

Economics dictates that if the desired ends are increased wealth and the efficient allocation of resources, unhampered entrepreneurship – within a general institutional framework – is the means to achieve the ends. Economics can say nothing of substance regarding the ends in themselves. It cannot judge them to be good or bad, moral or immoral; all it can do is analyse the validity of means in achieving desired ends. It has nothing to say when those who may lose their jobs to international competition claim that this is 'unfair' or 'unjust'.

The fear then of 'destruction', meaning a loss of certain jobs, businesses and industries, is very real in the presence of unhampered international entrepreneurship. But it should be clear that this is the only way for a country (and mankind as a whole) to progress. Surely the producers of the horse buggy and whale oil could have been protected from the threat of entrepreneurship and the resulting innovations, but this would have been at the expense of modern forms of transport, electricity and economic and social progress. If economic and social progress are the desired ends, governments must be careful not to concern themselves with the 'distributions of globalization' at any one point in time. Rather focus must be placed on establishing a broad institutional framework which allows the market process – and the entrepreneur as the central figure of the process – to take its course.

THE WEAKNESS OF STRONG TIES AND THE STRENGTH OF WEAK TIES: THE ENTREPRENEUR AND SOCIAL CAPITAL[14]

One of the key issues in opening borders to international entrepreneurs is the issue of trust or social capital. Notions and levels of trust differ across regions and geographic locations. This leads to the critical issue: will those in one geographic region trust entrepreneurs from other regions given differences in institutions, *métis* and so on? Will there be a general deficiency of trust? And how will this affect the entrepreneurial process and the benefits of uninhibited entrepreneurship? In this section we will attempt to address these issues.

The issue of trust is an important one because it influences the social sphere in which one interacts and exchanges. If one trusts one's family or a close group of people, the extent of potential trading partners is severely limited. We refer to trust, and hence trade, within a small group of people as having strong bonds. The bonds are strong in that each party in a transaction knows the other quite well and deals with them on a frequent basis as part of their family or close social group. If, on the other hand, trust is more widespread, that is, beyond a small group of people, then trade can take place within a much larger group of people. This case is characterized by weak bonds. While there is a trading bond with many partners in this case, the relationship, or bonds between them, is weak in that they are not directly related in terms of a family or small community unit. It has been postulated that those countries with high social capital, that is, with weak bonds, are more successful than those with strong bonds because the range of potential trading partners is drastically increased (see Fukuyama, 1995). However a specific mechanism for developing weak bonds over strong bonds has not yet been explored. It is our contention that the entrepreneur is the mechanism through which weak bonds, and hence economic development, occur.

Before moving on to explore the connection between entrepreneurship and trust, we must clarify what exactly the notion of trust entails. The framework we employ to consider trustworthiness in the case of the entrepreneur is the encapsulated interest account as put forth by Hardin (2002). This analytical construct dictates that agent A trusts agent B because it is in agent B's interest to take agent A's interests into account. The requirements for trust, however, are more stringent: both parties must want a continued future trading relationship. It is a combination of encapsulated interests and the desire for continuous dealings that forms the concept of trust.

The link between the entrepreneur and trust is a logical one. The entrepreneur, driven by the profit motive, has the incentive to satisfy the consumer in such a way that repeated interactions take place in the future. Notice that the two requirements set out above are fulfilled. As the encapsulated interest theory dictates, the consumer trusts the entrepreneur because it is in the entrepreneur's interest to take the consumer's interests into account. The entrepreneur wants to maximize his profits and the only way to do so is to satisfy as many consumers as possible. Furthermore it is in the entrepreneur's interest to continue to meet the needs of the consumer over time (to engage in continuous dealings) in order to continue to gain profits.

In reality, the difficulty with the above theoretical rendering is that information is not perfect and therefore it is not always easy to determine if it is in the interests of others to take your interests into account. In short, there is an issue of credibility or trustworthiness due to a lack of information. How does one know that the entrepreneur is interested in continuous dealings, let alone in taking the interests of the other individual into account? The entrepreneur is continually attempting to solve this problem in three ways, two of which are direct and one of which is indirect.

The first is specifically related to the entrepreneur's own business endeavours. He is continually making efforts to signal to current and potential clients that he is credible, that it is in his interest to take their interests into account and that he wants a continued trading relationship.

He signals in a number of ways, including advertising, displaying testimony from past customers, offering warranties, memberships, credit, return/ exchange policies and so on. All of these efforts are aimed at fulfilling the two requirements for trust defined above.

In addition to the above, there is an indirect way in which entrepreneurs increase the general level of trust. Specifically we can link the discussion on the public good aspects of entrepreneurship to our discussion here of social capital. Recall that the activities of entrepreneurs, while not pure public goods, in many cases have significant spillover effects. The entrepreneur, via innovation, is continually lowering the costs and barriers to communication. By doing so, he makes it cheaper not only for himself, but for others, to communicate their credibility and trustworthiness to potential consumers. For instance, the entrepreneur who develops a new, creative form of advertising to market his business provides a spillover benefit to both other entrepreneurs and consumers who are able to benefit from the new advertising technique.

The issue of trustworthiness can also be linked to our discussion of *métis*. The knowledge gained from practical experience includes who is trustworthy and who is not. As economies and societies progress and *métis* expands, this information is known by more and more people. As progress occurs and new information technologies are introduced, the cost of obtaining information about others decreases, making trustworthiness more transparent. As borders are opened and entrepreneurs interact with consumers, the *métis* of each group, including the notion of trust, is altered in such a way that people learn how to 'get things done'.

The third way that entrepreneurs increase trust is by directly entering the business of information dissemination. These entrepreneurs offer customers transparency and information regarding others. Examples include *Consumer Reports* magazine, industry and product newsletters and consumer credit agencies. Certain entrepreneurs also offer customers a rating system for a specific industry to signal trustworthiness, credibility and quality. Standard and Poor's and Moody's, for example, rate companies on the basis of their investment quality. Michelin is famous for its reviews of hotels and restaurants in various countries throughout the world. Underwriters Laboratory is a non-profit business that objectively tests products for a fee and offers a seal of approval to those products deemed safe. Where enough consumers demand information regarding others, entrepreneurs, driven by the profit motive, will rise to meet the need.

One can now see why we have chosen the title for this section. While strong ties are beneficial in that one has specific and detailed knowledge of one's trading partner, they are costly in that there are severe limitations on the range of potential trading partners and, hence, economic progress. Weak ties, on the other hand, despite the lack of specific information, provide strength in terms of the economic fabric of social cooperation. They allow for an increased range of trading partners and, hence, more opportunities for mutually beneficial exchanges and economic progress. We have argued that the entrepreneur serves as the mechanism through which weak ties are extended. He is constantly introducing new technologies that reduce the costs, and hence barriers, to communication and trust. Moreover there are significant spillover effects of the introduction of such technologies that allow many parties to benefit. Of course the success of the entrepreneur in carrying out this function of establishing weak ties is directly linked to the institutions – rule of law, private property and so on – that allow him to operate productively in the first place.

THE ROLE OF GOVERNMENT IN THE NEW ATLANTIC ECONOMIC PARTNERSHIP

Possible Roles of Government

The role of government is, without a doubt, of utmost importance to the success of the transatlantic relationship between the EU and the USA. The critical question is what specific roles and activities the governments should undertake in this context. There are two issues that will be covered here. The first is the creation of an environment that allows entrepreneurs to act successfully towards productive ends and the second is the fear of monopoly and/or collusion due to the opening of borders. It is with these concerns in mind that we must consider the role of the government.

One can consider two possible roles for the EU and US governments: they can either assume the role of a referee or that of a player. As a referee, the government is limited to enforcing general, endogenously emergent, institutional rules. Its capacity as 'institutional builder' is restricted to the mechanisms of enforcement and its presence in the social order is passive. As a player, on the other hand, the state not only enforces endogenously emergent rules of the game but also actively creates these rules and the institutional composition of society itself. In this capacity, government intervenes and exogenously imposes institutional order from above instead of merely providing a network of enforcement for indigenous institutional arrangements that evolve spontaneously from below.

It should be obvious that the role assumed by the government has a direct impact on the level of entrepreneurship that manifests itself in a specific economic environment. If the government takes an active role in shaping the economic environment, this will potentially suffocate some aspects of productive entrepreneurship and direct entrepreneurial efforts towards perverse ends via unproductive entrepreneurship. For instance, when the government assumes the role of player, it makes itself vulnerable to pressures from special interest groups seeking favours via direct interventions in the economy.[15]

For example, both the US and the EU governments are subject to lobbying on the part of the agriculture and aerospace industries and provide them with subsidies and other favours.[16] Another example that is relevant for EU policy is the powerful unions and their concern with competition from lower wage workers from East and Central Europe. The divide between Old and New Europe can in fact be rendered intelligible by reference to the power of interest groups to block the dynamic force of markets as instruments of social change. The Old Europe is committed to taming the transformative thrust of markets, while the New Europe has embraced markets as a prime vehicle by which to destroy the old institutional structures which produced economic backwardness and political repression for two generations. The battle line being drawn concerns whether government will be a force for change or a force for interest groups. Paradoxically government as a force for beneficial social change is best conceived as a referee. If the government assumes the role of a referee and enforces the general rules of the economic game – a well defined and enforced private property structure, a stable rule of law, minimal intervention in the economy and so on – one would expect productive entrepreneurship to flourish and unproductive entrepreneurship to decline.

The Market Process and the Role of Government

Having defined the two potential roles for government, it is beneficial to clarify the context in which governments operate to better understand their impact on entrepreneurship. Recall that market process theory dictates that we view the market as a continuous process which requires one to recognize that temporality and uncertainty are fundamental categories of all economic action. Furthermore, uncertainty, due to changing conditions and data, is purely a market phenomenon, one which all economic actors must deal with and one which cannot be removed. The entrepreneur must be recognized as an intricate part of the market process. He is continually discovering previously unknown data and removing the uncertainty inherent in the market.

Inherent uncertainty must be differentiated from created or structural uncertainty, which results from instability in man-made institutions. Such things as unstable political institutions, unstable economic institutions and unstable legal institutions would all serve to illustrate the notion of structural uncertainty. When the government becomes a player in the market, it runs the risk of undertaking activities that lead to structural uncertainty. If the goal is increased economic progress via entrepreneurship, the focus of government should be on creating a stable environment for the market and hence productive entrepreneurship. This requires stable and generalized institutions rather than continuous interventions.

Government Intervention

Both the US and the EU governments may feel the need to intervene actively as players in the transatlantic relationship. Gains in European productivity may be seen as a threat by the USA, whose policy emphasizes relatively open markets with the underlying expectation that they will be advantaged by relatively higher efficiencies. On the other hand, the EU is concerned about the concentration of US firms in Europe. It is feared that European firms lag behind the US in technological innovation and are disadvantaged by unfavourable taxes and labour-related costs. This fear of creative destruction was discussed in an earlier section. If the goal is to promote economic progress, governments should undertake activities that minimize structural uncertainty. That is, they should provide a general framework of secure and enforceable property rights and a stable rule of law.

Yet another perceived intervention and regulation is to protect consumers of each geographic region. This issue is made more difficult because of differences in culture and values as well as regulatory objectives which make convergence a moving target. Examples include the EU's ban on beef hormones that are critical to US beef production, the EU's greater restrictions on genetically engineered crops as compared to the USA and differences in environmental protection. For example, the USA has much more stringent laws protecting dolphins and turtles, while the EU has stringent laws regarding eco-labelling (Vogel, 1997).[17] It may be argued that what is necessary is a harmonizing of regulations, but, to the extent that the differences are due to differences in public opinion, such attempts will be difficult. For example, the populace in the EU places a higher value on fuel conservation and food purity than is the case in the USA, which could result in difficulty coordinating on laws that appease all involved (ibid., p. 61).

While there is no doubt that such disputes will continue, the government bodies must be sure not to use regulations as trade barriers or to favour interest groups. Regulations should protect the property of those within a geographic area. Where health, safety and protection of private property are at stake, there is potential for government involvement. However there should be great caution as to the extent of government involvement in this area. Where health, safety or property issues are not at stake, the government should remove itself from the process. Furthermore, where there are private means of safety and/or health certification, government need not get involved.

To illustrate this, consider EU Commission regulation No. 1677/88, which states the degree of curvature of EU cucumbers as part of their quality standards. This regulation clearly does not deal with safety, health or property rights and, as such, is an unnecessary intervention. Of course, this does not illustrate all government involvement, but is rather meant to illustrate what can happen when governments take on the role of player. When political favours and rent seeking characterize the political and social environment, entrepreneurship shifts from productive to unproductive ends. Instead of innovating, efforts are expended on rent-seeking activities. The market has an inherent mechanism for quality control as manifested through the preferences (and hence purchases) of consumers and the impact on profits and losses. This mechanism should be free to operate to the greatest extent possible. Finally, by myopically restricting policy choices to regulatory and interventionist options, the potential for government agents to further entrepreneurial learning and coordination will not occur. One example of these potentialities is SEMATECH, which is a collaborative effort among the leading US semiconductor companies with government. The programme has been relatively successful and has been singled out as a role model for government–industry collaboration (see Spencer and Grindley, 1993).[18]

Collusion and Monopoly

The fear of increased collusion and/or monopoly is yet another issue related to the increase in complementary entrepreneurship between the USA and the EU (see Boyd and Rugman, 2003). The EU has laid out its regulation of cartels in Article 85[81] of the European Community (EC) Treaty which prohibits agreements that affect trade between the member states where they have as their objective the prevention or distortion of competition within a single market. Likewise the EU has clarified its competition policy as it relates to monopoly and has specified a list of abuses in Article 86[82] of the EC Treaty, including selling at extremely high prices, predatory pricing, restricting production, discriminating against certain customers, refusing to supply the product in particular cases, imposing exclusive purchasing agreements and strengthening a dominant position via merger with a competitor. It is our contention that the fear of collusion and monopoly has been overstated in both the USA and the EU.[19] The market process approach offers key insights into the issues of collusion and monopoly.

To reiterate, the key is to view the market, not at a static point in time, but rather as a continually evolving process.

The common argument against cartels is that they restrict output or restrict competition. Such restrictions, it is claimed, injure consumers. However, as long as there are free entry and exit from an industry (that is, the lack of government enforcement of the cartel agreement), a cartel is unstable for several reasons. The first is the chiselling effect of members cheating to obtain more of the profits from the cartel. In the absence of an effective enforcement mechanism, the cartel, as a result of the chiselling effect, will eventually break down. Furthermore, if there are increasing profits in an industry, one would expect a tendency for others to enter that field. The critic may vociferously object and claim that entry is not really free because not anyone can enter at any moment they choose. This, of course, confuses freedom of entry with the ability to enter. Just because there is free entry does not mean that each and every person is able to enter for reasons of personal capabilities, monetary or capital resources and so on.

Turning to monopoly, the neoclassical price doctrine states that a certain quantity of a good, when produced and sold, leads to a competitive price. A monopolist or cartel can, if the demand curve is inelastic at the competitive price, restrict quantity and raise the price. However the market process approach demonstrates that there is no such thing as a competitive price as neoclassical theory dictates. And, if no competitive price is discernible, there is no possible way to determine a monopoly price which is higher than the competitive price.

The reason why no competitive and hence monopoly price is discernible is that, while neoclassical theory assumes a given supply and demand curve with a resulting competitive price, in reality the demand curve is not given to the producer. Rather the producer must discover demand through the market process and continuous discovery of changing information and data. As this discovery process continually unravels, there is no way of telling if a producer, in changing output and price from period to period, is moving above or below the competitive price.[20] In this sense, even what one would term a monopolist is an entrepreneur, as he is continually discovering new data and meeting the demands of consumers to avoid new entrants eroding his market share.

It is true that the efforts of government must focus on maintaining a competitive environment, but what this requires is not monitoring of the market environment at a specific point in time to determine the degree of competition. Rather, to truly foster an environment of competition, all barriers to entry must be removed by government. This means that all subsidies, tariffs and other special political favours which restrict the entry of competitors must be removed. Until the ultimate goal of removing barriers is met, any efforts by both the USA and the EU in this area should be to lower the costs and resource misallocation resulting from multijurisdictional antitrust enforcement. As long as standards differ across borders, inefficiencies will continue to exist (Evenett *et al.*, 2000, pp. 20–23).[21]

CONCLUSION

We have argued that unhampered entrepreneurship is critical to fully capturing the positive-sum gains that exist in the transatlantic relationship. Toward this end, we explored the role of entrepreneurship in economic progress, in the context of a public good and in the development of *métis* and trust. We also discussed the role of government and the potential impact of assuming various roles. We can now put forth some general guidelines for the achievement of a successful transatlantic relationship in the context of entrepreneurship.

1. *Focus must be placed on the market process* instead *of the planning process.* The entrepreneurial–competitive market process serves systematically to ensure a tendency towards an allocation of society's resources which reflects consumer preferences, as well as alerting consumers to hitherto unattainable possibilities for fulfilling those preferences. Given the inherent uncertainty of the market and localized knowledge of specific geographic areas, entrepreneurship and the allocation of resources cannot be planned by central governments. Rather governments should focus on creating an institutional framework that allows the entrepreneurial aspect of human action to manifest itself.
2. *There is a tradeoff between economic progress and other, competing ends.* Economics dictates that, if efficiency and economic progress are the ends, unhampered entrepreneurship is the means. If other ends (protecting domestic jobs, maintaining a current 'way of life' and so on) are valued more highly than efficiency and economic progress, the transatlantic relationship will fail both to yield 'economic development' and to contribute to the expansion of 'world trade and closer economic relations'.[22]
3. *The consumer is the captain of the economic ship.* It must be remembered that, in an unhampered market, entrepreneurs are at the whim of consumers. It is only through serving the consumer that the entrepreneur makes a profit. The allocation of resources and the resulting changes in 'ways of life' cannot be blamed on entrepreneurship per se, but are solely due to consumer preferences. As Mises wrote, 'They [entrepreneurs] are at

the helm and steer the ship. A superficial observer would believe that they are supreme. But they are not. They are bound to obey unconditionally the captain's orders. The captain is the consumer' (1996, pp. 269–70).

4. *Differences in* métis *are only short-term barriers to development.* It is critical to remember that *métis* is not static. When borders are opened, the indigenous populace gains experience from interacting with foreigners. As these interactions continue, there is synergy between the domestic and foreign *métis* that creates a new and unique *métis*. It is true that this may take time, but it must be realized that this unique *métis* is beyond the grasp of any single mind (or group of minds) and cannot be planned.

5. *Opportunities for unproductive entrepreneurship must be minimized.* Unproductive entrepreneurship does not result in increased efficiency or economic progress. Rather it results in transfers of existing wealth as well as large-scale deadweight losses. In order to avoid unproductive activities, the payoffs to productive entrepreneurship must be relatively higher than unproductive entrepreneurship. It is critical to realize that, when government takes on the role of a player, these opportunities increase. Instead, the focus should be on a general framework (private property, a stable rule of law and so on) that applies equally to both private citizens and political agents and which allows productive entrepreneurship to serve its function.

NOTES

*   We would like to thank Gavin Boyd, Peter Leeson and participants in the conference on Alliance Capitalism in the New trans-Atlantic Economy, St. Mary's University, September 26 and 27, 2003 for helpful comments. We acknowledge the financial assistance of the J. M. Kaplan Fund to support our research. The usual caveat applies.
1.   Source: http://europa.eu.int/comm/trade/bilateral/data.htm.
2.   Source of employment data: http://www.eurunion.org/partner/usstates/usstates.htm.
3.   For detailed expositions of the market process, see Kirzner (1992) and Boettke and Coyne (2003).
4.   We follow the New Institutional use of the term 'institutions' to mean both formal and informal institutions.
5.   For more on the institutions necessary for entrepreneurship, see Boettke and Coyne (2003).
6.   In standard welfare economic theory, the term 'efficiency' is equivalent to Pareto optimality.
7.   A negative externality occurs when a voluntary exchange between two agents negatively affects the utility of a third agent. The third agent bears some of the cost without compensation and hence the outcome fails to meet the Pareto optimal standard.
8.   For a critical examination of Grossman and Stiglitz's argument in light of the Austrian theory of the entrepreneurial market process, see Esteban Thomsen (1992, pp. 29–62).
9.   For more on this, see Minkler (1994), Powell (1998), Amin and Wilkinson (1999), Cohendet *et al.* (1999), Dulbecco and Garrouste (1999), Fu-lai Yu (1999), Lewin and Phelan (1999), Maskell and Malmberg (1999) and Nooteboom (1999).

10. For a discussion of national values and culture and how they affect cooperative and competitive interaction between firms, see Boyd (2003, pp. 26–9).
11. For a discussion of the trends in expanding the international production system, see the 2000 *World Development Report* by the United Nations Conference on Trade and Development.
12. One can see a connection with the discussion here of *métis* and Dunning's (2003) discussion of R-assets.
13. One could take issue with the use of the term 'coordinated market economies' to describe those situations where non-market mechanisms are used, given that it is the very presence of a price system – a market mechanism – that coordinates the activities and plans of economic actors.
14. This terminology is borrowed from Granovetter (1973).
15. For an example of this, see *The Economist*, 26 July 2003, which addresses the excessive business regulation in the USA: business regulation is a $1 trillion annual industry of rent seeking. The article also addresses the influence of special-interest groups on business regulation (page 12) and the excessive financial regulations in the EU. The EU regulations are so cumbersome that, in many cases, even the government fails to follow them (page 51).
16. Under the Uruguay Round Agreement the ceiling for domestic farm subsidies is $19.1 million for the US and $62 million for the EU. Furthermore, it is estimated that the EU spends approximately $5 billion in subsidizing exports each year, while the US spends around $200 million. (Source: US Embassy Press release #66/02, June 25, 2002, available at http://www.usa.or.th/news/press/2002/nrot066.htm).
17. It should be noted that there are many areas where the USA and EU cooperate: for example, regarding mutual recognition of standards in the areas of drugs and medical devices.
18. For more on technocratic contributions to the evolution of technology based corporate linkages, see Macher *et al.* (1998) and Ham *et al.* (1998).
19. Although we do not go into detail here, the USA has competition/anti-trust policies similar to those of the EU. For more, see the Department of Justice, antitrust website at http://www.usdoj.gov/atr/. See also, Boyd and Rugman (2003).
20. Note that the fact that the demand curve is not given leads to problems not only with determining the competitive price but also in regulating monopolies. For more on the problems of neoclassical monopoly theory as well as applied case studies, see Armentano (1982).
21. Venit and Kolasky (2000) contend that there has already been considerable convergence between the competition policies of the USA and the EU.
22. These are a few of the 'major fields', as laid out at the EU–US Summit in Madrid, 3 December 1995.

REFERENCES

Amin, Ash and Frank Wilkinson (1999), 'Learning, proximity and industrial performance: an introduction', *Cambridge Journal of Economics*, **23**, 121–5.

Archibugi, Daniele, Jeremy Howells and Jonathan Michie (eds) (1999), *Innovation Policy in a Global Economy*, Cambridge: Cambridge University Press.

Armentano, Dominick T. (1982), *Antitrust and Monopoly: Anatomy of a Policy Failure*, New York: John Wiley & Sons.

Audretsch, David B. (2002), 'Entrepreneurship: a survey of the literature', paper prepared for the European Commission, Enterprise Directorate General (available at http://europa.eu.int/comm/enterprise/entrepreneurship/green_paper/literature_survey_2002.pdf).

Baumol, William J. (1990), 'Entrepreneurship: productive, unproductive, and destructive', *Journal of Political Economy*, **98**, 893–921.

Baumol, William J. (2002), *The Free-Market Innovation Machine*, Princeton: Princeton University Press.

Boettke Peter J. and Christopher Coyne (2003), 'Entrepreneurship and economic development: cause or consequence?', *Advances in Austrian Economics*, **6**, 67–88.

Boyd, Gavin (2003), 'Alliance capitalism and macroeconomic policies', in John H. Dunning and Gavin Boyd (eds) *Alliance Capitalism and Corporate Management: Entrepreneurial Cooperation in Knowledge Based Economics*, Cheltenham, UK and Northampton, MA, USA: Edward Elgar, pp. 24–44.

Boyd, Gavin and Alan M. Rugman (2003), 'Corporate alliance and competition policies', in John H. Dunning and Gavin Boyd (eds), *Alliance Capitalism and Corporate Management: Entrepreneurial Cooperation in Knowledge Based Economics*, Cheltenham, UK and Northampton, MA, USA: Edward Elgar.

Brenner, Reuven (1985), *Betting on Ideas: Wars, Inventions, Inflation*, Chicago: University of Chicago Press.

Cohen, Stephen S. and Gavin Boyd (eds) (2000), *Corporate Governance and Globalization: Long Range Planning Issues*, Cheltenham, UK and Northampton, MA, USA: Edward Elgar.

Cohendet, Patrick, Francis Kern, Babak Mehmanpazir and Francis Munier (1999), 'Knowledge coordination, competence creation and integrated networks in globalised firms', *Cambridge Journal of Economics*, **23**, pp. 225–41.

Cowen, Tyler (2002), *Creative Destruction: How Globalization is Changing the World's Cultures*, Princeton, NJ: Princeton University Press.

Dulbecco, Philippe and Pierre Garrouste (1999), 'Towards an Austrian theory of the firm', *The Review of Austrian Economics*, **12**, 43–64.

Dunning, John H. (2003), 'Relational assets, networks and international business activity', in John H. Dunning and Gavin Boyd (eds), *Alliance Capitalism and Corporate Management: Entrepreneurial Cooperation in Knowledge Based Economics*, Cheltenham, UK and Northampton, MA, USA: Edward Elgar, pp. 1–23.

Dunning, John H. and Gavin Boyd (eds) (2003), *Alliance Capitalism and Corporate Management: Entrepreneurial Cooperation in Knowledge Based Economics*, Cheltenham, UK and Northampton, MA, USA: Edward Elgar.

Evenett, Simon J., Alexander Lehmann and Benn Steil (eds) (2000), *Antitrust Goes Global: What Future for Transatlantic Cooperation?*, Washington, DC: Brookings Institution Press.

Fischer, Thomas C. (2000), *The United States, the European Union and the 'Globalization' of the World*, Westport, CT: Quorum Books.

Fu-lai Yi, Tony (1999), 'Toward a praxeologial theory of the firm', *The Review of Austrian Economics*, **12**, 25–42.

Fukuyama, Francis (1995), *Trust*, New York: Simon & Schuster.

Garrouste, Pierre (2002), 'Knowledge: a Challenge for the Austrian theory of the firm', in Nicolai J. Foss and Peter G. Klein (eds), *Entrepreneurship and the Firm: Austrian Perspectives on Economic Organization*, Cheltenham, UK and Northampton, MA, USA: Edward Elgar, pp. 72–87.

Granovetter, Mark S. (1973), 'The strength of weak ties', *American Journal of Sociology*, **78**, 1360–80.

Grossman, Sanford J. and Joseph Stiglitz (1980), 'On the impossibility of informationally efficient markets', *American Economic Review*, **70**, 393–408.

Hall, Peter A. and David Soskice (eds) (2001), *Varieties of Capitalism: The Institutional Foundations of Comparative Advantage*, Oxford: Oxford University Press.

Ham, Rose Marie, Greg Linden and Melissa M. Appleyard (1998), 'The evolving role of semiconductor consortia in U.S. and Japan', *California Management Review*, **41** (1), 137–63.

Hardin, Russell (2002), *Trust and Trustworthiness*, New York: Russell Sage Foundation.

Kasper, Wolfgang and Manfred Streit (1998), *Institutional Economics: Social Order and Public Policy*, Cheltenham, UK and Lyme, USA: Edward Elgar Publishing.

Kirzner, Israel M. (1973), *Competition & Entrepreneurship*. Chicago: University of Chicago Press.

Kirzner, Israel M. (1985), *Discovery and the Capitalist Process*. Chicago: University of Chicago Press.

Kirzner, Israel M. (1992), *The Meaning of the Market Process: Essays in the Development of Modern Austrian Economics*, London: Routledge.

Leff, Nathaniel (1979), 'Entrepreneurship and economic development: the problem revisited', *Journal of Economic Literature*, **17**, 46–64.

Lewin, Peter and Stephen E. Phelan (1999), 'An Austrian theory of the firm', *The Review of Australian Economics*, **13** (1), 59–80.

Loasby, Brian J. (2002), 'Explaining firms', in Nicolai J. Foss and Peter G. Klein (eds), *Entrepreneurship and the Firm: Austrian Perspectives on Economic Organization*, Cheltenham, UK and Northampton, MA, USA: Edward Elgar, pp. 11–23.

Lundvall, Bengt-Ake (1999), 'Technology policy in the learning economy', in Daniele Archibugi, Jeremy Howell and Jonathan Michie (eds), *Innovation Policy in a Global Economy*, Cambridge: Cambridge University Press, pp. 19–34.

Macher, Jeffrey T., David C. Mowery and David A. Hodges (1998), 'The recovery of the U.S. semiconductor industry', *California Management Review*, **41** (1), 107–36.

Maskell, Peter and Anders Malmberg (1999), 'Localised learning and industrial competitiveness', *Cambridge Journal of Economics*, **23**, 167–85.

Minkler, Alanson P. (1994), 'The problem with dispersed knowledge: firms in theory and practice', *Kyklos*, **46**, 569–87.

Mises, Ludwig von ([1949] 1996), *Human Action: A Treatise on Economics*. San Francisco: Fox & Wilkes.

Mokyr, Joel (1990), *The Lever of Riches: Technological Creativity and Economic Progress*, New York: Oxford University Press.

Nooteboom, Bart (1999), 'Innovation, learning and industrial organization', *Cambridge Journal of Economics*, **23**, 127–50.

Powell, Walter W. (1998), 'Learning from collaboration: knowledge and networks in the biotechnology and pharmaceutical industries', *California Management Review*, **40** (3), 228–41.

Rothbard, Murray N. ([1962] 1993), *Man, Economy and State*. Alabama: The Ludwig von Mises Institute.

Schumpeter, Joseph A. (1950), *Capitalism, Socialism and Democracy*, New York: Harper & Brothers Publishers.

Schumpeter, Joseph A. (1961), *The Theory of Economic Development*, New York: Oxford University Press.

Spencer, William J. and Peter Grindley (1993), 'SEMATECH after five years: high technology consortia and U.S. competitiveness', *California Management Review*, **35** (4), 9–24.

Thomsen, Esteban (1992), *Prices and Knowledge: A Market-Process Perspective*, London: Routledge.

United Nations Conference on Trade and Development (2000), *World Investment Report 2000: Cross-border Mergers and Acquisitions and Development*, New York: United Nations.

Venit, James and William Kolasky (2000), 'Substantive convergence and procedural dissonance in merger review', in Simon J. Evenett, Alexander Lehmann and Benn Steil (eds), *Antitrust Goes Global: What Future for Transatlantic Cooperation?*, Washington, DC: Brookings Institution Press, pp. 79–97.

Vogel, David (1997), *Barriers or Benefits? Regulation in Transatlantic Trade*, Washington, DC: Brookings Institution Press.

8. Institutionalizing Atlantic structural partnering

Gavin Boyd

The clear imperative to build a coordinated Atlantic interregional political economy, through policy-level and corporate endeavours, requires planning to ensure that these endeavours will develop in a spirit of solidarity, with fairness, reciprocity and social justice, in line with insights in behavioural macroeconomics (Stiglitz, 2002), and will be sustained through institutional development. Economic cooperation across the Atlantic is often thought of only in terms of government functions, understood in liberal perspectives, but what is required in the common interest has to be expressed in terms of structural logic. The necessary collaboration has to be transnational, that is, between corporate managements across borders, within larger processes of policy cooperation. Liberal philosophy guiding policy, moreover, has to become more comprehensive through responses to challenges in structural interdependence. These are challenges to evolve new forms of consultative statecraft, for extensive entrepreneurial coordination. Such statecraft is becoming more and more necessary because of technological advances that are making firms more and more interdependent in the development of their production capabilities and because of the increasing scale of sectoral and intrasectoral linkages that are associated with the formation of international production systems.

Sustained policy cooperation, with wide ranging entrepreneurial collaboration aided by consultative statecraft, could be made possible by the establishment of an Atlantic structure, which, while representative, would independently contribute to policy-level and corporate coordination. This could be done through the sponsorship of conferences for technocrats and corporate managements, to build broad understandings about potentials for entrepreneurial complementarities and the harmonization of economic policies. Projections of economic trends by the Atlantic structure would aid the conference activity. Economic policy management by the USA and the EU could thus become more consensual, with more significant accountabilities, and more interactive learning. Corporate planning would develop with increasing awareness of opportunities for concerting new initiatives and for building relational assets. The development of Atlantic corporate associations, moreover, would be aided, and these could be sources of vital inputs into policy-level cooperation.

The commonly recognized deficiencies of international organizations may be considered to be all the more serious in a context which would require much consultative interaction within and between technocratic and corporate groups. The innovative entrepreneurial coordination to be hoped for could be prevented by incompetence, distrust and opportunism. Moreover all the dangers of fraudulent managerial collusion that have been evident in the USA since the last years of its speculative boom could be seen as warnings. The external reach of regulatory tightening in the USA has been limited by surveillance problems, and accordingly there have been incentives for managements to move questionable operations to offshore locations. Furthermore, while the moral deficiencies of numerous managements have drawn attention to major corporations allowing much scope for managerial discretion, the losses of integrity have apparently been factors in a larger problem of decline that has affected levels of dedication in national and international bureaucracies.

Nevertheless the rationale for establishing the proposed Atlantic structure remains valid. The interregional public good of large-scale entrepreneurial coordination has to be provided through the institutionalized sponsorship of managerial learning linked with policy learning. This must be affirmed as a joint responsibility for interregional welfare, that is, for growth, employment and distributional objectives, to be served through orderly patterns of production and exchange. A key element of the rationale will have to be emphasis on the basic responsibility of financial sectors to support growth in the interdependent real economies through productive funding. Comprehensive orientation towards this responsibility will be essential, with effective restraints on the tendencies of financial enterprises to generate and exploit volatility in markets for financial assets.

PROMOTIONAL TASKS

The formation of an Atlantic consultative structure could be seen to require detailed political designing to guide negotiations towards a hard and precise agreement, rather than to establish a basis for highly innovative relational cooperation. A low-trust culture of adversarial legalism, evident in the Uruguay and North America Free Trade Agreements, could be expressed in a drive for hard and precise understandings about the formation of the consultative structure, but this would prevent the development of the intended consultative role. The approach required for such a role would be that appropriate for the establishment of a consortium of economic policy research institutes.

The institutional design would have to take account of similarities and differences in the orientations of American and European economists, and would have to assert imperatives for solidarity-based Atlantic entrepreneurial coordination and collaborative macromanagement. The urgency of financial sector reforms for the productive funding of growth in the real economies would have to be stressed. The principal elements of the design would be an economic policy research team, comprising US and European scholars; a technocratic group of Atlantic structural and trade policy bureaucrats; a high- and medium-technology roundtable of industrialists; and an advisory section staffed by representatives from the Bank of International Settlements. Collegial coordination of the challenging interactions between members of the institution would be vital for its efficiency, and could be motivated by common focus on the key issues of Atlantic interdependence: the problem of stability in the US economy, the prospect of increasing European vulnerability to further destabilization of the US economy and the danger of a stronger speculative rather than productive propensity in the operations of international financial enterprises gaining world oligopoly power. European economists tend to have a stronger sense of responsibility than their American counterparts for contributing to the development of economic policies, and have been less interested in abstract modelling, which contributes too much ambiguity in economic analysis, but more conscious of policy-level obligations for macromanagement. European initiatives for the establishment of an Atlantic consultative structure could thus be hoped for, especially in view of general awareness of slow growth in Europe increasing asymmetries in Atlantic interdependence. Decisional problems in the EU, however, could make agreement in support of the proposed interregional consultative institution very difficult. There could be concerns, moreover, that interactions within such an institution would provide opportunities for increased US exploitation of rivalries between European governments. The central axis of Franco-German political cooperation in the EU could be subjected to strains because of diverging perspectives on relations with the USA.

European policy-level and corporate views of proposals for Atlantic structural cooperation would certainly be influenced by the national attachments and loyalties which hinder collaboration within the Union. There would be mixed effects, as unevenly shared concerns to limit the scope for potentially divisive US initiatives would be linked with competition between member governments and national firms to assert active roles in the consultations. The common European interest in the growth and employment effects of interregional entrepreneurial coordination and policy harmonization could be obscured, especially by the fears of less industrialized Union members, including the countries that became members of the EU in 2004, that the more advanced and larger members would benefit most.

The logic of very active and concerted European governmental and corporate involvement in the consultative venture, however, is tending to become more persuasive because of the increasing gravity of the threatening issues in Atlantic interdependence. A further boom and recession sequence in the USA has to be reckoned with. US international firms will have increased capacities for expansion in Europe during the boom and increased incentives for such expansion during the recession, while throughout the sequence Europe's significance as a destination for foreign direct investment will become greater because of the EU's enlargement. Meanwhile Atlantic exchange rate management will demand more attention because of the volatility associated with downward pressures on the US dollar. Furthermore, during the phase of speculative asset appreciation in the USA, increased outflows of European investment to the USA will reduce funding for regionally based growth in the Union. Another consideration of wider significance is that the global pattern of interactions between financial sectors and real economies will be changed by stronger speculative propensities in world financial enterprises gaining additional oligopoly power. Declines in monetary policy capabilities and capacities for financial market regulation will have to be anticipated.

The perspectives of US policymakers and corporate managements would be extremely diverse because of strong individualism in the business culture and its consequences in the fragmented pattern of economic associations. Corporate distrust of government and lack of confidence in intercorporate goodwill would tend to prevent positive responses to the rationale for a consultative structure that would be seen to have a structural policy role. Concern would tend to develop about the potential for increasing policy-level influence in such a structure, and about the probability that a small number of very large enterprises would have preferential access to the deliberations. Promotional endeavours for the establishment of the consultative institution would thus have to place great emphasis on the common interest and on the vital importance of extensive entrepreneurial coordination for the US economy. Because levels of trust have been pushed lower by numerous corporate scandals since the end of the speculative boom, a drive to build support for the concept of entrepreneurial coordination would encounter serious difficulties, but a core group of major entrepreneurial figures could be formed for interaction with the European Round Table of Industrialists. A challenging initiative from the European side could be very productive.

The rationale that would have to be stressed by a US promotional group, in agreement with European colleagues, would have to stress that the increasing importance of striving for greater entrepreneurial coordination in the USA is part of a larger imperative for Atlantic entrepreneurial coordination. What may be achieved domestically will depend on the development of Atlantic complementarities, and this will have to be emphasized because of the high and rising levels of structural interdependence between the USA and the EU, and the prospect of increasing uncertainties affecting entrepreneurial decisions, as a result of business cycle changes in the USA and exchange rate volatilities.

Corporate links across the Atlantic, in networks and alliances, are assuming greater significance for interdependent growth than connections between political groups and organizations. Competing and complementary interests are active in the intercorporate interactions, largely to the exclusion of concerns with public goods. The common focus is on increasing the efficiencies of corporate strategies in competitive and cooperative contexts. US enterprises are advantaged by generally larger capabilities and market positions, but their increasing significance as agents of structural change has an unfortunate aspect relating to the home country's business cycle. The recent history of this destructive cycle has shown that recoveries from US post-boom recessions are likely to involve weak employment growth, especially because of the movement of production processes to foreign locations. Instability in the US economy, contributing to corporate emphasis on expanding transnational production, increases problems of deindustrialization which do not draw attention from the corporate managements focused on their international strategies. In the absence of strong peak economic associations the public goods problem is a challenge for a highly pluralistic system of government that lacks structural policy capabilities.

CORPORATE ORIENTATIONS

Intensifying competition, driving concentration trends in the Atlantic and the world economy, tends to cause narrow corporate focus on opportunities for expansion in global markets, while weakening home country attachments and loyalties. The US corporate presence in Europe, however, is politically and economically challenged to achieve cohesion within a pattern of EU corporate collaboration focused on consultations with the European Commission. The main effect of these consultations is a growth of support in European business associations for Union policies intended to promote more complete integration in the regional market, despite the efforts of member governments to favour and retain the political loyalties of major national firms.

As a dynamic force in the Union pattern of business associations the US presence has a capacity to build consensus in those organizations on imperatives for extensive Atlantic corporate cooperation, to promote orderly interdependent growth on a scale which has not been possible for rival member governments. The potential for such a role tends to be obscured by corporate interest in encouraging the European Commission's market integration efforts, but there clearly is scope for conference activity that would open the way for collaborative engagement with structural issues of common interest and long-term significance.

In the dynamics of corporate interest representation managements of large firms tend to combine in elite groups for coordinated privileged access to policy levels while avoiding the accountability that could result from active organizational links with corporate associations comprising large numbers of smaller enterprises. The European Round Table of Industrialists is such an elite group, and could work with the Union's larger business associations for consensus on the development of Atlantic entrepreneurial consultations. Political will to provide leadership in cooperation with the American presence in the regional business associations, however, does not appear to be developing. Members of the Round Table are major national firms with special interests in their consultative links with member governments and with the European Commission, which can be effective if these remain exclusive, so that relative bargaining strengths are not weakened by advocacy for larger assortments of interests.

Elite preferences for privileged access to policy levels are also evident in the USA's Business Council, which stands above a large number of industry associations with which it has no organizational links. Informal advisory connections provide opportunities for influence on policy orientations, but the promotion of broad consensus is difficult. Leadership for Atlantic entrepreneurial consultations could well be viewed as an inappropriate option because the likely activation of assertions of interests by the country's industry associations could weaken the Council's high level advisory role, while resulting in the formation of strong rival business associations.

Managerial focus in major US and European corporations on strategies for increased oligopolistic strengths is thus likely to continue as a dominant trend, with the neglect of opportunities for entrepreneurial coordination. Policy-level failures to grasp the importance of such coordination as an urgently required public good are allowing the trend to become more probable. Entrepreneurial coordination does develop in alliances, especially because of the logic of combining specializations based on advanced technologies, but alliances tend to be short-lived, leading to mergers and acquisitions.

The corporate oligopolistic strategies, motivating competitive representations of interests to governments, contribute to policy-level failures to promote production complementarities aligned with the common good. A basic problem for advanced knowledge-intensive political economies is that corporate associations have not developed sufficient capabilities for the promotion of spontaneous order through entrepreneurial collaboration. Overall balances between competition and cooperation are being tilted against the latter. With this change, moreover, the public interest is being adversely affected by the stronger speculative propensity in financial sectors which limits productive funding and causes destabilizing sequences in business cycles. Meanwhile declines in the economic sovereignty of national administrations are in effect making corporations and corporate associations more responsible for growth and general welfare. Imperatives for corporate learning, then, are becoming more significant: concepts of corporate social responsibilities for employment and growth have to be expanded and given greater motivational force. This can be affirmed because obligations to serve the common good increase with the structural power acquired by large enterprises.

The political philosophy of corporate governance that has become relevant with the expansion of transnational operations by large enterprises has to be based on the multiplication of civic interdependencies and risks in structurally linked liberal market economies. Vast numbers of relatively passive and uninformed investors have implicit interests in the performance of wide ranges of firms other than those in which they hold stocks, because of specific and general intercorporate production and exchange linkages. Managerial obligations to coordinate entrepreneurial ventures and to compete constructively have to be recognized and made effective through business associations. Such discipline in the common interest, moreover, clearly has to be reinforced by the regulatory functions of governments, despite their losses of economic sovereignty. Furthermore, spontaneous entrepreneurial coordination by firms has to be given encouragement and assistance from policy levels through consultative interactions, in service to the common interest.

The numerous cases of large-scale corporate fraud in the USA during recent years have drawn much attention to stakeholder interests at risk because of wide scope for managerial discretion, especially in the pursuit of speculative opportunities. The fortunes of vast numbers of stakeholders in closely and distantly related firms, and of greater numbers of vulnerable individuals, have also been affected. All this makes the entire pattern of civic interdependencies a demanding challenge for corporate associations across the Atlantic. Hence it must be reiterated that corporate learning about social responsibilities has to be much wider than what would appear to be appropriate for greater efficiencies in the direct service of markets. Policy-level obligations in this context also have to be affirmed as more than just matters of instrumental rationality serving purposes of structural competitiveness.

POLICY ORIENTATIONS

The strong liberal political tradition in the USA, widely seen to have been given increased validation by the superior efficiencies of its private sector, sustains beliefs that the state must allow very extensive freedom for market forces, and that these will provide solutions for problems of growth and welfare. Slow growth and high unemployment in Europe thus tend to be viewed as consequences of excessive governmental intervention in and regulation of the continental economies and of efforts to maintain welfare systems that induce dependence. European governments have been obliged to recognize the high costs of their welfare systems, which are making fiscal discipline very difficult and limiting the growth potential of the substantially integrated regional market.

The established US economic policy orientation is being challenged by the effects of corporate shifts of production to foreign locations, with degrees of deindustrialization that have not evoked concerted structural adjustment. An acute problem of external imbalance, moreover, has been made worse by fiscal expansion and investment inflows that have increased domestic demand in excess of domestic production. Currency overvaluation has been a major factor in the imbalance, and has been followed by depreciation, but, as noted, the corporate emphasis on foreign production has reflected the continuing strength of major incentives. Altogether the free implementation of corporate strategies, extending more and more into the world economy, is not generating solutions for the manifest problem that has emerged in asymmetric structural interdependence. Recognition of this challenge to liberal economic policy has been hindered by pragmatism and subjective preferences for continuity, as well as by awareness of adversarial corporate attitudes to administrative authority, seen to be prone to manipulation by ambitious politicians.

Moderate welfare obligations are recognized in the established liberal tradition, with beliefs that increased welfare allocations will reduce labour productivity and cause overall growth to decline to European levels. Competition for political support necessitates affirmation of the moderate welfare obligations. Policy-level deliberations, however, tend to exclude recognition of the problem of external imbalance and of expanding outward direct investment as a factor contributing to that imbalance. Prolonged neglect of very large current account deficits has evidenced this failure in knowledge-intensive government tasks, especially as an example of pragmatic short-termism.

The welfare challenge, however, is becoming more serious, because of the rising costs of deepening integration in the world economy and of the recessions following speculative booms, as well as of stronger speculative orientations in financial sectors and of increasing oligopoly power in world product markets. These difficulties confronting the USA have special significance in the Atlantic context because of the size and entrepreneurial dynamism of the US economy and because of problems affecting its learning potential as well as that of the European Union.

A much more knowledge-intensive policy orientation is needed in the USA to meet the challenges of its structural interdependencies, and to deal constructively with the effects of its policy failures. The present state of policy-level dynamics has serious implications for the planning of Atlantic initiatives and for European engagement with the area's macromanagement tasks. The mix of policy orientations on each side demands careful analysis for the development of productive dialogue.

The European mix of policies exhibits degrees of cooperative macroeconomic logic and of competitive microeconomic functionalism, with political exchange motivations. Potentials for leadership are quite limited because of national rivalries which tend to motivate efforts to enhance structural competitiveness, notably in Germany and France; political will to increase the structural competitiveness of the Union as a whole is lacking, as noted, and may be more seriously lacking because of stronger decisional pluralism after the enlargement of the Union.

Cooperative macroeconomic logic is expressed in qualified observance of fiscal discipline under the Stability Pact of the European Monetary Union. Recent breaches of this pact by Germany and France evidence the costs of welfare state burdens and of aids to industry to strengthen structural competitiveness, motivated in the French case by concerns about lagging behind Germany. European competitive microeconomic functionalism is encouraged by prospects for increased market access in the East and Central European states entering the Union. A resulting focus in German policy, together with stronger interest in strengthening the nation's leading role as an exporter to the USA, may well further reduce consideration of possibilities for Union-level structural development. Meanwhile German views on any institutionalized entrepreneurial cooperation with the USA are thus likely to favour an informally exclusive relationship rather than an arrangement open to all Union members. US corporate penetration of the less industrialized European states would be a likely German concern if Atlantic entrepreneurial collaboration were in prospect.

European and US policy communities, challenged by advocacy of major initiatives to increase cooperation that has been weakened by trade disputes, have been urged to launch new initiatives for economic collaboration that will build solidarity and thus resolve current frictions (Bergsten and Koch-Weser, 2003). Imperatives for deeper understanding of Atlantic structural and policy linkages have been affirmed, in terms that can be taken to imply some recognition of interdependencies in advanced political development and in the management of interregional integration, and therefore of requirements for very profound policy learning. An increasingly clear imperative is for this necessary policy learning to become open to absorption of the entrepreneurial significance of knowledge diffused in technology-based corporate networks. Official technology enhancement projects in the USA and Europe result in increasing understanding within specialized policy groups, but there is much scope for deeper and wider policy learning to aid entrepreneurial innovations. Advances could thus be made towards the formation of an interregional market economy with production patterns more coordinated through US and European policy-level contributions to concerted entrepreneurial applications of new technologies. Ventures into more extensive structural cooperation could then be possible, that is, with more knowledge-intensive corporate and technocratic interaction.

Cooperative Atlantic macroeconomic policy achievements would be made more feasible with the technology-based knowledge-intensive entrepreneurial collaboration. Effective monetary cooperation, it must be reiterated, has been made more difficult but more necessary by the long neglect of the USA's balance of payments problems and its sequences of speculation and recession. External balance will be attainable if there is extensive intercorporate collaboration to increase domestic production and to promote reform in the financial sector, to enhance productive funding and curb speculative market manipulation. The EU does not yet have a serious external imbalance but will have to anticipate one if large firms shift high-volume production to external locations. Disruptive business cycle sequences, moreover, will be in prospect if a stronger equity culture develops in the Union's gradually integrating financial market without innovations to promote wide-ranging coordinations of corporate production strategies. Atlantic fiscal policy management meanwhile will be assisted by the disciplinary effects of entrepreneurial coordination on each side, including the reduced diversions of investment away from productive funding.

POLITICAL AND FUNCTIONAL LINKAGES

Issues of Atlantic economic policy cooperation are linked functionally and politically with issues in US and European relations with the rest of the world and with questions of common defence and security. At the transnational level, major corporations reckon with and endeavour to influence the management of US and European policies while implementing production and marketing strategies that tend to assume global dimensions. In the absence of extensive corporate entrepreneurial cooperation, policy makers confront many uncertainties about the functional significance of measures affecting trade, investment, taxation and infrastructure development. Corporate managements also have to cope with many uncertainties about the operations of rivals and potential alliance partners, but are better placed to acquire commercial intelligence.

The political linkages to be considered with proposals for conferencing on Atlantic entrepreneurial coordination would be subject to media- and policy-level distortion; moreover they would be vulnerable to propaganda attack by non-governmental organizations. An obvious danger is that numerous discussions at different levels of expertise and responsibility would obscure basic analysis and cause pragmatic procrastination by policy makers and corporate leaders. European political figures, influenced by media coverage, could view US policy-level involvement in the sponsorship of the entrepreneurial conferences as an indicator that dialogue would be used to press for cooperation with US proposals for accommodating changes in Union trade, investment, and industrial and taxation policies, and that there would be divisive effects, open to US exploitation. European corporate managements, sharing the same concerns, could see cohesion in their associations being diluted while the preferences of many Union medium- and high-technology firms for alliances with US enterprises were becoming stronger.

Continuing strains in Atlantic trade relations, due particularly to conflicts over subsidies to export industries, would tend to make European caution more likely, despite the potential for achieving greater harmony in trade policy management through understandings and goodwill generated in the proposed entrepreneurial conferences. Leadership for building a constructive consensus could certainly be lacking in the Union because of the absence of a strong central economic authority apart from the European Central Bank, and because of the multi-country structure of Union business associations. Meanwhile, despite the absence of consensus on Atlantic issues, there may well be common tendencies to hope for more regionally based growth because of the enlargement of the Union, which, as noted, will ensure greater bargaining strength in trade negotiations with the USA.

While in Europe proposals for Atlantic entrepreneurial conferencing would be seen to have complex implications for each government's structural policies, in the USA a major concern for corporate managements and policy makers would be the likely extension of state power in the economy. Because of the strength of the established liberal tradition this would be viewed as an innovation opening the way for misuses of power and for virtual restrictions on entrepreneurial freedom that would weaken economic growth. The logic of promoting entrepreneurial coordination could be regarded with suspicion because of expectations that oligopolistic collusion and administrative favouritism would dominate the proposed conferences.

Enlightened and dedicated policy-level and corporate advocacy of consultative entrepreneurial coordination would be needed to cope with the actual and expected linkages on each side of the Atlantic. The necessary leadership is not developing in US and European political and business groups, but could be encouraged and given orientation by policy research institutes and by the International Monetary Fund, through contributions to policy learning focused on linkages between microeconomic and monetary policies. Assertion of a role in this area of international policy learning would be a vital contribution by the Fund to global collective management.

The promotion of entrepreneurial coordination for dynamic balance in Atlantic structural interdependencies, it must be stressed, would be seen in Europe with much awareness of vulnerabilities. The advocacy would have to inspire much trust, while opening up possibilities for knowledge-intensive policy learning and corporate learning about efficiencies and equities in balancing competition with cooperation in market economies with complex structural linkages. An extremely important advantage of *exploratory* conferences on potentials for entrepreneurial coordination would be that informal exchanges would facilitate friendly interactions through which trust could develop. This consideration would also be very significant for the promotion of the concept in the USA. One aspect, it must be reiterated, is that US managements would tend to be confident of being able to interact with European representatives from positions of strength in world markets, while nevertheless being reluctant to contribute to increases in governmental involvement in the economy.

A supportive role for the International Monetary Fund can be suggested because its assessments of trends and issues in industrialized states that relate to the international monetary system can contribute more substantially to policy learning by examining closely linkages between microeconomic and monetary policies, with special interest in the overall effects of interactions in those linkages. The Fund's surveillance responsibilities concentrate on trends in financial markets and their effects on real economies, which have been increasingly severe in the USA: a key problem identified is high-volume and high-risk speculation in financial markets under weak regulation – misallocations of capital away from productive use, adding to the complexities and uncertainties of these markets. The regulatory issue, the toleration of potentially destabilizing misallocations of investment for market manipulation, is becoming more serious because of concentration trends in international financial markets. This subject is rather avoided in Fund publications, despite indications that market discipline, as well as regulatory discipline, is weakening in those markets.

There is highly significant scope for Fund studies that would examine the problems for structural policies and for macromanagement caused by regulatory deficiencies in financial markets. A key consideration is that such studies could enhance policy-level and corporate understanding of potentials for entrepreneurial coordination by producer enterprises, to reduce dependence on funding by financial markets that is open to manipulation, and to build political will for effective regulation of those markets. A further purpose of the studies would be to increase general understanding that monetary policies, seriously weakened by the vast growth of speculative manipulation in financial markets, could be made more effective for growth and stability by the direct and indirect consequences of a general shift towards entrepreneurial coordination by producer enterprises.

Assertion of a major role by the Fund in the assessment of linkages between macroeconomic and microeconomic policies in Europe and the USA, because of the centrality of Atlantic interdependencies in the world economy, would be a very important service to Atlantic and global collective management. Encouragement of such a role by European and US policy communities and corporate associations would help the development of Atlantic networks capable of promoting active consensus on issues of interregional economic cooperation. On the European side a special reason for taking initiatives is that stronger Fund contributions to policy learning in the USA, with increased external accountability, could motivate efforts by US policy communities to work with more resolve for stability in the American economy. Europe, it must be stressed, is threatened by further boom and decline sequences in the USA, during which unsustainable fiscal and current account deficits will be made more dangerous by increases in speculative market manipulation by financial enterprises, with relative declines in productive funding.

Altogether the diverse connections which proposals for Atlantic entrepreneurial coordination would be seen to have with other policy areas and with issues of corporate responsibility indicate requirements for a comprehensive rationale, and for a common institution dedicated to consensus building, on the basis of that rationale. The European Central

Bank, with concerns for stability and growth in the real economies of its area, may well be able to provide exceptional clarity and orientation for comprehension of the principal issues, because of research and decisional capabilities, and relative independence from political pressures. This must be reaffirmed because of the importance, for Europe, of working for a well planned Atlantic consultative institution that will assist the development of balanced structural interdependencies with the USA. It must also be affirmed that Europe will benefit substantially if the European Central Bank assumes greater status and influence by asserting an advisory function in the structural policy area, where member governments operate individually while the European Commission remains narrowly focused on working for the development of a liberal Union market economy, except in aerospace.

NEW ECONOMIC DIPLOMACY

The scale and complexities of structural and financial interdependencies are obliging knowledge-intensive political economies to engage in new economic diplomacy (Bayne and Woolcock, 2003). Very active consultative links with firms and corporate associations secure access to large flows of commercial intelligence (Hocking and McGuire, 2002) which aids identification of potential complementarities and conflicts of interest in negotiations over market access, direct investment, competition policy and institutional change. Extensive knowledge of structural linkages across borders increases sensitivities to issues affecting the development of these linkages in the common interest. Interest group pressures for trade protection or opening and for investment liberalization have to be assessed with understandings of trends in the transnational linkages. The management of interdependencies thus tends to be seen in terms of transnational interest aggregation through knowledge-intensive dialogue, for sustained cooperation. Bargaining, with offers of cooperation and threats of discrimination, is recognized to have relational costs; its prospective gains, moreover, are understood to be affected by multiple uncertainties, due to shifts in the operations of international enterprises, advances in applied frontier technologies and the destabilizing effects of speculative market manipulation by large financial enterprises.

New economic diplomacy accords with efficiency and welfare imperatives for pervasive coordination in knowledge-intensive political economies, for the development of coordinated market economies (Hall and Soskice, 2001). While the expanding structural roles of transnational corporations increasingly affect domestic economic management, the new economic diplomacy has to be directed not only at other governments but at those international firms; their large cross-border production systems are becoming more and more significant as structural linkages between industrialized countries. There are general requirements for coordination that will benefit the world economy, and there are more immediately visible requirements for the promotion of complementarities of special significance for countries and regions. In the Atlantic configuration of structural linkages shaped by transnational corporations, the new economic diplomacy clearly has to be, increasingly, a process of US–European collaboration.

Problems of advanced political development hinder management of the new economic diplomacy in the Atlantic context. These problems are basically difficulties in interest aggregation, consensus formation and institutional performance. National business associations and firms use political leverage to secure protection for domestic market positions and aids for export expansion while setting up informal entry barriers that restrict opportunities for new national and foreign enterprises. Political competition, it must be reiterated, drives fiscal expansion that in varying degrees diverts investment from productive use and tends to increase domestic demand while limiting domestic output, in conjunction with corporate movement of production operations to foreign locations. Meanwhile, it must be stressed again, administrative toleration of speculative market manipulation by large financial enterprises causes destructive business cycles, bringing into prominence the dangers of declines in productive funding and of shifts to speculative activities by managements of producer enterprises.

With the highly visible problems of advanced political development there is also uncritical policy-level acceptance of liberal economic thinking about the efficiencies of free market forces. This entails failures to understand the critical importance of *coordinating* production and marketing activities, that is, without resorting to interventionist measures that would reduce entrepreneurial freedom. There is, however, ambivalence about expressing liberal economic thought in policy, because of common governmental concerns with drawing political support from major corporate groups and with managing trade policy to secure substantial gains from involvement in the world economy.

The increasingly vital functional significance of entrepreneurial coordination in highly industrialized structurally interdependent market economies has been obscured in studies of macromanagement options. Some have focused on growth strategies relying on the attraction of direct investment by transnational enterprises through the provision of location advantages, including highly developed infrastructures and minimal regulation.

Competitive enhancement of location advantages has been seen to be rewarded by concentrations of multinational direct investment, but the growth effects can be less than anticipated because of the cost advantages of production in less developed countries with less burdensome tax systems. Moreover geographic dispersals of process stages in the building of international production systems (Arndt and Kierzkowski, 2001) can limit sectoral and intrasectoral complementarities. Domestically oriented studies have seen difficult policy choices between fiscal discipline, employment growth and income equality (Iversen and Wren, 1998), suggesting that employment can be increased only with income inequalities unless there is public sector expansion, with relaxed fiscal discipline. The scope for these choices, however, has to be recognized to be very restricted in view of work which has shown that the expansion of multinational production systems imposes burdens of adjustment on governments and workers (Rodrik, 1997).

Macromanagement choices, it is also clear, have to be made in contexts distinguished by the effects of past failures. Accumulations of government debt represent the consequences of losses of fiscal discipline, including growth prevented by diversions of investment away from productive use, and the taxation of productive ventures at levels that in effect restrict entrepreneurship. These problems have been especially visible in the USA, and the dynamics of its political economy generate pressures to impose adjustment costs on other states with weaker bargaining strength. In Atlantic relations an established trend has been pressure on European governments to resort to expansionary policies that will increase domestic demand for US exports.

Rodrik's insights are especially relevant for clarification of the major macromanagement options. Competition between governments in industrialized states to provide locational advantages for transnational enterprises has diminishing significance as multinationals construct international production systems with dispersals of manufacturing phases, and as Third World locational advantages increase. In the USA, corporate emphasis on international production has contributed to low employment growth during the slow recovery from the 2000/2001 recession. Increased fiscal expansion has of course made possible some employment growth, but has not significantly altered overall corporate interest in offshore manufacturing, which has highly significant cost and tax advantages and offers gains in potential bargaining leverage when dealing with large numbers of host governments. It must be reiterated, moreover, that business cycle uncertainties in the USA add to the incentives of corporations to spread their risks internationally.

Changes in the political balance within the USA can be expected because of overall employment losses attributed to production abroad and to post-recession cost cutting; public sentiment favouring the Democratic Party because of its image as a force for protection of the internal market and for boom-promoting fiscal expansion may well increase and some influential sections of the US media are promoting this anti-outsourcing message. Nevertheless the corporate focus on opportunities for foreign production may become even stronger in view of the longer term tax implications of likely changes in the political balance.

A key problem for the USA in the development of knowledge-intensive new economic diplomacy is that its present liberal orientation entails excessive reliance on unguided market forces, resulting in neglect of an acute danger of external imbalance. This, it must be stressed, entails increasingly serious vulnerabilities for the EU, and also stands as a warning to the Union about the dangers of macromanagement failure to engage with what is likely to become a similar problem of external imbalance. More has to be said, however, because the new economic diplomacy's expectations about the efficiency effects of free market forces are challenged as well by the emphasis of large financial enterprises on quests for speculative gain through market manipulation rather than on revenue from productive funding. Here also the issues confronting the USA are more immediate than those for the EU.

CORPORATE OPERATIONS

The structural contexts of new economic diplomacy are being shaped increasingly by transnational corporate activities. The changing fragmented patterns of growth and employment, as well as allocative and dynamic market effects, extending across borders, tend to cause vicious circles in which real economies experience concentration trends and are endangered by the speculative manipulation of financial enterprises which offsets the growth effects of their productive funding. In the Atlantic region the scope for US producer and financial corporations is especially significant because of their sizes and resources and their degrees of independence from policy-level influence and regulation, as well as their entrepreneurial dynamism. Within Europe, US firms building international production systems are well placed to assume larger structural roles, while European enterprises in the USA constitute a fragmented and less active pattern. US financial enterprises meanwhile are consolidating positions in Europe stronger than those of their European counterparts in the USA. Concentration trends in the US international corporate pattern tend to be preceded by the formation of alliances, resulting in phases of entrepreneurial coordination that typically lead to mergers and acquisitions.

The phases of entrepreneurial coordination do not endure because of the intensely competitive orientations of managements, which motivate quests for rapid gains in market strengths, managerial rewards and stock values through differing types of takeovers. Steady managerial rewards through relational cooperation tend to be considered less attractive, especially where there are visible threats of investor activism, which can be encouraged by the routine market manipulation strategies of major financial enterprises. Financial market pressures on the managements of producer enterprises in the USA drive expansion in Europe and at home, and this trend is understandably stronger during speculative booms in the USA.

If there is spontaneous development of broadly representative corporate associations across the Atlantic there may be more relational and longer-term entrepreneurial collaboration, with restraint on concentration trends. Such progress toward the formation of a more coordinated interregional economy, however, is not likely without guidance and support from highly constructive new economic diplomacy. Policy-level responsibilities in the USA and the EU therefore have vital significance. Losses of economic sovereignty have to be regained through statecraft seeking corporate understanding and goodwill.

The management of infrastructure network services is a key area in which economic sovereignty has to be regained, and this can be done with policy-level advantages in interactions with manufacturing and non-financial service firms whose entrepreneurial coordination has to be promoted in the common interest. There are complex choices for producer enterprises with varying degrees of dependence on infrastructure network services and with actual or prospective holdings in such services. Efficiencies in network services are major factors determining location advantages, and national policies on the control and development of the services can influence governmental efforts to induce entrepreneurial cooperation by manufacturing and non-financial service firms. European infrastructure network services constitute a disorderly pattern of mostly liberalized industries, changing with strong concentration trends; a lack of Union-level coordination has allowed numerous market failures to persist (European Network Infrastructures, 2001). Substantial advances in regional integration and coordination are not expected, because of problems of collective decision making in the EU. With the persistence of structural policy rivalries in the Union a coherent regional effort is needed to link infrastructure issues with endeavours to promote entrepreneurial coordination between producer enterprises. A common Union infrastructure policy, however, is becoming more and more necessary, and its development could be facilitated by very active consultations with European and US manufacturing and non-financial service firms. Assessment of the potential for constructive policy-level and corporate initiatives is difficult, but, while the general lack of coordination persists, US and Union enterprises will continue to have opportunities to exploit investment bidding by European governments.

European producer enterprises have much less significant potentials for productive interaction on issues of infrastructure development in the USA; the fragmentation of the European corporate presence is tending to become more pronounced, a reflection of the persistence of national attachments and loyalties in Union firms, and of their individual interests in ties with US corporations rather than with other European companies. US policy-level involvement in entrepreneurial consultations with European and national enterprises could exert influence on the basis of infrastructure trends and plans, but coherent use of this capacity would depend on political will that could be difficult to form because of the strong pluralism at the policy levels.

The strategies of US and European manufacturing and non-financial firms, responding principally to financial sector pressures for higher returns, and thus focusing on international expansion for the acquisition of stronger market positions, with extensive risk spreading, tend to become highly self-reliant. This is a major effect of intensifying competition in the global process of deepening integration. The ties of national business associations weaken, together with home country political bonds, and interactions with large numbers of foreign governments, firms and corporate associations have to be managed concurrently, adjusting to constant changes. Alliances based on production interdependencies tend to be managed instrumentally, across generally long social distances, because of proliferating uncertainties. Substantial reductions of uncertainties are achieved mainly through mergers and acquisitions, and the scope for these is extensive because of general failures in competition policy cooperation. Where such cooperation does develop, moreover, it is rather ineffective against tacit collusion.

Atlantic securities enterprises, competing for speculative gains through the manipulation of markets for financial assets, similarly drive concentration trends. The pattern reflects the attractions of higher and faster returns from speculation than from productive funding that benefits real economies. The speculative operations, as forms of opportunism, contribute to the multiplication of uncertainties in product markets and exchange rates which obligate the expansionary and risk reduction strategies of producer enterprises. While these enterprises can gain from entrepreneurial coordination, however qualified by instrumental concerns, the financial enterprises tend to benefit more, on balance, from the uncertainties, strains and disruptions that result from competition and conflict between producer enterprises.

NEW REGIONALISM

New economic diplomacy, with dynamics linking policy and corporate levels, is active in new regionalism and in the interregional Atlantic context. A large integrated market, providing extensive scope for production specializations, tends to achieve high growth, thus attracting outside states: they seek entry, or privileged trade and investment access. The attraction can be especially strong if there are prospective developmental and distributional benefits, as has been evident in the recent history of the EU's expansion. If such benefits are not in prospect, but high growth has been achieved in the integrated market, the benefits attraction can nevertheless be quite potent, as has been illustrated by Latin American and Canadian quests for favourable terms of liberalized trade with the USA.

New European regionalism is a case of concerted new economic diplomacy to achieve an advanced form of integration, a single internal market, under a system of collective management which includes a monetary union. This new regionalism generates a dynamic to achieve deeper integration, through the removal of remaining barriers to trade and investment in the single market, and through the establishment of a stronger form of federalism, for more functional collective management in the common interest. Progress in these respects provides wider scope for the development of transnational production linkages between member states. Secondary features of the new European regionalism are the persistence of national structural policies, but these are gradually losing significance because of cross-border investment between member states and the growth of a regional US corporate presence.

The European regionalism is being obliged to respond to problems of interregional structural interdependence, because of large-scale production, trade and financial links with the USA, an economic union committed only to elementary levels of integration with neighbouring states through liberalized trade and investment. This regionalism is a form of shallow integration which perpetuates asymmetries in structural and policy interdependence, allowing little scope for functional logic to activate advances towards integration at higher levels. Imbalances in the spread of gains thus tend to be more pronounced than in the new European regionalism.

While the dimensions of Atlantic structural interdependence are being increased by the EU's admission of East and Central European states, other increases are resulting from the consolidation of the USA's role as the central member of the North America Free Trade Area and its negotiation of trade liberalization agreements with Latin American countries. Brazil and Argentina, the two key partners in negotiations for a Free Trade Area of the Americas, have strong trade and investment links with the European Union.

Atlantic interregional structural links are being extended on a vast scale through US, European and Latin American corporate operations and financial flows. Cultural affinities facilitate the expansion of structural links and the development of commercial networks, but institutions for policy-level and corporate cooperation have yet to be formed. Challenges to build such institutions are apparent in the trend of market efficiencies and failures in the vast pattern. There is, moreover, a special structural challenge demanding recognition. This is the regional and interregional spread of corporate production operations, including infrastructure network industries. Multiple forms of structural power are extending more and more across borders, through the expanding activities of transnational enterprises shaping and linking sectors on scales which decrease national economic sovereignty and set requirements for broadly cooperative macromanagement. Growth, employment and stability in Europe and the western hemisphere depend increasingly on the overall effects of the transnational production. Here there are challenges for the new economic diplomacy and the new regionalism. Economic sovereignty, weakened by the multiplication of structural interdependencies, has to be shared, in consultative interaction with the multinational enterprises whose independent activities are shaping those structural links.

New imperatives for institution building thus have to be recognized. Collective liberal administrative guidance, well institutionalized for consultative engagement with corporate managements, has to be planned for, in conjunction with the building of peak representative European and US corporate associations. Vital roles in the necessary institutional arrangements will have to be played by the European Central Bank and the Federal Reserve. The shared vision, a coordinated Atlantic Market economy linking Europe with the western hemisphere, will have to attract loyalties that have long been too national, for acceptance of the logic of widening circles of multi-level cooperation, in line with sound concepts of natural law and welfare economics.

International competition policy cooperation, however, will be necessary. Transnational enterprises using structural and marketing capabilities with much autonomy will tend to set up entry barriers and resort to collusive practices. The necessary Atlantic institutions will have to acquire competition policy functions, and these will have to become effective with the support of the peak corporate associations facilitating entrepreneurial coordination. The institutional designing and performance, then, will depend very much on high, principled dedication.

REFERENCES

Arndt, S. W. and H. Kierzkowski (eds) (2001), *Fragmentation: New Production Patterns in the World Economy*, Oxford: Oxford University Press.

Bayne, N. and S. Woolcock (eds) (2003), *The New Economic Diplomacy: Decision Making and Negotiation in International Economic Relations*, Aldershot: Ashgate.

Bergsten, F. and C. Koch-Weser (2003), 'Restoring the trans Atlantic alliance', *Financial Times*, 6 October.

European Network Infrastructures (2001), *Oxford Review of Economic Policy* (Symposium), **17** (3), Autumn.

Hall, P.A. and D. Soskice (eds) (2001), *Varieties of Capitalism: Institutional Foundations of Comparative Advantage*, Oxford: Oxford University Press.

Hocking, B. and S. McGuire (2002), 'Government–business strategies in EU–US economic relations', *Journal of Common Market Studies* **40** (3), September, 449–70.

Iversen, T. and A. Wren (1998), 'Equality, employment and budgetary restraint', *World Politics*, **50** (4), July, 507–46.

Rodrik, D. (1997), *Has Globalization gone too far?*, Washington, DC: Institute for International Economics.

Stiglitz, J.E. (2002), 'Information and the change in the paradigm in economics', *American Economic Review*, **92** (3), June, 460–501.

9. The development and structure of financial markets in the European–American economy

George G. Kaufman[*]

1. INTRODUCTION

Empirical evidence clearly demonstrates that financial institutions and markets that maximize the flow of funds from savers (lenders) to investors (borrowers), allocate the funds efficiently and permit diversification of risk for lenders both within countries and across countries are a prerequisite for lasting real macroeconomic development and growth. (For a recent summary of the evidence, see Levine, 1997; Wachtel, 2003.) In addition the evidence also demonstrates that the performance of the financial sector importantly affects the performance of the macro economy both domestically and across national boundaries. Moreover breakdowns in banking and financial markets feed back to cause or intensify breakdowns in macroeconomic activity (Bank for International Settlements, 2002). As a result, the current financial public policy focus of many countries and official international organization centres on improving financial sector efficiency by reforming financial regulations and reducing extant barriers that restrict freedom of entry and operation, including pricing, in financial markets both within and across countries.

At the same time, recent and continuing rapid advances in computer and telecommunication technology have greatly increased the volume of domestic as well as cross-border (transnational) capital flows by both reducing the operational cost and increasing the speed of transmitting funds across great distances, including across national boundaries. It is now as cheap and as fast to transfer funds from Chicago to London, Frankfurt, Tokyo or Singapore as it is to transfer them from Chicago to New York. As a result, large financial markets throughout the world are almost fully integrated. To the extent that increased efficiencies in finance increase the efficiency and volume of domestic and international trade, these increases in international integration have enhanced aggregate welfare in the countries affected. It has been estimated recently that accelerated financial integration in the European Union (EU) could increase the level of GDP by more than 1 per cent (OECD, 2003a).

In addition to barriers to the cross-border flow of funds that decrease the amount of such flows, and advances in communications and computer technology that increase the speed and reduce the cost of cross-border financial flows, the volume of such flows also depends on a number of other factors, including the size of the country, government regulations imposed on financial institutions and markets in the country, the structure of institutions and markets in the country, relative levels of interest rates and corporate profitability. Other things equal, the smaller the country, the fewer government restrictions on prices and quantities, and the larger the banks, the greater will be cross-border financial flows relative to a country's GDP. In large measure because the recent advances in communications and computer technology have made it progressively easier to circumvent regulatory barriers to cross-border financial flows, explicit capital barriers have tended to be greatly reduced or removed altogether in most countries. A recent IMF study reports that while increases in international financial openness since 1985 have been dramatic, international trade integration, where barriers are more difficult to evade and thus more difficult to remove, has advanced at a much slower pace (Brooks *et al.*, 2003).

But transferring funds across national boundaries involves a number of other costs that affect the volume of the flows and have economic and financial consequences. For example, if the boundary crossed separates two countries that use different currencies, the transfer of funds across the boundary is likely to involve both transaction costs in exchanging one currency for the other and the risk that the exchange rate may move adversely between the time of the initial funds transfer abroad and their subsequent repatriation. In addition, to the extent that other factors, such as labour, firms and goods, may not be transferred across these boundaries as rapidly as funds, shocks in some but not all countries will lead to adjustments primarily through the financial sector rather than through real sectors, as is likely to occur within a country. If so, such shocks are likely to amplify both the volume and rapidity of flow reversals and increase the volatility of international capital flows.

This chapter describes and analyses both the existing structure of financial institutions and markets in the developing North Atlantic economic community of the United States, Canada and Europe and the current changes in the financial sectors, particularly as they affect cross-border financial (capital) flows. On the basis of this analysis, the chapter evaluates both the success of the countries in the community in implementing reforms to achieve financial integration to date and the potential for further reform and integration in the future.

The North Atlantic community consists of two areas on opposite sides of the Atlantic Ocean that are roughly similar in population and GDP. But there the similarities end. The west side (North America) consists of two countries speaking the same language. The east side (Europe) consists of many countries, speaking many languages with the precise number depending on the area in Europe considered. At a minimum, the area is generally considered to include the member countries of the EU, which currently includes 15 countries, but is scheduled to expand to 25 countries and possibly more next year.[1] As currently structured, the 15-country EU is larger in population than the USA–Canada grouping by some 20 per cent but smaller in GDP by nearly 15 per cent. (Population and GDP data for the North Atlantic community countries and groupings as well as Japan are shown in Tables 9.A.1 and 9.A.2 in the appendix) As a result, in terms of GDP per capita, the EU is nearly 30 per cent lower than the two North American countries. If expanded to 25 countries, the EU's population jumps to nearly 50 per cent greater than the USA–Canada, but its GDP increases only slightly and remains smaller. Whatever the definition, Europe is far more heterogeneous than North America.

Because national borders often tend to serve as both explicit and implicit barriers to free movements in population, goods and services, the larger the number of countries in a given geographic area, the poorer is the aggregate allocation of resources likely to be and the lower aggregate economic efficiency and welfare. Thus, the west-side North Atlantic countries had an economic advantage over the east-side countries. To improve efficiency and welfare and thereby also reduce the disadvantage vis-à-vis North America, a number of European countries, primarily the west-most side countries, began in the post-World War II era to organize on a multinational basis to foster greater integration by reducing and eventually eliminating the barriers, first as the European Community (EC) in 1958 and then as the European Union in 1993. To further reduce barriers and improve efficiency, 12 of the 15 EU countries joined together, with effect from 1999, to use a single currency – the Euro (E) – and operate a single central bank, the European Central Bank (ECB), in a community commonly identified alternatively as Euroland, Euroarea or Eurozone. Nevertheless, in mid-2003, considerable barriers to free transfers remained, particularly among the countries still outside the community. Multiple currencies are used outside the ECB, political independence is strong and numerous languages are spoken.[2]

2.   CROSS-BORDER CAPITAL FLOWS

As can be seen from Table 9.1, international trade in financial services (less insurance) has tripled in dollar volume in the years between 1987 and 1997 for major industrial countries. This rate of growth is considerably faster than the increase in either inflation or GDP in these countries. In large measure, as noted earlier, this rapid increase reflects both the greatly reduced cost and increased speed of transferring funds across borders and the almost complete disappearance of barriers to cross-border financial flows, particularly for industrial countries.

As a whole, in 1997, these countries exported nearly twice the dollar volume of financial services to the rest of the world as they imported from those countries. The dollar amount of cross-border activity varied greatly among individual countries, reflecting both their absolute size and the depth and breadth of their financial markets. The USA is by far the largest exporter of financial services, accounting for one-third of the total exports of the nine reporting countries. The UK is a distant second. However, if the Euroland countries were summed, they would surpass the UK, although some of their exports are likely to be to other Euroland countries and thus involve double counting. The USA is also the second-largest importer of financial services behind Italy, but its imports are only some one-third as large as its exports while Italy's exceeded its exports. The USA was the largest net exporter of financial services in 1997. Germany was the only other net exporter, but on a much smaller scale. It is doubtful that any excluded country would rank as a significant net exporter of financial services, nor would the Euroland countries as a whole. These data confirm the major international roles of the financial markets in the USA and UK.

Funds are transferred from lenders (surplus spending units) to borrowers (deficit spending units) and receipts (securities) are transferred in the reverse direction either through the 'banking' or financial intermediation (indirect) market or the capital (direct) financial market. In the bank market, the institutions effectively transform the securities they buy from (loans they make to) borrowers into another security with different characteristics in terms of size denomination, maturity, term to repricing, credit risk, currency denomination and so on that enhance its value to the ultimate lenders. These new securities are liabilities of the intermediating institution. Thus, for example, loans are transformed into deposits by banks, into policy contracts by insurance companies and pension funds, and into shares by mutual funds. At the same time, the large pool of funds that these institutions are able to collect through offering 'personalized' securities to lenders also permits them to purchase personalized securities from borrowers. As the institutions obtain, process and store private information about the preferences and capabilities of their lenders and borrowers, the process is generally continuous and is often referred to as 'relationship banking'.

Table 9.1   *Cross-border trade in financial services, excluding insurance (billions of US dollars)*

	A Receipts (exports)	
	1987	1997
Canada	0.41	1.16
France	—	1.68
Germany	0.56	2.57
Italy	1.55	3.77
Japan	—	1.85
Netherlands	0.23	0.49
Switzerland	3.30	—
United Kingdom	—	7.47
United States	3.73	11.06
Total	9.78	30.05

	B Receipts (imports)	
	1987	1997
Canada	0.73	1.63
France	—	1.61
Germany	0.13	1.15
Italy	2.50	4.98
Japan	—	2.68
Netherlands	0.19	0.52
Switzerland	—	—
United Kingdom	—	—
United States	2.08	3.91
Total	5.63	16.48

Source: OECD, *Financial Market Trends*, March 2000, p. 28

In the capital market, the securities issued by borrowers, such as the loans advanced to household, corporate or government borrowers, are effectively sold in unmodified form to the ultimate investor or, if modified in form (for example, asset-backed securities), do not become liabilities of third parties. As these transactions are not personalized, they are more likely to be 'arms-length' and one-time rather than continuing. While most countries have both financial markets, which one is used to a greater extent varies substantially among countries and depends on the country's particular institutional history, including its legal system, form of government, degree of property rights, enforcement of contracts, quality of financial supervision and regulation, and sophistication and efficiency of its financial markets.

Table 9.2 provides a measure of the relative sizes of the bank and capital markets for corporate financing by country: bank loans to corporations as a percentage of total corporate financing. The larger the percentage, the more important relatively is the bank market. However, to the extent that corporations may obtain financing from bank-like institutions, such as insurance companies and pension funds, that also transform the nature of the security but are not included in bank loans, this measure understates the importance of the bank market. Recent evidence suggests that greatest aggregate welfare is achieved by having active bank and capital markets that compete with each other (Levine, 1997, 2002). In addition having two channels to direct funds from savers to investors provides protection in case one channel encounters problems. Market participants can then turn to the functioning channel and lessen the pain to the economy. Table 9.2 shows a wide divergence among countries in the relative importance of the two markets.

Table 9.2   Relative size of bank and capital markets for corporate financing in select countries, 1990–2002

Bank corporate loans as % of total corporate financing

	1990	1998	2002
Euroland	—	88	87
France	84	81	78*
Germany	—	94	95*
Italy	67**	70	71*
Japan	74	70	64
United Kingdom	80	64	61
United States	52	44	41

Note: *2001, **1991.

Source: BIS, *Annual Report, 2003* p. 131.

In 2002, the USA had by far the least important relative 'bank' market and Germany the relatively most important. In the USA, the two markets were roughly equal in size, while in Germany the capital market was practically non-existent. The Euroland countries as a whole were basically bank market countries; only 13 per cent of corporate funding was provided on the capital market. Even the UK, with its well developed capital markets, was primarily a bank market, although not to the same extent as the Euroland countries. The changes in the relative importance of bank and capital markets between 1990 and 2002 indicate a possible decrease in the importance of bank markets, on average. Such a reduction occurred in France, Japan, the UK and the USA. Of the included countries with complete data, only Italy showed an increase in the importance of the bank market relative to its capital market. A possible explanation for the relative decline in the importance of the bank market is the rapid development of loan securitization, which increases the role of banks as originators of loans but may reduce their role as investors by broadening the market for these securities.

The total volume of cross-border financing by type in US dollars from 1992 to 1998, excluding equity financing, is shown in Table 9.3. The flows are classified according to whether they are bank- or capital market-transmitted and, if the latter, whether short-term (money market) or long-term. Total net international flows more than tripled from $245 billion in 1992 to $875 billion in 1997, before declining sharply to $565 billion in 1998 in the wake of the long-term capital management (LTCM) and Russian debt crises that greatly reduced liquidity in both domestic and international markets. Net flows increased in both the bank (which is primarily short-term) and bond markets in this period, but did not increase in the money market. Net international bond financing replaced bank financing as the major form of cross-border financing, particularly in 1998, when bank financing declined sharply, to one-quarter its 1997 amount and smaller than in 1992. Indeed, in 1998, bond financing increased sharply over 1997 and represented 85 per cent of total international financing, up from only 35 per cent in 1992. These changes were not unexpected and do not reflect any breakdowns in markets or cross-border financing. As has also been observed in other periods and in other crises, long-term international financing is less volatile than either bank or short-term capital market financing (Kaufman, 2000). In terms of stock outstanding at year-end 1998, however, bank claims slightly exceeded short- and long-term capital market securities combined. These data appear consistent with the apparent decline in the importance of the domestic bank market discussed above.

Table 9.3   Estimated net financing in international markets by type (billions of US dollars)

	Flows				Stock
	1992	1995	1997	1998	1998
Bank claims*	165.0	333.0	465.0	115.0	5 485.0
Money market instruments	40.4	17.4	19.8	7.4	194.5
Bond and note financing	111.1	245.8	553.5	670.3	4 121.6
Total international financing	316.5	593.1	1 038.3	792.7	9 801.1
Minus double-counting	71.5	48.1	163.3	227.7	1 456.1
Total net	245.0	545.0	875.0	565.0	8 345.0

Note: * International financing.

Source: OECD, *Financial Market Trends*, March 2000, p. 29.

Because they have counterparties to their activities on both sides of their balance sheets, the participation of banks in international financing can be measured on either side. The positions of all large banks in a country with bank counterparties in other countries as a percentage of the country's GDP are shown for select years from 1983–98 in Table 9.4(a) for assets (loans) and Table 9.4(b) for liabilities (inter-bank deposits and borrowings) and with non-bank counterparties in other countries in Tables 9.5(a) and 9.5(b), respectively. Bank cross-border activity has increased faster than GDP for all of the included countries, but, as in the previous tables, these ratios vary greatly from country to country and, to a lesser and more surprising extent, from year to year. Nor are the ranking of the ratios the same for the two sides of the balance sheet. In terms of assets/loans to foreign banks, Switzerland, which is geographically small and has large banks, had by far the greatest ratio in 1998, twice its GDP, followed by the UK. Not surprisingly in view of its geographic size and diversity, the USA had the lowest ratio of loans by its banks to foreign banks to GDP, less than 10 per cent.

In terms of deposits or borrowings from foreign banks, banks in the UK have the highest ratio, with Swiss banks next. The USA again has the lowest ratio. For most countries, cross-border inflows of funds were more important than cross-border outflows. Switzerland was the major exception. Its banks exported twice as many funds to banks in other countries as they imported from them. Cross-border bank lending and borrowing expanded faster than GDP for all countries between 1983 and 1998.

Table 9.4   *External positions of banks in individual countries* vis-à-vis
other banks (percentage of GDP)

	A Bank assets	
	1983	1998
Belgium	52.3	67.4
France	17.4	30.3
Germany	6.6	23.7
Italy	8.3	13.7
Netherlands	30.6	52.5
Sweden	5.7	15.8
Switzerland	—	200.0
United Kingdom	73.4	91.7
Canada	10.9	12.8
Japan	6.8	21.2
United States	7.9	7.9

	B Bank liabilities	
	1983	1998
Belgium	78.2	77.8
France	23.5	42.5
Germany	6.6	31.4
Italy	10.5	20.5
Netherlands	32.0	72.5
Sweden	13.7	31.3
Switzerland	—	87.9
United Kingdom	79.8	106.5
Canada	11.1	13.8
Japan	8.8	17.8
United States	6.9	10.5

Source: OECD, *Financial Market Trends*, March 2000, p. 30.

The ratios are lower on both sides of the balance sheet for bank counterparties with foreign non-banks than with banks for nearly all countries, suggesting that the inter-bank market is more internationally active than the bank–non-bank market. UK banks are the largest relative lenders to foreign non-banks, followed by Belgian banks. As it is for inter-bank flows, Switzerland is also the largest relative collector of foreign non-bank funds, followed by the UK and Belgium. The USA is again a very small participant in lending to or borrowing from foreign non-banks relative to its GDP. Moreover, unlike nearly all other countries, its participation in this market did not increase relative to its GDP between 1983 and 1998.

Table 9.5   External positions of banks in individual countries vis-à-vis *the non-bank sector (percentage of GDP)*

	A Bank assets	
	1983	1998
Belgium	22.6	38.2
France	9.5	15.8
Germany	3.1	15.1
Italy	0.1	5.4
Netherlands	12.2	21.5
Sweden	1.9	6.5
Switzerland	23.2	26.0
United Kingdom	32.8	44.8
Canada	1.9	2.6
Japan	2.4	11.8
United States	3.4	1.7

	Panel B Bank liabilities	
	1983	1998
Belgium	10.4	32.1
France	2.9	4.1
Germany	2.1	10.7
Italy	0.5	2.0
Netherlands	8.9	14.9
Sweden	1.4	6.6
Switzerland	—	99.0
United Kingdom	32.9	31.3
Canada	7.5	6.3
Japan	0.2	0.9
United States	1.5	1.5

Source: OECD, *Financial Market Trends*, March 2000, p. 31.

The above analyses suggest that cross-border financial flows in the aggregate have been increasing significantly in recent years relative to a country's GDP, but that individual country relative participation in this market varied greatly. UK, Swiss, Dutch and Belgian banks are the most internationally active relative to the economic importance of their home country, and US, Canadian, Italian, Swedish and Japanese the least. Swiss banks are by far the greatest net exporters of funds. Banks in almost all other countries are greater relative importers than relative exporters. Despite being a small international participant relative to its GDP, the USA is the largest absolute participant in the international financial market. Thus it is of interest to analyse its international financial flows in greater detail. This is done in the next section.

3. US INTERNATIONAL FINANCIAL FLOWS

As shown above, US cross-border financial investments have increased rapidly in dollar terms, if not relative to its GDP. Since 1980, US nationals have been purchasing increasing amounts of foreign securities and foreign nationals an increasing amount of US securities. In 2000, foreign investors held nearly $4.5 trillion of US securities (see Figure 9.1). In 1990, foreign holdings had totalled only $1 trillion in market value. Nearly 40 per cent of

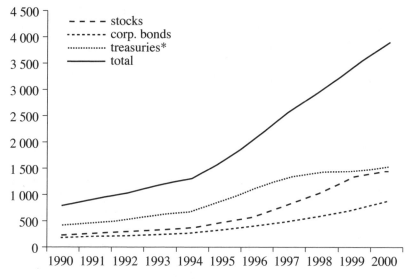

Source: Steil (2002, p. 19).

Figure 9.1 Foreign holdings of US securities, 1990–2000 ($ billions)

the 2000 holdings were in Treasury bonds and corporate stock, respectively, and 22 per cent in corporate bonds. As a percentage of the total value of all US equities, foreign holdings of equities nearly doubled, from 6 per cent in 1990 to over 11 per cent in 2001. However, the large amount of corporate stock and the rapid increase are probably overestimates of the long-run trend. They reflect in large part the rapid rise in stock prices in the period covered and are likely to have declined significantly in later years. Not only did the volume of foreign holdings of US corporate stock rise sharply, but trading in these stocks increased even faster from very small amounts in the early 1990s to some $3 trillion in 2000 by Europeans alone. The breakdown in US equity trading by select European country from 1990 to 2000 is shown in Table 9.6. The largest traders by far were UK investors, who accounted for nearly 50 per cent of all gross transactions by European Union countries in 2000. French investors were next highest, with only 13 per cent of total European gross transactions. Canadian investors ranked third.

Table 9.6   Gross transactions in US equities by foreign investors, 1990–2000 ($ billions)

	1990	1992	1994	1996	1998	2000
Canada	38	53	78	110	154	307
France	13	16	17	41	393	383
Germany	12	12	20	29	102	213
Netherlands	6	11	23	32	55	119
Switzerland	28	35	51	85	163	292
UK	93	122	197	318	629	1 410
European Union	144	184	292	498	1 356	2 631
Total Europe	178	226	353	587	1 535	2 958

Source: Steil (2002, p. 19).

At the same time, US investors increased their participation in foreign securities. The market value of US holdings of foreign equities alone increased from about $100 billion in 1985 to $250 billion in 1990, and nearly $2 trillion in 1999 before falling back again to $1.5 trillion in 2001. As a percentage of total US equities, foreign equity securities increased from 6 per cent in 1991 to 10 per cent in 1994 and remained relatively constant since. Thus the market value of foreign holdings of US equity securities were about the same percentage of total US equities in 2001 as US holdings were of foreign equities. US investors traded most heavily in UK securities.

In 2000, gross transactions in UK securities represented 65 per cent of all US investor transactions in European securities (Table 9.7). Transactions in German securities ranked a distant second, accounting for only 7 per cent of all transactions in European securities, slightly lower in dollar terms than US investor transactions in Canadian securities. These data suggest the relatively small and illiquid equity markets in Europe outside of the UK.

Table 9.7   Gross transactions in foreign stocks by US investors, 1990–2000 ($ billions)

	1990	1992	1994	1996	1998	2000
Canada	10	14	35	64	107	172
France	12	17	23	26	47	92
Germany	14	12	34	33	84	148
Netherlands	8	9	18	25	49	80
Switzerland	9	10	23	21	58	35
UK	93	134	279	373	787	1 350
European Union	141	182	387	492	1 057	1 937
Total Europe	154	199	436	536	1 155	2 063

Source: Steil (2002, p. 20).

4   INTRA-EU FINANCIAL FLOWS

As noted earlier, a primary purpose of both the EU and the Eurozone was to improve efficiency through reducing barriers to cross-border financial flows both within the area and between the area and outside areas, such as the USA. Among the policies adopted to achieve this objective were the introduction of a single corporate passport that permits financial firms chartered in any one member country to conduct business in other member countries under the same conditions and a reduction in regulatory barriers to cross-border mergers and acquisitions to encourage the creation of larger financial institutions that may be more likely to compete successfully with large outside financial institutions and thus engage in a greater volume of cross-border financing.

Although both the EU and Euroland are larger in population than the USA and the EU is almost equal in GDP, both are less efficient because of remaining barriers to cross-border financial flows and mergers and multiple currencies in the case of the EU. It was the removal of these restrictions that was a primary drive behind the development of the EU and particularly

Euroland. The EU's Second Banking Directive, which was adopted in 1989 and implemented in 1993, provided for the removal of all cross-country barriers to bank entry, mutual recognition of bank powers, equal prudential regulations and deposit insurance determined by the host country for all banks physically operating there (This was later modified to the home country). At the same time, although the USA had a single currency, until the mid-1990s it was not a true single market for all financial institutions. Some types of financial institutions, primarily banks and other deposit-taking institutions, were restricted from cross-state mergers and branching, not greatly different from the cross-country restrictions in Europe.

Table 9.8 shows that Euroland bank cross-border financing activities increased significantly between 1997 and 2002. The greatest relative increases were in investments in the short-term paper of foreign monetary financial institutions (MFIs) and in fixed income securities on the asset side of the balance sheet and in deposits from foreign banks on the liability side. Loans to both banks and non-banks remained primarily loans to domestic borrowers. Loans to domestic non-banks declined only from 91.6 per cent of all loans at year-end 1997 to 88.7 per cent in March 2002 and loans to other domestic banks declined only from 60.1 per cent in 1997 to 59.2 per cent in this period. Thus Euroland banks remained primarily domestic lending banks. Their international activities occurred in areas other than lending.

Interestingly enough, there appears to be a dichotomy in the non-domestic geographic areas experiencing increases. On the asset side (use of funds), the largest relative increases were with counterparties within the euro area, while on the liability side (source of funds), the largest relative increases were with counterparties outside the euro area. This suggests that the Euroland banks as a whole are attracting relatively more funds from the rest of the world and rerouting them to other Euroland countries. Banks in some Euroland countries appear less efficient in tapping funds from the rest of the world (ROW) than banks in some other Euroland countries and require a middleman bank.

5.   EUROPEAN BANKING INTEGRATION

In addition to cross-border financing, another measure of cross-border financial integration is the ability of foreign-owned banks to operate physically in a country. Table 9.9 shows the percentage of bank capital in Euroland countries owned by investors in both other Euroland and major non-Euroland countries. As year-end 2000, nearly one-quarter of the equity capital of banks in Euroland was held by investors outside the country in which the banks were chartered. But the degree of foreign ownership was

Table 9.8   Domestic and cross-border on-balance-sheet activities of euro area banks (€ billions)

	December 1997	March 2002
Total inter-bank assets[1]	*4 649.00*	*6 308.00*
Loans to MFIs	3 859.00	4 835.00
domestic business (%)	60.1	59.2
business with other euro area countries (%)	15.3	18.6
business with the rest of the world (%)	24.6	22.2
Other claims on MFIs (securities, money market paper)	790	1 474.00
domestic business (%)	80.5	62.5
business with other euro area countries (%)	12.7	20.2
business with the rest of the world (%)	6.8	17.3
Total loans to non-banks[2]	*5 905.00*	*8 046.00*
domestic business (%)	91.6	88.7
business with other euro area countries (%)	2.2	3.6
business with the rest of the world (%)	6.2	7.7
Fixed income securities issued by non-banks[2]	*1 380.00*	*1 745.00*
domestic business (%)	72.5	52.6
business with other euro area countries (%)	15.6	30.5
business with the rest of the world (%)	11.9	16.9
Equity holdings	*380*	*984*
Other assets	*1 069.00*	*1 231.00*
Total assets	13 383.00	18 314.00
Total inter-bank deposits	*4 057.00*	*5 534.00*
domestic business (%)	59.5	52.6
business with other euro area countries (%)	14.6	16.4
business with the rest of the world (%)	25.9	31
Total deposits from non-banks[2]	*5 104.00*	*6 586.00*
domestic business(%)	88	83.7
business with other euro area countries (%)	5.4	5.2
business with the rest of the world (%)	6.6	11.1
Fixed income securities[3]	*2 064.00*	*3 117.00*
Capital and reserves	*688*	*1 054.00*
Other liabilities	*1 470.00*	*2 022.00*
Total liabilities	13 383.00	18 314.00

Notes:
1. These items do not include shares.
2. Including general government.
3. The item includes money market paper.

Source: Cabral *et al.*, (2002).

Table 9.9   Capital of euro area banks owned by foreign residents, year-end 2000 (% of total equity capital)

Country of the Bank	Country of the owners*															Total
	BE	DE	GR	ES	FR	IT	LU	NL	PT	DK	SE	UK	JP	US	Other	
BE		1.11	0.00	0.23	0.47	0.00	0.04	27.04	0.00	0.00	0.00	0.00	0.00	0.24	0.37	29.5
DE	0.00		0.00	0.66	0.38	0.86	0.06	1.98	0.00	0.00	0.03	0.00	0.02	0.49	0.68	5.2
GR	0.00	0.00		0.00	1.16	0.00	0.00	0.00	0.00	0.00	0.00	0.96	0.00	1.25	2.72	6.1
ES	0.00	2.87	0.00		1.26	1.92	0.00	0.00	1.18	0.00	0.00	2.29	0.00	0.00	0.00	9.5
FR	6.17	2.54	0.00	1.44		1.09	0.19	0.58	0.02	0.00	0.00	1.56	0.67	0.00	0.00	14.3
FI	0.00	0.00	0.00	0.00	0.00	0.00	0.00	0.00	0.00	0.00	37.64	0.00	0.00	2.81	0.22	40.7
IE	2.88	26.30	0.00	0.00	0.00	2.79	0.91	5.82	0.00	0.00	0.00	1.14	0.00	0.01	0.38	40.2
IT	0.09	1.74	0.00	1.12	2.59		0.28	0.67	0.00	0.00	0.00	0.11	0.00	0.00	3.68	10.3
LU	18.40	47.30	0.32	0.00	9.80	4.28		1.49	0.00	2.17	0.27	0.79	0.00	0.00	1.02	85.8
NL	1.23	1.65	0.00	0.00	0.00	0.00	0.00		0.00	0.00	0.00	0.00	0.59	3.10	0.10	6.7
AT	1.01	9.03	0.00	0.00	0.02	0.11	0.00	0.00	0.00	0.00	0.00	0.00	0.00	0.00	0.00	10.2
PT	0.86	2.02	0.73	0.99	0.78	3.19	2.82	1.83		0.00	0.00	0.25	0.00	3.10	0.10	16.7
Average	2.79	8.60	0.10	0.40	1.50	1.29	0.39	3.58	0.11	0.18	3.16	0.59	0.11	0.92	0.77	22.9

Notes:
* No Finnish, Irish or Austrian investors owned capital in other Euroland banks; AT: Austria, IE: Ireland, IT: Italy, JP: Japan, BE: Belgium, LU: Luxembourg, DK: Denmark, NL: Netherlands, DE: Germany, PT: Portugal, GR: Greece, ES: Spain, FI: Finland, SE: Sweden, FR: France, UK: United Kingdom, US: United States.

Source: Cabral et al., (2002).

not uniform among the countries in either terms of banks being owned by foreign investors or of foreign investors owning banks in Euroland countries. Almost all the capital of banks in Luxembourg was owned by foreign investors, primarily German, followed by Belgians. Forty per cent of the capital of both Finnish and Irish banks was foreign-owned. In contrast, less than 10 per cent of the capital of banks in Germany, Greece, Spain and the Netherlands was foreign-owned. German investors were the most prevalent in investing in foreign banks, accounting for 8.6 per cent of the total equity capital of Euroland banks. They primarily invested in banks in Luxembourg and Ireland. Dutch investors held 3.6 per cent, primarily in Irish banks, and Belgian investors held 2.8 per cent of the capital of Euroland banks, primarily in Luxembourg and France. Non-Euroland investors held less than 6 per cent. Of these, Swedish investors held over one-half of the amount, almost all in Finnish banks. Thus foreign ownership of banks in Euroland countries is primarily ownership by other Europeans. That is, Euroland banking integration to date is primarily European integration and foreign banks invested primarily in neighbouring countries. This is consistent with the home bias reported by many researchers in international trade (Rugman and Verbeke, 2003). US investors held only 1 per cent of the capital of Euroland banks, divided primarily among banks in Finland, the Netherlands and Portugal.

One method of investing in the capital foreign banks is through merger or acquisition (M&A). M&A may also be used to expand within borders or into other industries. Larger domestic banks are more likely to engage in cross-border financing activities. Table 9.10 summarizes M&A activity of Euroland banks from 1990 to 2001, by type. Merger activity among Euroland banks has increased since the introduction of the Second Banking Directive in early 1993, particularly since 1998 with the coming of the ECB and a single currency. Seventy per cent of the overall value of bank mergers and acquisition from 1990 to the first half of 2001 occurred after 1998. Surprisingly, the large majority of these activities (nearly 80 per cent) were domestic. Only 22 per cent were cross-border and much of these occurred in the first half of the 1990s, and only in 2000 did cross-border M&As represent as much as 50 per cent of total M&As. But, by 2001, the percentage had declined sharply to virtually zero. It appears that M&A activity has been used primarily to grow domestic banks to a size that would discourage entry by foreign banks and possibly reduce domestic competition in the process. Seventy per cent of the M&As, both domestic and cross-border, were traditional within industry, although cross-industry M&As picked up sharply in the first half of 2001. Cross-border M&As were evenly divided between within- and cross-industry activity. The average size of M&As increased sharply in the period from 1997.

Table 9.10 Value of M&As involving banks in the euro area, (€ billions
or % of total)

	Total		Within-industry		Cross-industry	
	€ billions	Per cent	Domestic	Cross-border	Domestic	Cross-border
				(percentage of total)		
1990	15.4	5	45	7	45	3
1991	8.7	3	76	2	10	12
1992	5.2	2	17	4	19	60
1993	12.0	4	22	3	17	58
1994	6.1	2	73	5	22	0
1995	11.0	3	39	26	32	3
1996	6.4	2	74	1	6	19
1997	27.9	9	74	2	5	19
1998	72.4	23	70	3	17	10
1999	70.9	22	79	13	3	5
2000	49.7	16	38	42	12	8
2001*	31.3	10	31	1	67	1
Total	316.9	100	60	11	18	11

Note: * Up to August.

Source: Cabral *et al.*, (2002).

By far the most frequent foreign acquirers of Euroland banks in this period were acquirers in other Euroland countries (Table 9.11). This was particularly true for within-industry mergers. Acquirers from the three non-Euroland EU countries were the next largest acquirers for within-industry acquisitions and acquirers from ROW countries, primarily Switzerland, for cross-industry acquisitions. Both sets of acquirers were relatively far less important in the other classification. Surprisingly, US acquirers were relatively unimportant in both the within-industry and cross-industry classifications. Only in the first part of the 1990s and only for within-industry acquisitions did the USA represent an important acquirer.

In addition to entry in foreign countries through M&A, foreign banks can also enter Euroland and EU countries through branching. The number of cross-border branches opened by banks in EU countries in Euroland countries and by banks in Euroland countries in EU countries, is shown in Tables 9.12 and 9.13, respectively, for 1997 and 2000. The number of branches in both directions was greater in 2000 than in 1997, although not substantially so. By far the largest number of foreign branches operated by banks in EU countries in Euroland countries in 2000 were located in Germany, followed by France and Luxembourg. But the increases were not even. While the number of foreign branches opened by banks in EU countries in France almost doubled in the three years, the number in Luxembourg was smaller in 2000 than in 1997. Nearly one-quarter of the foreign branches in Euroland countries operated by EU country banks were from the three non-Euroland countries, presumably primarily from the UK. In terms of asset size, foreign branches of EU banks were not very important in any Euroland country. Only in Ireland and Luxembourg did these branches account for more than 10 per cent of the consolidated assets of all banks in the host country in 2000.

Table 9.11   Type and origin of acquirers in cross-border bank mergers in the euro area, 1990–2001

Acquiring country/area	Within-industry			Cross-industry		
	1990–1997	1998–2001	1990–2001	1990–1997	1998–2001	1990–2001
	(percentage of total €)					
Euro area	53	59	58	50	47	48
Other EU countries	9	38	31	1	0	1
USA	21	2	7	2	13	8
Rest of the world	17	1	4	47	40	43
Total	100	100	100	100	100	100

Source: Cabral *et al.*, (2002).

Foreign branches of banks in EU countries operated by banks in Euroland countries in 2000 were owned primarily by German and French banks (Table 9.13). Again about a quarter of all of these branches were in the three non-Euroland EU countries. In terms of asset size of all banks in the home Euroland country, assets were not very great. Assets in foreign branches of domestic banks were relatively most important in the Netherlands and Germany, but even in these two countries they were only about 15 per cent of total domestic bank assets. Almost all of the foreign branch assets of banks in Euroland countries in 2000 were in the three non-Euroland EU countries, presumably primarily in the UK, and almost all were acquired after 1997.

Table 9.12   Inward branching of banks from EU countries into euro area

| Host country | Number of branches from | | | | Assets of foreign branches as a % of total consolidated assets of host country | | | |
| | Euro area | | EU | | Euro area | | EU | |
	1997	2000	1997	2000	1997	2000	1997	2000
Austria	4	12	6	15	0.6	N.A.	0.7	0.8
Belgium	23	28	25	34	N.A.	N.A.	8.5	5.7
Finland	1	0	9	N.A.	0.0	N.A.	0.0	7.3
France	36	73	52	93	N.A.	N.A.	2.6	3.3
Germany	90	113	118	145	0.7	1.0	1.0	1.3
Greece	9	9	14	13	5.3	4.2	9.0	6.4
Ireland	N.A.	N.A.	N.A.	N.A.	N.A.	N.A.	N.A.	13.5
Italy	27	32	34	41	3.0	3.0	3.4	3.5
Luxembourg	55	47	62	55	N.A.	N.A.	17.9	16.6
Netherlands	6	0	9	N.A.	N.A.	N.A.	2.1	2.7
Portugal	13	18	15	22	N.A.	N.A.	4.0	4.2
Spain	28	33	34	41	4.0	2.8	4.7	3.4
Euro area average	27	33	34	42	2.3	2.8	4.9	5.7

Note: N.A. not available.

Source: Cabral *et al.*, (2002).

The above analysis suggests that the EU and Euroland countries have been increasing cross-border banking through both branching and M&As, but the pace of cross-border expansion has been relatively slow and foreign banks and branches remain relatively unimportant as a percentage of assets of all banks in either the host or home country, particularly in comparison to similar changes in the USA. Much of the cross-border banking involved UK banks. US banks do not appear to be increasing their relative physical participation in either the EU or Euroland countries. Thus it appears likely that further cross-border invasion of other countries by financial institutions on both sides of the Atlantic is likely, and probably at an accelerated pace, particularly within the EU, as this area attempts to catch up in structure with the USA as a single market. Nevertheless, the ECB recently predicted

> [cross-border] integration in the banking industry [in Euroland] is more likely to occur through liquid integrated markets for interbank funding and through developed markets for loan securitization and credit derivatives … rather than just through cross-border mergers of banks. (ECB, 2002b, p. 19)

That is, the future will not differ greatly from the past.

Table 9.13   Outward branching of banks from euro area countries into EU

Host country	Number of branches from				Assets of foreign branches as a % of total consolidated assets of host country			
	Euro area		EU		Euro area		EU	
	1997	2000	1997	2000	1997	2000	1997	2000
Austria	9	14	13	17	0.2	0.3	0.2	3.5
Belgium	19	23	24	28	0.6	0.4	0.6	5.0
Finland	0	1	4	2	0.0	0.0	0.4	0.0
France	61	68	72	83	2.5	2.0	2.6	7.4
Germany	64	83	78	109	0.2	0.4	0.2	15.1
Greece	3	6	7	11	0.2	0.3	0.2	9.9
Ireland	1	7	10	16	0.9	0.2	0.9	9.0
Italy	35	41	48	57	1.0	0.9	1.0	5.6
Luxembourg	35	39	38	40	0.1	0.0	0.1	0.0
Netherlands	24	35	29	44	2.6	1.6	2.9	16.6
Portugal	10	12	14	16	0.9	0.4	0.9	3.0
Spain	31	36	37	42	1.9	2.2	1.9	4.3
Euro area average	24	30	31	39	0.9	0.7	1.0	6.6

Source: Cabral *et al.*, (2002).

The relative slow pace of cross-border M&A activity for European banks may be explained in part by noting that where these banks, particularly in Euroland countries, compare unfavourably with US banks is not in size but in capital and profitability. In 2001, European banks accounted for 14 (nine in Euroland countries) of the world's largest 25 commercial banking companies in total assets compared to only three US banks and five Japanese banks (Table 9.14).[3] In terms of book value tier 1 capital (equity), 12 European banks, including seven Euroland banks, were ranked in the top 25, only double rather than nearly five times the six US banks. In terms of market capitalization, which reflects market perception of longer-term profitability, 12 European banks again ranked in the top 25, but only five were from Euroland countries, while US banks accounted for nine, three times the number of US top 25 banks by asset size. Thus it appears that, with the possible exception of British and Swiss banks, European banks have been chasing asset size and market share rather than profitability. Indeed the profitability of large German and French banks in recent years exceeded only that of large Japanese banks of the large banks in ten countries analysed by the BIS, despite an upward bias from below average provisions for loan losses (Bank for International Settlements, 2002). Partly as a result, they did not generate the book or market capitalizations required to purchase more profitable foreign banks. A policy of chasing market share over profitability and capital accumulation appears also to have been followed by Japanese banks in the 1980s, with disastrous financial results in the 1990s and beyond.

Table 9.14   Number of largest 25 banks in the world domiciled in USA, Europe and Japan, 2001

Measure	USA	Europe			Japan
		Total	ECB	ROE	
Total assets	3	14	9	5	5
Tier 1 capital	6	12	7	5	4
Market capitalization	9	12	5	7	2

Source: The Banker (July 2002).

6.   EUROPEAN CAPITAL MARKET INTEGRATION

The move towards financial integration among the Euroland countries is also reflected in changes in the capital market as evidenced by increases in the volume of new securities issuance and decreases in fees on such issuances. This is shown in Table 9.15. Three times as many new bond issues were issued by borrowers in Euroland countries in 2001 denominated in euros as in 1995 denominated in the predecessor currencies. In addition, the average size of issue increased fivefold, from €100 million in 1995 to €520 million in 2001. Increases of a smaller magnitude occurred for new Euro equity issues and syndicated bank loans. The larger these markets, the more likely they are to reflect cross-border activity. Between 1995 and 2000, fees on the issuance of large new Eurobonds declined by two-thirds, from 1.9 per cent to 0.6 per cent and less sharply on large Euro equity issues, from 2.8 per cent to 2.4 per cent. The reduction in gross fees on the issuance of new bonds and stocks is an indicator of increased competition in underwriting presumably at least in part from underwriters in other countries. A similar reduction was not observed for syndicated bank loans, however.

It should be noted that the establishment of the ECB and Euroland provided a fundamental change in the market for national government bonds of the member countries. Before the ECB, each country had a central bank with the power to 'print' that country's domestic currency. As a result,

Table 9.15   *Issuance of Eurobonds and Euro equities by Euroland corporations: number, volume and underwriting fees, 1995–2001*

	Number	Bonds Funds (billion euros)	Fees[*] (%)	Number	Equities Funds (billion euros)	Fees[*] (%)
1995	53	5.3	1.9	56	20.6	2.8
1999	123	37	1.3	301	76.1	2.6
2001	161	83.5	0.6	119	44.7	2.4

Note: [*] Large issues.

Source: Cabral *et al.*, (2002).

at least the government's domestic currency-denominated debt was credit risk-free as it could be bought in unlimited amounts by the central bank. But the establishment on the ECB with a new unified currency in 1999 removed the power to print money from the national central banks. There is no guaranty, indeed probably only a small likelihood, that the ECB will provide full support for the government bonds of any member country that is experiencing financial difficulties. Similar to bonds issued by states in the USA, bonds issued by Euroland country governments now assume credit risk, the amount depending on the financial, economic, political and other characteristics of the particular issuing national government. Thus national government bonds need not all have the same credit rating, even when denominated in euros, their domestic currency. In March 2003, for example, Standard and Poor's rated the domestic currency denominated sovereign debt of only seven of the 12 Euroland countries AAA (Table 9.16). Greece received only an A rating. This change makes it difficult to compare the Euroland government bond market with that of the USA and other countries, such as the UK, that have central banks authorized to 'print' domestic currency and therefore can issue domestic currency bonds effectively free of credit risk.

7. CONCLUSIONS

This chapter has reviewed recent changes in cross-border financing and financial activities of banks, primarily on the European side of the North Atlantic. These changes have been stimulated both by changes in computer and communications technology that have increased the speed and decreased the cost of transmitting funds over long distances and by the desire of the numerous, relatively small, European countries to establish a single larger economic market, including, for some, a single currency. The drive for a single market is motivated by, among other things, the promise of achieving the more efficient allocation of resources that exists in the larger two North American countries that are less handicapped by numerous cross-border barriers and making Europe more competitive.

Table 9.16   S&P sovereign debt ratings for Euroland countries, March 2003 (long-term, domestic currency)

Country	Rating
Austria	AAA
Belgium	AA+
Finland	AAA
France	AAA
Germany	AAA
Greece	A
Ireland	AAA
Italy	AA
Luxembourg	AAA
Netherlands	AAA
Portugal	AA
Spain	AA+

Source: OECD (2003b).

The chapter documents the increases in cross-border transfers of financial services and in cross-border financing, but the increases have not been homogeneous across countries. Different countries have specialized in different types of cross-border financial activities. Banks in most of the countries, particularly in Euroland, appear geared more to borrowing from other countries than to lending to them. Although large and growing rapidly in absolute dollar size, US cross-border activity is relatively small when measured against its GDP. The chapter also examines cross-border activity in Europe in pursuit of a single market. It concludes that, while on the upswing, such activity, particularly through bank M&A and branching, is occurring at a relatively slow pace and in terms of bank lending is primarily an inter-bank market. In the limited cross-border expansion through branching or acquisition that occurred there is a strong home bias: investment in neighbouring areas. The European financial market is currently still a long way from being a single integrated market.[4]

To date, most of the increase in European cross-border financial activity appears to reflect technological improvements rather than deliberate reductions in explicit and, more importantly, implicit government imposed barriers. M&A activity, in particular, has been used primarily to grow domestic banks to forestall rather than to encourage cross-border invasions.[5] Moreover the continuing domination of financial markets by banks in Euroland is also likely to block more rapid development of capital markets, which have expanded sharply from a low base and has become more competitive. Continued expansion is important as cross-border transactions are more common in this market and its expansion would intensify competition and increase efficiency. But because current technological advances are reducing the effectiveness of the barriers, additional financial market reforms that formally recognize these changes are likely in the near future. Thus many barriers may be expected to be lowered or removed altogether at a quicker pace and progress towards a single European and then a North American economic community market is likely to pick up in future years. However today's structure of financial markets on the east side of the North Atlantic community is not greatly different from what it was a decade ago and Europe will continue to play catch up for some years to come. In the meantime the financial sector is not contributing as much to economic growth in the area as it could.

NOTES

*   This paper was prepared for presentation at a conference on 'Alliance Capitalism in the New Trans-Atlantic Economy' at St Mary's University in Halifax, Canada on 26 and 27 September 2003. I am indebted to the participants at the conference as well as Tom Mondschean (DePaul University) for helpful comments and suggestions.
1.   The 15 current EU members are Austria, Belgium, Denmark, Finland, France, Germany, Greece, Ireland, Italy, Luxembourg, Netherlands, Portugal, Spain, Sweden and United Kingdom. The UK, Sweden and Denmark are not currently members of the ECB and Euroland. The ten countries scheduled to join the EU in 2004 are Cyprus, the Czech Republic, Estonia, Hungary, Latvia, Lithuania, Malta, Poland, the Slovak Republic and Slovenia.
2.   Mitchener (2003) provides a good summary of the current political divisions.
3.   The rest of Europe (ROE) banks represented are in the UK and Switzerland.
4.   Likewise recent news articles have provided other examples of implicit cross-border barriers to financial transactions in Europe. One article reported that cross-border use of euro bank transfers at the retail level in Euroland represents only 3 per cent of total euro retail transfers. The article attributes this small percentage to the complexity involved in making such transfers through the domestic clearinghouses. An integrated Euroland clearinghouse is being developed (Freudmann, 2003). Another article describes the difficulty in selling the same mutual fund in different European countries: 'Only 31% of the 24,982 funds sold somewhere in Europe are sold in more than one country' (Ascarelli, 2003, p. C1).

5. This may be less true for the 'new' EU countries, many of whose major banks have been acquired by banks in 'old' EU countries. I am indebted for this point to Tom Mondschean.

REFERENCES

Ascarelli, Silvia (2003), 'Mutual Funds Run a Maze of Rules in Europe', *Wall Street Journal*, 3 September C1, 11.

Bank for International Settlements (2002), *Annual Report, 2002*, Basle, 8 July.

Bank for International Settlements (2003), *Annual Report, 2003*, Basle, 30 June.

Brooks, Robin, Kristen Forbes, Jean Imbs and Askoha Mody (2003), 'Dancing in unison', *Finance and Development* (International Monetary Fund), June, 46–9.

Cabral, Ines, Frank Dierick and Juilia Vesala (2002), 'Banking integration in the euro area' *Occasional Paper Series, No. 6* (European Central Bank), Frankfurt, December.

Freudmann, Aviva (2003), 'Euro still gets tripped at borders', *Wall Street Journal*, 27 August, p. B3C.

Kaufman, George G. (2000), 'Banking and currency crises and systemic risk: a taxonomy and review', *Financial Markets, Institutions, and Instruments*, **9** (2) May.

Levine, Ross (1997), 'Financial development and economic growth', *Journal of Economic Literature*, June, 688–726.

Levine, Ross (2002), 'Bank-based or market-based financial systems: which is better?', *Journal of Financial Intermediation*, October, 398–428.

Mitchener, Brandon (2003), 'As Europe unites, religion, defense still stand in way', *Wall Street Journal*, 11 July, A1, A6.

OECD (2000), 'Cross-border trade in financial services', *Financial Market Trends*, March, 23–60.

OECD (2003a), 'European banking and stock market integration', *Financial Market Trends*, March, 99–117.

OECD (2003b), 'Convergence in euro area government debt markets', *Financial Market Trends*, March, 121–35.

Rugman, Alan M. and Alain Verbeke (2003), 'Multinational enterprises and public policy', in T. Brewer et al., *The New Economic Analysis of Multinationals*, Cheltenham, UK and Northampton, US: Edward Elgar, pp. 122–44.

Steil, Benn (2002), *Building a Transatlantic Securities Market*, New York: Council on Foreign Relations and the International Securities Markets Association.

'Top 1000 World Banks' (2002), *The Banker*, July.

Wachtel, Paul (2003), 'How much do we really know about growth and finance?', *Economic Review* (Federal Reserve Bank of Atlanta), first quarter, 32–47.

APPENDIX

Table 9.A1 Population and GDP, various countries and groupings, 2002

	Population	GDP*	
		Total	Per capita
	(millions)	(billion $)	(dollars)
USA	280	10082	36007
Euroland	306	7598	24830
EU (current)	380	9501	25003
EU (expanded)	455	10313	22666
Canada	32	923	28844
USA and Canada	312	11005	35272
Japan	127	3550	27953

Note: * Current US dollars at 2002 exchange rate.

Source: *CIA World Factbook 2002* (www.cia.gov/cia/publications/factbook/).

Table 9.A2   Population and GDP, European Union countries, 2002

A   European Union members

	Population	GDP*	
		Total	Per capita
	(thousands)	(billion $)	(dollars)
Austria	8170	226	27666
Belgium	10275	298	28966
Denmark	5369	156	28968
Finland	5184	136	26278
France	59766	1540	25768
Germany	83252	2184	26234
Greece	10645	201	18891
Ireland	3883	111	28663
Italy	57716	1438	24916
Luxembourg	449	20	44643
Netherlands	16068	434	27012
Portugal	10084	182	18048
Spain	40077	828	20660
Sweden	8877	227	25620
United Kingdom	59778	1520	25427

B   Candidate European Union members

	Population	GDP*	
		Total	Per capita
	(thousands)	(billion $)	(dollars)
Czech Republic	10257	156	15201
Cyprus	767	9**	11864
Estonia	1416	15	10742
Hungary	10075	135	13370
Latvia	2367	20	8453
Lithuania	3601	29	8109
Malta	397	7	17632
Poland	38625	368	9530
Slovenia	1933	36	18634
Slovakia	5422	66	12173

Note: * Current US dollars at 2002 exchange rate; **2001 figure.

Source: *CIA World Factbook 2002* (www.cia.gov/cia/publications/factbook/).

Index